ROCK GETS RELIGION

"All art (rock music) that endures reveals truth: that which conforms to reality—whether sacred or secular—ultimately glorifies God. G. K. Chesterton said that the most beautiful part of every picture is the frame. In my work, it is the Judeo-Christian worldview that has brought meaning to the music, and I'm in good company in today's music scene, where a counter-counterculture is making some noise. Mark Joseph has been a key voice in the transformation of American popular music; in this book, his final in a three-part series, he shows us how the transformation happened and outlines a vision for the future of the unlikely alliance of rock music and serious faith."

—GARY CHERONE, LEAD SINGER OF EXTREME AND VAN HALEN

"Rock is at its most exhilarating when it's asking those big questions of our existence, and I've been honored to have my songs of praise to [Jesus] happen in the center of the rock music culture and not in the religious basement of pop culture. *Rock Gets Religion* is a stirring call to all of us to occupy until His return, and work hard to make the greatest music the world has ever heard."

—SCOTT STAPP, LEAD SINGER OF CREED

"Mark Joseph is someone whom I gladly call my friend, and although I don't like outwardly promoting this personal side of my life, I feel that Mark 'gets it,' and at the very least, he certainly 'gets me.'"

—DAVE MUSTAINE, LEAD SINGER OF MEGADETH

"How does Mark Joseph know all these things? Better question: Why does he care? I've struggled so many times just trying to keep up with it all myself. My personal faith has been tried and tested. I believe he cares for the same reasons I do. At the end of it all he wants God to receive His due glory and to reveal God's hand in all the details whether you or this industry choose to acknowledge it or not. Thank you, my friend. Well written."

—SONNY SANDOVAL, LEAD SINGER OF P.O.D.

"*Rock Gets Religion* is a long overdue and brilliantly written book about art that expresses relationships not just with a higher power but in many cases with Jesus Christ. Although many tried to ignore it, the success and income being generated were noticed by the secular music industry and could no longer be ignored. Faith being incorporated into rock is not going away any time soon, and it will become even more prevalent as the world continues to decline. Mark Joseph has written a must-read book that brings to light the kind of music that has been etched forever in time."

—JOHN ELEFANTE, FMR. LEAD SINGER OF KANSAS

"From someone who's been in the mines, *Rock Gets Religion* is a very engaging and accurate depiction of the history and state of the union between faith and rock music."

—LEIGH NASH, LEAD SINGER OF SIXPENCE NONE THE RICHER

"Mark Joseph's research into the lives and accomplishments of artists reveals some very poignant discoveries, such as the roots of faith and the diverse detours that lie ahead for those pursuing their dreams. We are spiritual beings, and what and who we worship must come out into the open eventually. I am thankful that God our Creator cannot be boxed in or limited because of tradition and status, or the approval of a few. Sit back and enjoy *Rock Gets Religion*."

—PHIL KEAGGY, RECORDING ARTIST

"Rock, pop, and rap now have a growing number of artists who make compelling and thoughtful music that doesn't leave faith at the door. I am happy to call many of them my dear friends. In ways that challenge me deeply, Mark Joseph shakes up the philosophical foundations of the notion of separation of music and faith with the third volume of his rock trilogy, making a strong case to reenter the world of rock with great music and a compelling story of faith."

—TOMMY COOMES, LOVE SONG

"Music is a powerful tool to touch hearts and change lives. And to that the power of rock and it is a force unlike any other. I've known Mark since 1985 and have seen his passion and knowledge firsthand and it's been inspiring to say the least. Together, we've seen what happens when rock and religion collide and it's been nothing short of miraculous. Mark's new book *Rock Gets Religion* is a first hand look at the power of music and the effect it can have on a dark and desperate world when it delivers a message of hope, love grace and peace."

-MICHAEL SWEET, LEAD SINGER OF STRYPER

FOR EMILYN MARTHA

ROCK

GETS

RELIGION

THE BATTLE FOR THE SOUL
OF THE DEVIL'S MUSIC

———

MARK JOSEPH

 BP BOOKS    WND Books

ALSO BY MARK JOSEPH
The Rock & Roll Rebellion
Faith, God & Rock 'n' Roll
The Lion, the Professor and the Movies

Published by BP Books in association with WND Books, Washington, D.C. WND Books is a registered trademark of WorldNetDaily.com, Inc. ("WND")

Editorial assistance by Drew Lawson, Matthew Little, Kaelynn Timmins, Bethany Thompson, Catherine Dinius, and Joseph Olvera.
Unless otherwise noted, Scripture quotations are taken from the *Holy Bible,* New Living Translation, copyright © 1996, 2004, 2015 by Tyndale House Foundation. Used by permission of Tyndale House Publishers Inc., Carol Stream, Illinois 60188. All rights reserved.
Scriptures marked BBE are taken from the Bible in Basic English (public domain).
Scripture quotations marked DARBY are taken from the Darby Translation (public domain).

Book designed by Mark Karis

WND books are available at special discounts for bulk purchases. WND Books also publishes books in electronic formats. For more information call (541) 474-1776 or visit www.wndbooks.com.

Paperback ISBN: 978-1-944229-18-4
eBook ISBN: 978-1-944229-19-1

Library of Congress Cataloging-in-Publication Data
Names: Joseph, Mark, 1968- author.
Title: Rock gets religion : the battle for the soul of the devil's music / by
    Mark Joseph.
Description: Washington, D.C. : WND Books, [2017] | Includes bibliographical
    references and index. |
Identifiers: LCCN 2017019612 (print) | LCCN 2017021188 (ebook) | ISBN
    9781944229191 (e-book) | ISBN 9781944229184 (pbk.)
Subjects: LCSH: Contemporary Christian music--United States--History and
    criticism. | Popular music--Religious aspects--Christianity.
Classification: LCC ML3187.5 (ebook) | LCC ML3187.5 .J68 2017 (print) | DDC
    781.66088/27--dc23
LC record available at https://lccn.loc.gov/2017019612

Printed in the United States of America
17 18 19 20 21 22 LBM 9 8 7 6 5 4 3 2 1

Contents

Foreword   ix

1   Rock Gets Religion   1

2   God's Idols   26

3   Relationship Status: It's Complicated   33
The Preacher's Daughter • Losing Her Religion • The Simpsons
Avril Love • The Wrong Path • Going West • The Evanescence Explosion
The Rapper Chancelor • Pimping A Butterfly

4   A Cross and a Song Where I Don't Belong   98
Oh, Mercy! • Stacie's Ride • The Great Battle
Cars, God, and Rock 'n' Roll • Best Foot Forward

5   Rock In A Hard Place   139
Return to Megadeth • A Passion for the Christ • Another Cold War
Mum's the Word • God-Relient • Into the Fray • Finding God's Will
God's Paramore • In the Flyleaf

6   Hiding in Plain Sight   203
A Swift Rise • The Realest Thing You've Ever Seen
Nothing Left to Lose • The Bedingfields • The True Belieber
Sons of Jonas • The Hunter • This Year's "Model" • Lecrae's Reach
Taking the Hill • Unbreakable • Stressed Out

7   Into the Great Wide-Open   282

Notes   294

Index   317

Pure and genuine religion in the sight of God the Father means caring for orphans and widows in their distress and refusing to let the world corrupt you.

—JAMES 1:27

FOREWORD

"PERSONALLY I DON'T BELIEVE IN ATHEISTS. I think God's imprint is in our DNA, on our hearts, and in our souls. We are a tribe of disobedient children. Rock and Roll is just another voice from the tribe screaming out with our fists raised at the heavens to some god that may or may not exist. Rock and Roll is healthy. Every rock lyricist is confessing all the time or bragging about their sinful past or delivering psychosexual babble. But what the rocker is really doing is giving a gigantic yell for help. Sheryl and I sometimes give talks to church youth groups. I'm sure I've raised some eyebrows when I ask everybody in the audience to think of their favorite song. It could be Lady

Gaga, the Beatles, or the Sex Pistols. I then challenge them to think of the lyrics. As a Christian knowing what they know, I ask if they can buy in to what that artist is selling. Everybody is preaching something. Then I tell them it's okay to love that song—Marilyn Manson or the Cowsills. Just know where you stand. Jesus did not come to condemn. He came to seek and save those who are lost and to give them life to the full. Jesus did not turn away from the world, He embraced it. Understand that Satan's hand is everywhere. Do not judge the black metal and death metal bands too harshly. They are the ones who are crying out to God the loudest. Rock has *always* had religion. After all, it started as gospel music. Elvis Presley knew every gospel song ever made. I'm not an alarmist or nihilist, but the world gets more dangerous every day. I think our natural survival instinct makes us question where we stand with God even if some claim atheism. Mark Joseph's *Rock Gets Religion* is a great read and may answer some of your deep dark questions. Enjoy Mark's book. Read on and Rock on!"

—ALICE COOPER

1

ROCK GETS RELIGION

In 1999 my first book on the subject of rock music and religion, *The Rock & Roll Rebellion: Why People of Faith Abandoned Rock Music—and Why They're Coming Back,* was released, followed in 2003 by a second book on the subject, *Faith, God & Rock 'n' Roll.* As I was putting the finishing touches on it, I began to notice an acceleration in the pace of what I had just finished documenting—the mass influx of devout young Christians into popular mainstream music. Although it was a topic I had written about for more than a decade, I was stunned at the burst of activity in early 2003, and a decade later it has only accelerated. Rock music, once the domain of hedonism and debauchery of every kind, is now populated by thousands of upstanding citizens who create all different kinds of music, but are animated by religious ideas that would have been completely alien to rock stars of yesteryear.

For years Christians had *occasionally* appeared on the nation's pop music charts with songs that reflected their beliefs—from Edwin Hawkins's "Oh Happy Day" to Amy Grant's "Find a Way"; from Jars of Clay's "Flood" to Stryper's "In God We Trust." But in the last decade, what was once a trickle became a flood as dozens of artists who were also professed Christians and Christian-themed songs exploded onto the popular music scene.

Between songs like Switchfoot's challenging "Meant to Live," and MercyMe's blatant "I Can Only Imagine," it seemed that the dream of those artists who had begun performing what was then known as Jesus Music in the late 1960s and early '70s was finally coming true: true believers were making music about their faith in God, but doing so in a way that allowed them to reach audiences of both Christians and non-Christians alike.

Four major phenomena seemed to be occurring simultaneously: First, a whole new crop of artists who had once been ensconced in the world of contemporary Christian music, or CCM, were, thanks to the guidance of a new generation of more savvy executives, bursting out of that scene and into the musical mainstream while still remaining at their current labels. These included the likes of MercyMe and Bob Carlisle, who experienced major crossover hits with "I Can Only Imagine" and "Butterfly Kisses," even as they continued to be signed to Christian-oriented labels.

Second, established artists who had once rocked the CCM world were leaving those labels behind, signing with mainstream recording companies, such as Atlantic, Epic, Universal, and others, and reemerging as mainstream artists without substantively changing their message. Among this group were the San Diego, California-based rockers Switchfoot, the Chicago-based band Chevelle, and the hard rocking Pillar, all of whom had once been signed to labels associated with the CCM industry, but who had moved on to the mainstream giants Columbia, Epic, and Universal, respectively.

The third major trend was the continuing phenomenon of young artists who were also Christians bypassing the "Christian music" business altogether and simply pursuing and being signed directly to mainstream labels. Among this group were the likes of Flyleaf, Paramore, Evanescence, and scores of other artists.

Finally, there was the stunning turn of events that found the hit television series *American Idol* producing winners who claimed to be Christians and would then be signed to mainstream labels—again, bypassing the Christian music world altogether.

As I worked on the final draft of *Faith, God & Rock 'n' Roll*, I wasn't sure whether to plunge into the task of thinking and writing about this phenomenon or to let some time pass before figuring out just what was going on and how strong the trend would be. Writing about popular music, religion, and pop culture, while not as weighty as writing about, say, presidential administrations, nevertheless does have at least one thing in common with such historical analyses: sometimes it's difficult to see trends and understand the historical context and ramifications of those trends when they are still developing. So after discussing it with my publisher, I decided to leave the new wave of God-rockers out of *Faith, God & Rock 'n' Roll* and revisit them another day, after some time had passed.

But the surprising marriage of rock and religion was just beginning—soon afterward, Prince, the most unlikely of artists when the term "religious conversion" comes to mind, announced his conversion from hedonism to the Jehovah's Witnesses: "I embarked on a journey more fascinating than I could ever imagine," he said. "Without spiritual guidance too much freedom can lead to spiritual decline."[1]

In 2015 Prince further confounded his fans when he released a cover of a song by artist Nichole Nordeman, who had long been a part of the Christian music scene, "What If."

What in the world was going on?

Rock, birthed in hedonism, was being overtaken by religion. Pop culture would never be the same again, and plenty of people were noticing. Some of the keenest observations came from across the pond, where British rock writers noted, sometimes with incredulity, the shocking transformation of American popular music:

> "Perhaps the Devil doesn't have all the best tunes after all," declared a reporter for one of Britain's largest papers, *The Independent*, and adding that "religion has always been crucial to American music. From the earliest spirituals to today's most threatening rappers, God is always there, even if only on the 'thanks' list on the sleeve notes, usually just before Moms get a shout."[2]

The paper also wryly noted that the trend had first been spotted in an episode of *The Simpsons*:

> Rachel Jordan, the Christian country singer who occasionally passes through *The Simpsons* was asked where her band had

gone. "They switched to regular pop," she replied. "All you do is change Jesus to Baby."[3]

American reporters were not far behind as a number of U.S. newspapers and magazines commissioned major pieces on the growing trend. VH1 aired a special in late 2004 about the growing presence of the devout in pop culture, as did CBS News' *60 Minutes*. The trend was unmistakable, and there were no signs that it was going to end anytime soon. *USA Today* noted:

> At a time when Christian music is one of the hottest niches in the business, a small wave of artists who cut their teeth there is pushing beyond its borders. As a result, more artists with Christian leanings are flying under the religious radar, showing up everywhere from MTV to the Billboard charts.
>
> Two trends are behind the musical moves. First is the tenor of the post-Sept. 11 music business, which has mainstream labels more accepting of music that reflects faith. Second is a brewing aversion by some artists to the church-state separation of Christian musicians into their own sub-genre.
>
> In recent weeks, the Billboard charts have been peppered with secular-label releases by bands that started in the Christian music industry.[4]

The *Christian Science Monitor*'s Kim Campbell weighed in with a story of her own, likening the movement to the strong presence of Christians in the sporting world:

> "Driving the trend is a generation of young artists who don't want their music marginalized simply because they read the Bible," she wrote. "Many don't consider their music as being

suitable only for Christians and would like to be part of a broader cultural discussion. It's the idea that if movie stars and running backs who talk about their faith aren't relegated to Christian movie studios or football leagues, why should musicians be? The way that one band, Switchfoot, has put it: 'We're Christian by faith, not by genre.'"[5]

In its take on the growing trend, however, the *Chicago Tribune* saw trouble on the horizon for the CCM industry, a subset of the larger music industry that had been quietly making and marketing records to the Christian populace for the better part of thirty years. Writing that it was in the midst of an "identity crisis," the *Tribune* observed:

> Contemporary Christian music—which includes rock, pop, gospel and R & B styles—is at a crossroads. Some believe it should be music made by Christians, largely for Christians, to encourage Christians. Others counter that entertainers need to heed Christ's call to go out into the world and preach the gospel and that to do that, they need the resources to compete with the Madonnas and Matchbox Twenties of the world.[6]

The *Tribune* correctly saw two paths forming as a result of the growing movement of artists of faith into the mainstream, and the resulting controversy, and chronicled the split:

> Christian music is developing along two distinct lines: a traditional "music ministry" path where artists record songs for the church and other Christians, and "message music," where a Christian point of view comes through in content that might address any subject. Perhaps the best example of the latter is U2, which began its career playing church shows. Why the

distinction? Much of that has to do with the Nashville-based Christian music industry. Nashville houses a host of Christian record labels—many of them owned by major-label parents—that sign artists marketed primarily via Christian bookstores, record stores and Christian music festivals.[7]

By 2004 the trend had grown to include the unlikeliest of all communities, the sometimes misogynistic world of hip-hop, where rappers paid tribute to women, cars, money, and success but rarely to God beyond the requisite shout-out. While there had been some notable Christians in the rap business, like MC Hammer and Run-D.M.C., for the most part it had not been a hospitable genre for those young African-Americans who placed great importance on their faith in God. But one hip-hop artist, named Kanye West, aimed to change all of that with an ode to his Savior, and the trend was not limited to rap: "Today, alongside 'Jesus Walks,' which has spent 16 weeks on the Billboard Hot 100, are the Los Lonely Boys' hit single, 'Heaven,' and Switchfoot's even bigger hit, 'Meant to Live,'" noted the *Baptist Standard*.

But as the *Standard* noted, with success would also come problems as the lines between the sacred and the secular blurred to the point of being difficult to discern which was which: "Singer R. Kelly presents other issues for the religious community," the paper noted:

> He recently released a double album and, according to many critics, a double message. The record, titled "Happy People/U Saved Me," is at once a sanguine party album and a penitent spiritual album. In one song called "The Greatest Show on Earth," the singer reportedly has clothes dropping to the floor.

Kelly's lifestyle also has come into question. Child pornography charges against him were recently dropped in Florida after a judge ruled that detectives illegally seized allegedly illicit photographs. He still faces similar charges in Illinois.[8]

While some pop culture observers were surprised by the trend, others were not, arguing that rock may have been overdue for such a makeover in light of the long history of intermingling between pop culture and religion: "Religion and American culture almost dance with each other," observed Philip Goff, director of the Center for the Study of Religion and American Culture. "Culturally, Americans are very comfortable having their pop culture served with a side of religion."[9]

Indeed, in America religion had traditionally refused to be contained in churches. But, it could be argued, for most of the twentieth century, religion had not had much of an effect on either politics or popular entertainment. Devout Christians had long considered politics to be a den of iniquity and avoided full participation en masse until a Southern minister, fed up with Supreme Court decisions legalizing abortion and banning school prayer, created the Moral Majority and registered millions of churchgoers, who turned out to vote for a fellow Christian named Ronald Reagan. Pollster Louis Harris, doing his postelection analysis in 1980, had come up with this stunner: without Jerry Falwell and his Moral Majority, Reagan would have lost to President Jimmy Carter by one percentage point.

Believers were on the march.

In the world of popular entertainment, however, devout Christians were a few decades behind their political brethren. Before the battle could be joined and the invasion begun, opposition among Christians toward things like popular music, television, film, and novels would first have to be broken down. To "beat them," the thinking went, they were going to have to "join them" first. As in politics, that opposition to various forms of entertainment and storytelling would largely dissolve as a direct result of a general coarsening of the mainstream media and entertainment culture, as well as a realization that if Christians did not get into media and tell their stories, the stories the culture produced would reflect their values even less.

In the early 1980s, objectionable content in popular music mostly consisted of double entendres, such as Olivia Newton John's mildly suggestive "Let's Get Physical." But within a few years, heavy metal and hip-hop cultures had introduced far more disturbing images of misogyny, degradation, and in a few cases, Satanism. American pop music culture was primed for a backlash that would begin in the cloistered world of contemporary Christian music in the mid-1990s and eventually leak out into the primary, secular culture. By the turn of the century, artists in that often self-contained world were in full revolt, demanding access to the cultural mainstream and doing everything possible to avoid being labeled in a way that would reduce their attempts to influence it. A revolution was under way, but that revolution was often inaccurately measured by the very industry—the Christian music industry—that the artists were seeking to escape from, an industry that was eager to show growth that was not actually taking place in order to stay relevant.

On one episode of the popular quiz show *Jeopardy*, the three contestants were caught off guard by a question that none would guess correctly, and with good reason—the answer was inaccurate: "Which genre of music grew the most last year?" Alex Trebek wanted to know.

"Hip-hop," answered the first contestant to hit the buzzer—a logical answer for those who hadn't been bombarded with press releases from Nashville, the headquarters of the "Christian" and "gospel" music industry. But since *Jeopardy* researchers were not among these, Trebek dutifully responded that it was gospel music, which had supposedly grown by 18 percent in the previous year. It was another example of how misleading statistics, repeated often enough, appeared to become facts and made it into prime time.

The alleged "growth" in so-called gospel music was actually not growth at all. Rather, the Christian music business was reporting a vastly exaggerated growth by expanding the definition of gospel music to include sales of music that was either not considered "gospel" by the musicians who created it or wasn't released on a "gospel" label, and in some cases didn't even have lyrics.

For years gospel music sales were measured by sales of artists who were signed to CCM labels—the big ones being Word, Provident, and Sparrow. These sales had traditionally been reported as sales of "gospel" or "Christian music." But the Christian Music Trade Association happened upon a brilliant way to pad those numbers when the traditional CCM labels began to function as the distribution agents for certain mainstream titles to Christian-owned bookstores which at the time constituted the CBA or Christian Booksellers Association. Thus, those stores started selling product from artists signed to mainstream labels, like Anne Murray, Andy Griffith, Mannheim Steamroller, Lifehouse, the writers of *O Brother, Where Art Thou?*, P.O.D., 12 Stones, Yolanda Adams, Mary Mary and others, and the CMTA (Christian Music Trade Association) decided to label those sales at Christian-owned bookstores as sales of "gospel music."

P.O.D. was the first to decry the categorization of their music as "gospel" simply because they refused to keep their faith out of their music. But the CMTA, in conjunction with Christian SoundScan, the religious arm of the group that registered point of purchase sales of music, took things a step further by counting not just the sales that occurred in CBA stores but all of the mainstream sales of these artists as sales of "Gospel/ Christian music."

Thus, when a band like P.O.D., which was signed directly to Atlantic Records, sold, for example, two million copies in the mainstream rock market and another 100,000 in the Christian-owned bookstore circuit, the Gospel Music Association was able to take credit for 2.1 million "gospel" records sold. Correspondingly, a huge increase in genre would—on paper, anyway—be realized. The same thing occurred for the *O Brother, Where Art Thou?* record and Mannheim Steamroller's Christmas record, among many others.

Dreamworks likely had no idea about the scheme when it subsequently made a deal to allow Sparrow/EMI to distribute Lifehouse's music into the CBA market. Lifehouse, which had also regularly objected to the categorization of its music as "Christian rock" and purposefully avoided signing with CCM labels, stood to help the CMTA show more phantom growth when every single sale of Lifehouse's record *Stanley Climbfall* both in and out of Christendom was used to show more alleged growth in sales of gospel music.

The only problem with the arrangement was that it just

wasn't true. Gospel music, or Christian music, as a genre was not growing—in fact, without the artificial numbers these "crossover" records provided, using straight sales of artists signed directly and only to self-identified CCM labels, it would likely actually have shown a steep decline along with the rest of the music business. What *was* growing was a phenomenon that couldn't be measured or taken credit for by the CMTA or any other trade group: the rise of serious Christians who were going straight to mainstream rock and refusing to stay sequestered in the Christian subculture that their forefathers had neatly constructed and subsequently sought to keep them in.

That the traditional CCM labels were creating pathways into their world for mainstream music that met the standards of their subculture was a good thing. That they sought to use these artists' sales to show phantom growth and present an inaccurate picture to their "secular" owners was not. The trend lines were clear: *Christian rock* was giving way to *Christians in rock*. That in itself was a far cry from CCM's guiding principles, which were forged in a Southern California church called Calvary Chapel, the headquarters of the so-called Jesus movement. The church produced Saturday night concerts that featured up-and-coming "Jesus music" musicians, created a record label called Maranatha! Music, and even had a bustling book and music store where the music could be purchased. Dozens of bands emerged from this movement, with names such as Love Song, Sweet Comfort Band, Mustard Seed Faith, The Way, and Parable.

But if you had asked these artists whether they had started playing music in order to create a separate music industry that would be walled off from the mainstream music business and secular fans, most would have adamantly objected. But with few exceptions, that's exactly what happened. One such artist was Tommy Coomes, leader of one of the most important bands of the era, Love Song.

"The minute the members of Love Song were awakened by the truth of the gospel, we knew we had to make an album to tell our generation," Coomes remembered. "We were artists and songwriters—that was our skill and trade. It was natural to continue in music, but now with new meaning and focus. Maranatha! Music was an upstart label out of our church and did not have the funds to make the kind of album we envisioned, nor did it have the mechanisms to get it out."[10]

If Calvary Chapel wasn't equipped to help artists like Coomes and Love Song fulfill their mission, neither were their mainstream counterparts, who weren't excited about their messages, leaving Coomes and hundreds of other Jesus music–era musicians in a bind: "There was no CCM music industry in 1970. The only kind of gospel music we could find was either southern gospel or black gospel," Coomes recalled. "We instinctively knew that we had to find another path. We spent the first two years doing concerts, writing songs and learning more about the Bible. We did showcases for Columbia and Atlantic records and finally signed a deal with a new label that had funding and distribution with United Artists Records. The mainstream media was hip to spiritual themes and looking for artists who were compelling. The frustrating thing was that they didn't know how to promote the music. It was too close to the culture for religious radio and too gospel for regular radio."[11]

Coomes's predicament was summed up by one of CCM's prophets, Mark Heard: "We were too saved for the sinners, and the saved didn't want us around."[12]

Parable, an early Jesus music favorite led by a talented musician named Chuck Butler, released its debut album in 1977 on Maranatha! with dreams of affecting the wider culture with its members' faith. But Maranatha!—like most other CCM labels—was simply not equipped to take the artists on its label to the world—nor, it could be argued, did it ever *intend to*. Functionally, it was music by the church, for the church. Butler's dreams of affecting the culture with his music in the same way that the Eagles or Led Zeppelin had, died as his band faded from the scene.

Or did they?

Nearly three decades later, his son, Chad Butler, better known as the drummer of a dynamic rock band named Switchfoot, hit the top of the charts with a song called "Meant to Live," which included this line that hinted at the connection between Parable and Switchfoot: "We want more than the wars of our fathers."[13]

What were the "wars" Switchfoot was referring to? The war in Vietnam, or perhaps the war between those who wanted the churched to stay in the church and those who wanted the gospel to be free to travel on life's highways without being held hostage in a single musical genre?

Chad Butler's own contribution to the ongoing debate, perhaps the most succinct quote of the last thirty years, clearly representing those who have argued that rather than forming a separate genre, Christians should focus instead on being present in the musical mainstream with a clear message of faith, was this: "We're Christian by faith, not by genre," a phrase repeated later by Switchfoot bassist Tim Foreman.[14]

Over the last three decades, others had attempted to say the same thing, but the words never rolled off the tongues of the artists who said them as smoothly as they did from Butler's and Foreman's. From B. J. Thomas's tortured attempts to say that he was an entertainer who happened to be a Christian and not a Christian entertainer, to Creed's lead singer's denial that he was in a "Christian band" even as they filled their songs with tributes to the only Deity who had ever claimed that His yoke was easy and His burden light, to U2 members' endless attempts to explain what they *didn't* believe instead of what they *did*, and Evanescence's plea to be removed from Christian-owned bookstores, artist after artist failed to hit the right note in their attempts to be *in the world but not of it.*

And then came Switchfoot.

Originally signed to musician Charlie Peacock's label, Re:think, the band was clearly disappointed when Re:think folded into the CCM label Sparrow Records. The band with the big vision decided it had to start all over again with a new mainstream label, Columbia, and a separate agreement with their old home, Sparrow (now EMICMG), that would essentially make them a band with two separate label homes—just the kind of arrangement many had argued was necessary to effectively function in both the secular and sacred worlds. And very quickly Switchfoot's album *The Beautiful Letdown* made history.

But timing is everything, and Switchfoot was ready to make their splash when the times were ready to meet them. There is little disagreement that for years mainstream music was not very hospitable to those musicians who wanted to sing about orthodox religious or spiritual ideas. But by the turn of the century, as numerous bands, such as Stryper, King's X, Jars of Clay, and others, each took their shots at chipping away at the wall that had mostly kept God and his followers out of rock music, that wall seemed to be collapsing. The phenomenal mainstream success of songs such as "Place in This World," (Michael W. Smith), "The Christmas Shoes" (NewSong), "Butterfly Kisses" (Bob Carlisle), and others showed that what had been dreamed of by the early Jesus music musicians was indeed possible. By the time Switchfoot released *The Beautiful Letdown*, the mainstream music business was open, as never before, to a band with a clear spiritual vision that knew how to express it with care. For at least three decades, what Switchfoot had managed to pull off had seemed to elude so many other artists. What had changed? Plenty, it seemed, beginning with a change in the way people of faith viewed themselves. For decades, Christians had all too often circulated stories among themselves showing how difficult it was to make an impact in the cultural mainstream, and over time it had become a self-fulfilling prophecy.

"Certain spiritual concepts can't cross over," said the late Dana Key, founder of DeGarmo & Key, one of Christian rock's seminal bands, and Ardent Records, a small, independent label. "Talk about God, talk about love—no problem. Talk about Jesus, his death, sin . . . those concepts are very offensive. The cross is still a stumbling block. The mainstream rejects music that is straightforward Christian."[15]

The problem was that such declarations assumed a static situation—and didn't take into account the X factor—that as more and more avowed Christians got involved in the mainstream culture at every level, their very presence in the corridors of media power would forge a path for themes that would have once been anathema. They also often had the effect of frightening away those who sought mainstream impact. As more and more young Christians came to believe such statements, they were discouraged from entering occupations where their influence could be felt—radio programmers, DJs, music critics, music executives—and where they could actually play a role in ensuring that such themes made it to the mainstream.

Artist and author Charlie Peacock, in his book *At the Crossroads*,[16] praised the efforts of the Calvary Chapel movement to embrace hippies and other "Jesus rock" artists, but also detailed the negative effects of the group's philosophy, which too often had resulted in cultural withdrawal. Although Calvary Chapel was by no means the only Christian denomination that was convinced that Christ's return would take place within a matter of months at any given time in the 1970s, the notion of the imminent return of Jesus Christ to rapture His church didn't exactly create an environment in which young Christians were encouraged to go into culture-shaping careers in broadcasting, journalism, film, the music business, or other industries where their impact would be felt not within *months*, but in *decades*.

In addition to a rapture theology that frowned on higher education and careers that would require planning and forethought since Christ's return to rapture or evacuate true believers to heaven was imminent, the theology of the 1970s all too often encouraged separatism from the world, which was not conducive to large masses of believers entering mainstream venues from which to affect the larger culture. Thus, when rock stars converted to Christianity, they were often encouraged to leave their careers at mainstream record companies and record for CCM labels.

"We had just left Egypt, and we didn't want to go back," remembered Mike MacIntosh, one of the leaders of the

Maranatha! Music label, the music arm of the Calvary Chapel movement.[17] A prime example of this was when Leon Patillo, the lead singer of Santana, left the group and began recording solo albums for Maranatha! However, not all artists followed that model. Two notable exceptions were artists who were under the tutelage of a pastor/teacher named Al Kasha. Kasha, a former CBS Music executive who had helped launch Bob Dylan's career, mentored artists such as Donna Summer and Dylan, both of whom experienced Christian conversions and yet stayed at their respective record labels instead of jumping ship to CCM.

The theological underpinnings of Kasha's quiet movement have also imbued many artists of faith who have sought to keep a presence in the mainstream music scene. While it's clearly not a theology that rejects the notion that Christ's return *may* indeed by imminent, it reflects German theologian Martin Luther's view, expressed when he was asked what he would do if he knew Christ would be returning that very day. "Plant a tree," Luther is said to have remarked, indicating that he lived his life as if Christ could return at any moment, yet would continue to invest in the future.[18] That theology has played itself out in the tendencies of the current crop of artists, who don't feel as if every song has to be evangelistic or present the entire gospel in a few minutes, instead allowing songs to reflect their faith in varying degrees.

The theology of separation that created the CCM business has also been modified by many artists who seem to have rejected the notion that physical separation from the world inevitably leads to holiness. Rather, a theology of spiritual separation without physical separation has taken hold, which allowed artists such as Jars of Clay to tour with mainstream artists, or P.O.D., led by its front man Sonny Sandoval, to appear regularly on MTV or *The Howard Stern Show.*

An unfailingly humble young man sporting dreadlocks and covered in tattoos, Sandoval was the star of not one but two of the most unforgettable confrontational moments in American pop culture between devout Christian rockers and their jaded critics. When Sandoval visited the atheist Bill Maher's talk show, *Politically Incorrect,* Maher characteristically wasted no time asking Sandoval how he could believe in a God who would allow cancer to exist. Without batting an eye, Sandoval responded that he was brought to faith in God precisely through his mother's death from cancer. Maher, dumbfounded, quickly broke away to a commercial.

Sandoval had a similar impact on shock jock Howard Stern when the band appeared on his radio show. Determined to get to the bottom of why the band wouldn't sleep with its female fans, Stern was met with Sandoval's quiet but firm contention that he and his bandmates wanted to be faithful to their wives back home. A befuddled Stern was left to ponder aloud: "You actually respect the chicks in your audience and you will not have sex with them and just do them . . . Well, that's unusual, that's a new point of view I gotta tell you . . . I respect you if you can do that."[19]

For some, like MercyMe singer Bart Millard, the change in attitude came about after interacting with non-Christians, including a DJ named Big Gay Steven:

"I'll tell you what God is teaching me, I'm totally changing my perspective," he told an interviewer. "I was one of those guys that if you weren't a Christian or you weren't in the church, I didn't have anything to do with you. Not that I was being rude, but I just didn't know how to interact. I'm just a worship leader. Steven is one of the first experiences like this I ever had, and the funny thing is, he's the kind of person that you're really drawn to his personality. He's just an all-around great person. And I tell him—I tell Big Gay Steven—that he's 'a Christian waiting to happen.' I tell him that all the time."[20]

Another factor that cannot be overlooked is a greater openness to Christian ideas on the part of many mainstream media gatekeepers, in part a direct result of Christians rejecting the subculture and joining mainstream institutions where they can effect change and have become cultural gatekeepers themselves.

Michael W. Smith's top-five smash hit song "Place in This World," for instance, came about because a young Christian named Claire Parr (nee West) happened to be working in radio promotions at Geffen Records and insisted on working the single to pop radio on her off hours. Other Christians have gone to work at MTV, VH1, *Entertainment Weekly*, the *Chicago Tribune*, and dozens of other mainstream institutions, and have paved the way for more accessibility for these artists through their mere presence. It's also the case that as more and more Christians tune in to mainstream entertainment media, their voices are increasingly heard and sometimes result in shaping the content. MercyMe's hit song "I Can Only Imagine," for example, experienced strong success initially when a Dallas pop station began playing it and many listeners—including Christians—began to request the song. The chicken-and-egg phenomenon continues: the more believers participate in the cultural mainstream by requesting Christian songs on pop radio, complaining about Janet Jackson's Super Bowl incident, or going to work for a mainstream company, the more the wider culture begins to recognize Christians' views. But it's also undeniable that world events and the general flow of popular culture have left more people open to hearing more direct spiritual messages.

"I think the rules changed after 9/11," said Millard. "Because before then, this wouldn't have really been an issue, but now a lot of people are scrambling for any kind of answers after that. Our certainty became uncertain. I really think we're now playing by a whole different set of rules as ministers, and I think it weighs heavily in our favor in regards to being able to share the Gospel and people being open to it. As Christians, we have these preconceived notions that if we try to share Christ, we'll get dogged for it. There are those people out there. There's a lot of people that don't want to hear it, but there's a lot of people who just haven't heard."[21]

It also appears that the rock music establishment of yesteryear, which was often plainly hostile to music made by Christians, is giving way to a more tolerant younger generation that is far more open to giving Christian ideas the time of day—so long as the music is compelling. That generational shift became apparent when *Rolling Stone*, a legend of the old guard of rock music criticism, refused to run an advertisement for a modern translation of the Bible in its magazine, though it violated no guidelines. *Blender*, on the other hand, representing a new and more tolerant generation of the music business, readily agreed to run the ad. The old guard of rock, schooled in the fires of battles between the church and rock music, was giving way to a new group of rock executives, journalists, and radio programmers who, though not necessarily supportive of the effort to blend Christian ideas into the mainstream music industry, at least weren't as openly hostile as their forbears. All of this has made the efforts of young artists and executives who love God and want the world to hear their music infinitely easier.

Still, despite the strides made toward integrating artists of faith into the fabric of American popular culture, popular culture was littered with the bones of those artists who had never gotten a fair hearing because of the faith they espoused, the subculture their side created, *and* the intolerance of a secular culture that didn't want them ruining their party.

Andraé Crouch, known as a gospel legend, but whose music was actually more along the lines of R & B, began recording for Light Records in the early 1970s. Though one of his earliest records was titled *Take the Message Everywhere*, his music rarely made it beyond the CCM world. And though he had a song called "Satisfied," an answer to the Rolling Stones' song "(I Can't Get No) Satisfaction," it was likely never heard by a mainstream music fan. Dana Key wrote a stunning response to Eric Clapton's tearjerker "Tears in Heaven," called "Dear Mr. Clapton," that also went mostly unheard. If a great song was written and recorded but essentially went unnoticed by the watching world, would it matter? That was the question that haunted a generation of God-rockers and the executives who seemed unable or unwilling, in the words of the originator of the Prayer of Jabez, to "enlarge their territory."

When Dan Haseltine of Jars of Clay sang "I wanna love the world but I don't know how" in the pounding rock song "Revolution,"[22] it was a challenge to executives in the Christian music business to change the way they did business—to create and forge new pathways for artists like Jars into the musical mainstream, to keep making strong music with lyrics that spoke about faith in Christ but create avenues for the average American non-Christian listener to comfortably access their music. And many executives had clearly begun to rethink the traditional models.

Not insignificantly, the Gospel Music Association, then led by John Styll, made an important change in the group's mission statement, changing the traditional goal of promoting gospel music to a new goal of promoting the gospel *in* music, whatever genre that might be. Although late to the party, some in the Christian music establishment at least understood the change that was happening. Despite its critics, it was undeniable that CCM had done some important things—its very existence helped to galvanize and organize a group of artists and fans who may not otherwise have found one another, and helped dozens of artists hone their craft and prepare to affect the wider culture:

> "Some good things have happened along the way," noted LoveSong's [Tommy] Coomes. "Michael Omartian, Seawind, Amy Grant, Michael W. Smith, Steve Taylor, Steven Curtis Chapman, Steve Green, Dann Huff and Tommy Sims paved a path. Many more opportunities are available today because of artists who've followed their hearts. I rejoice at the success of MercyMe, Kirk Franklin, Mary Mary, Switchfoot and Jars of Clay. They're courageous and confident and have made great records that have connected with millions of listeners. Those who are culturally relevant may always be suspect to some folks, but who did Jesus hang out with? Does the church have to be 30 years behind to feel safe?"[23]

The movement of Christians into the cultural mainstream has been slow and steady, with many fitful starts and stops, but with its multipronged approach it is strongly impacting the music scene, which is today home to hundreds of artists who are having an impact on the wider culture and the wider world. But these artists stand on the shoulders of their forefathers—literally in some cases, as in the Butler family—a generation of artists whose purpose in creating Jesus music was to have that music heard by a generation of fellow unbelievers, in the hope that their music would provide hope and transformation. And today, older and wiser, they have advice to give to their musical offspring:

"We pretty much abandoned Hollywood," John Fischer, an early Jesus music artist and former *CCM* columnist recently noted. He continued:

> That's where putting all of our talent and time and money and energy into a Christian media, and a Christian version of Hollywood, is, I think, a detriment to our wider witness in the world. It's creating a catch-22 kind of thing. Christians have left the positions of influence, in places that really create a cultural understanding, a cultural impact. We've left those influential places, and then we sit over in our safe zone and complain about how bad the world is becoming. That's the catch-22: it is bad, but why shouldn't it be when there aren't Christians there to influence it from the inside? But I think that if Christians had stayed in places of influence, there might be more realistic Christian characters and worldviews out there.[24]

"It seems like we need to rethink many things," added Tommy Coomes, who recently started a nonprofit company to mentor artists, called Music Compass. "It's time to ask the five *W* questions: who, what, where, when and why? We've accomplished a lot over the last thirty-five years, but, as my friend

Reggie McNeal says in his book *The Present Future* [Jossey-Bass, 2009], we need to get outside the bubble.

"My two sons, Tyler and Erick, find no meaningful place of service in what we call CCM," he went on. "They have no interest in preaching to the choir—they want to communicate to their generation in the language that they speak. They believe that their place is in the rap, hip-hop, and R & B world. They have recorded and toured with soul singer Anthony Hamilton, played on the new Daniel Bedingfield CD, Chingy records, and lots more cool stuff. I dig it. I'm proud of them. They're making hit records and trying to be the salt and light. They're good at it."[25]

Many other artists appear to be doing just the same. And like Moses, who never made it to the promised land but was at least given a glimpse of Canaan, the land that had been promised to his people, from a distance, today these Jesus music–era artists can look on with satisfaction as their children and children's children take their music and their beliefs to all, for all to hear.

2

GOD'S IDOLS

he long-held philosophy of cultural separatism that had once kept Christians from the mainstream of American pop culture life was rapidly fading, and nowhere was that more apparent than in the world of the *American Idol* television series, which created numerous superstars, such as Carrie Underwood, Daughtry, Jordin Sparks, Ruben Studdard, Fantasia, Kris Allen, Clay Aiken, RJ Helton, Diana DeGarmo, and many other winners who were vocal about their Christian faith. But had the governing philosophy that created the Christian music industry still been in place, the result would likely have been the creation of a separatist Christian *American Idol* contest, walled off from the main show and likely featuring Christian artists facing off against one another, performing gospel songs.

Diana DeGarmo's second-place finish in particular was of symbolic import because her uncle was the legendary '70s CCM pioneer Eddie DeGarmo, who had been a fierce champion of cultural separation and had at times encouraged young rock bands not to cross over and record for a mainstream audience. His sixteen-year-old niece, on the other hand, had pointedly skipped the Christian music circuit where her uncle worked as a label vice president, and gone straight to *American Idol* instead. But there were other challenges for Christian performers who aspired to make it to the top of the heap on *Idol,* for outside the safe and comfortable walls of friendly Christian music executives, they would face pressures to change their music and please their musical mentors. In the case of Clay Aiken, for example, that meant having to listen to legendary music mogul Clive Davis, who had signed the likes of Janis Joplin, Billy Joel, Whitney Houston, and others. But when it came to the intersection of God and rock 'n' roll, most notable was the artist Davis *hadn't* signed: a singer named Keith Green, who is to the CCM community what John Lennon is to mainstream music: a legend who died too young. Green was a child prodigy who had become a born-again Christian intent on taking his message to the "secular" world he had once been a part of. Although he was flown to New York for a meeting with Davis, Green's hopes were dashed by an executive who likely couldn't fathom what Green was trying to do.

"Clive Davis . . . kept me waiting for almost two hours," Green wrote in his journal. "It was a failure, but I took it so well I couldn't believe it . . . [I] kept telling myself that the

Lord wanted me to do a Christian album. It depressed me, but I kept my chin up."[1]

Passed over by Davis, Green was picked up by Davis's Christian world counterpart, a canny record executive named Billy Ray Hearn, who quickly signed Green to make "Christian" records, which he intended to market exclusively to fellow Christians. Three decades later, Davis would face a new crop of Christians, but this time he wouldn't be able to keep them down since they were winners of a contest that he couldn't control. *American Idol* had circumvented the process of rock stars being picked by a handful of typically secular executives, and stars were now being picked by the American people themselves.

Davis was there to sign *American Idol* winners to his label, yet despite his weakened position, he still appeared to have definite ideas about the direction artists like Aiken should take. Recounting conversations with Davis, Aiken gave fans a peek into the kinds of pressures that are put on artists who want to bring their beliefs into a mainstream setting: "Clive tried to tell me that saying certain words in a song—or as he says, 'putting some balls into it'—isn't bad, it's just strong emotion," Aiken recalled to *Star Magazine*. "Well there are certain words and emotions I don't want kids hearing, and I'm not changing because they think it's going to sell better."[2]

Behind his innocence and boy-next-door demeanor lay a sharp and strategic thinker who knew when to pick fights over important things and when to go with the flow: "I try not to get upset about all this marketing stuff because I'm saving it for the time that they tell me that I need to do a song about 'Let's hook up and have sex.' But I'm like, 'Do not—ugh!—don't pretend that the public are a bunch of idiots!'" said Aiken. "'Don't pretend that you know what they want and they don't know what they want.' That's the stupidest thing I've ever heard of in my life!"[3]

CNN noted Aiken's successful pushback: "Aiken's had a couple of victories," the network noted. "He refused to go along with one concept for the 'This Is the Night' video, and it was his idea to call the album 'Measure of a Man,' though Davis hated the title."[4]

Aiken had given outsiders an inside look into the process by which innocent wannabe pop stars were sometimes turned into the musical equivalent of sexual predators. Some suspected that it was likely a similar process of industry peer pressure that had transformed Janet Jackson in the space of a few years from a sweet teenager arguing for virtue to a lusty lounge singer begging for sex. In the late '80s, in her hit song "Let's Wait Awhile," Jackson had sung confidently about her desire to save herself for marriage. Seven years later, the wait was over, and Jackson, either by virtue of her own personal evolution or, more likely, by the kind of pressure from music industry insiders Aiken had faced, was getting down and dirty with the song "That's the Way Love Goes."

The fact that professing Christians like Aiken bothered to show up at the *American Idol* tryouts was because clever Christian marketers hadn't yet gotten around to creating their own "Christianized" version of *American Idol*, which would then have likely drawn these talented artists away from *American Idol* and ushered them into the Christian format. But it wasn't for lack of trying. In 2004 came the announcement that a Christianized competition to *Idol* would soon go live, with the likely effect that any future DeGarmos and Aikens with a talent to sing and a professed Christian faith would, given the choice, sign up to compete on the easier-to-win and more comfortable Christian show. Thus, future *American Idol* winners would not be drawn from a pool of artists that would include people of devout faith.

"*Gifted*, a Christian version of the popular *American Idol* TV show, is scheduled to debut in October [2004] on Trinity Broadcasting Network, the Costa Mesa, CA–based conglomerate that features such well-known evangelists as Benny Hinn," noted Yahoo! News in a story on the venture. "The Orlando-based Wright Entertainment Group is part of a joint venture with Matt Crouch, son of the founders of Trinity Broadcasting Network, to create the talent search show, Wright spokesman Philip McIntyre said. McIntyre said the joint venture, called Wright Generation, is negotiating with a private investor to finance the project."[5]

According to news reports, the group planned to tour Trinity Network stations, where auditions would be conducted, and the results would later be aired on the network. The winners were to be managed by Wright and Crouch, the Christian versions of Simon Cowell. And thus, once again, just at a moment when mainstream popular music had been infused with talented artists of faith who had put their talent to work in a mainstream venue, short-sighted religious businessmen who drew more inspiration from Madison Avenue niche marketing than from the Great Commission, which emphasized taking the Christian message everywhere, were sentencing artists of faith to cultural obscurity.

In addition to the savvy religious businessmen, it was likely that there would be others who would be thrilled when the future stars of *American Idol* failed to show up for the tryouts because they were too busy competing in the subpar Christian version. Executives who wanted to sex up their artists' music would likely face little opposition from future, more secular winners, and mainstream media outlets wouldn't have to put up with artists like Aiken who spoke publicly about his status as a virgin. (Aiken would later come out as gay.)

By 2009 the impact of *American Idol* on the Christianization of American pop music was crystal clear, even to the most casual observer, when it produced a showdown between two artists, Kris Allen and Adam Lambert. Allen, it turns out, was a "worship leader" at his church, which in non-evangeli-speak roughly translates to "guy who leads the singing," while Adam Lambert was the contestant who had seen photographs of himself kissing men splashed across the Internet. Although Lambert didn't exactly confirm his sexual orientation at the time, it was widely seen as the showdown between the gay guy and the Christian guy, with a judgment to be rendered by middle America. Apparently it took the Allen-Lambert showdown for media outlets such as *Newsweek* to figure out what had been happening all along with *American Idol*—the return of people of faith into the mainstream of American popular music, both as voters and performers.

"Most of [Lambert's] groupies have overlooked a possible roadblock to the title," the publication observed. "*Idol* is the No. 1 show on TV at least in part because it's so family-friendly, and it also appeals to a large demographic of Christian viewers. . . . Many of *Idol*'s previous winners—Jordin Sparks, Carrie Underwood, Ruben Studdard—are devout Christians. Coincidence? Perhaps. But we don't know much about Lambert's faith, and that might hurt him with Christian voters. He could be extremely religious, but he's kept his religious beliefs quiet."[6]

The votes of millions of average Americans put Allen over the top, and he went on to secure a recording contract and sell millions of records while Lambert, who would easily have been the choice in a pre-*Idol* world, in which rock stars were picked by the likes of Davis and David Geffen, finished in second place. It was quickly becoming obvious to even the most casual observer that *American Idol* had become the conduit for dozens—perhaps hundreds—of Christian-oriented artists, including Carrie Underwood and Chris Daughtry, to reach the heights of fame by serving as a sort of farm team. This resulted in young Christians from around America being able to directly access the big leagues of pop culture, bypassing the gatekeepers and short-circuiting the system that had reigned for half a century, where secular white males from the coasts picked America's pop stars. One of the founders of the Christian rock industry, Billy Ray Hearn, who had taken the sincere desires of young and devout artists to bring their beliefs and their music to the mainstream and effectively silenced them by marketing to fellow believers, once remarked, "I didn't want to be a part of the world and I got out."[7] He had gotten his wish and dragged with him a generation of talented but stifled artists who would have little meaningful impact on the mainstream music world. But *American Idol* was changing the equation and giving these artists a shot at taking their music and their message to the world.

3

RELATIONSHIP STATUS:
IT'S COMPLICATED

THE PREACHER'S DAUGHTER

"I hate the song. It clearly promotes homosexuality and its message is shameful and disgusting.

"Katy knows how I feel. We are a very outspoken family and she knows how disappointed her father and I are. I can't even listen to that song. The first time I heard it I was in total shock. When it comes on the radio I bow my head and pray."[1]

That was the reaction of Mary Hudson, mother of one of the biggest pop stars of the twenty-first century, Katy Perry, who skyrocketed to stardom on the strength of her debut smash hit song "I Kissed a Girl." While most parents of nascent pop stars might be thrilled at such success, the rise of Perry—and her parents' reaction—added another wrinkle to the tug-of-war between religion and pop music. Many Christians spoke with pride about the cultural prominence achieved by artists such as Switchfoot or any number of Christian *American Idol* winners, but some performers, like Katy Perry, were met with consternation and bewilderment. One needed to look no further than Perry's own mother to hear the angst:

> Katy is our daughter and we love her but we strongly disagree with how she is conducting herself at the moment.
>
> We cannot cut her out of our lives as she is our child, but she knows we disagree strongly with what she is doing and the message she is promoting regarding homosexuality, which the Bible clearly states is a sin.
>
> But the Bible also promotes understanding and forgiveness, which I keep reminding myself.
>
> Katy is not a homosexual but I fear she has been led astray by the Hollywood crowd. I pray all the time that God will work through her and help her find salvation.[2]

Not only was Perry raised in a devoutly Christian household by parents who were both ministers and evangelists, but she first signed to a Christian-run music label as a teenager and released a minor hit album under her given name, Katy Hudson. As she entered the pop world, things began to change rapidly, prompting her mother to unleash a torrent of cautionary comments to reporters:

> Katy was raised in a very strict Christian household. She started performing in church at nine. She was a special child;

she loved to sing and had an angelic voice. That is why this is all so disappointing and sad.

I think she acts and says certain things to be provocative and to shock. . . .

Katy was spotted by a music producer who invited her to LA. That's when she started to change. . . .

I was worried she'd start doing drugs and drinking alcohol. I still am. I spoke to her only recently. She said, "Oh Mom, I'm not going to turn into Amy Winehouse.". . . .

Like any child she is going through a period of rebellion.[3]

But the case of the wayward Perry and her freaked-out Christian parents represented something far larger than the typical parent-child angst experienced by millions of families around the world. It spoke to the larger issues and challenges that would inevitably arise when devout American Christians attempted to reintegrate into the mainstream culture—a process that would inevitably lead to fireworks and confusion, both in the Christian subculture and in the mainstream world. An article at MTV.com noted that "Katy Perry is quite the conundrum. While she likes to pose in lingerie, like she did for her upcoming cover for *Rolling Stone*, she is also quite vocal about her religious upbringing. In fact, she's even tweeted about other pop stars using religion as part of their acts."[4]

"I am sensitive to Russell taking the Lord's name in vain and to Lady Gaga putting a rosary in her mouth," she said in the August 19, 2010, issue of *Rolling Stone*. "I think when you put sex and spirituality in the same bottle and shake it up, bad things happen."[5]

"Russell" referred to another source of confusion, which

Perry herself helped to perpetuate when she married British comedian Russell Brand in a Hindu wedding ceremony in India. Brand, a notorious womanizer whom Perry claimed was "basically a 'professional prostitute'" before he allegedly embraced Perry (and monogamy), was miles away from the strict Christian upbringing Perry hadn't completely walked away from. In fact, in her interactions with Brand, it became clear that Perry still retained elements of that upbringing, even as she challenged it and made decisions that upset her parents. Perry the wayward daughter was now playing the role of scolding parent to Brand, and she jumped into it with relish:

> He was a heroin addict and now he's not. He was addicted to all kinds of things and now he's not. And he basically used to be a professional prostitute and now he's not . . .
>
> So he's an extremist, which can be both good and bad.
>
> I always needed someone stronger than me and I am, like, a f****** strong elephant of a woman.
>
> I say that hopefully in the humblest way I can. When we have an argument he knows I'm not just gonna throw my hands up and say, "okay, you win.
>
> Let's get into it. Let's start debating. Let's wrestle, Russell.[6]

Perry's confusing mix and match of traditionalism with modernism extended to her views on pop culture and its penchant for mixing the sacred with the profane, something that caused Perry to take aim at fellow pop star Lady Gaga, who followed Madonna's well-worn path of intermingling the two. MTV noted:

> This isn't the first time that Perry has taken a stab at Lady Gaga. After the premiere in June of Gaga's "Alejandro" video,

which features the singer seemingly swallowing a rosary whole, Perry tweeted, "Using blasphemy as entertainment is as cheap as a comedian telling a fart joke." . . . For those who are raising an eyebrow at Perry, a pop star who has participated in her share of provocative photo shoots and videos— her "California Gurls" wardrobe includes a whipped-cream cone bra—she fired back a few words in response, telling *Rolling Stone*, "Yes, I said I kissed a girl. But I didn't say I kissed a girl while f---ing a crucifix."[7]

Rock 'n' roll and religion had too often been mortal enemies, and Katy Perry's experience pointed clearly to the perils of mixing the two, for her tortured soul still seemed to be rooted in the strict upbringing that the singer often dished about: "I wasn't ever able to say I was 'lucky' because my mother would rather us say that we were 'blessed,' and she also didn't like that 'lucky' sounded like 'Lucifer,'" Perry once told an interviewer. "Deviled eggs were called 'angeled' eggs. I wasn't allowed to eat Lucky Charms, but I think that was the sugar. . . . I think my mom lied to me about that one."[8]

Perry, who claimed to have a tattoo of Jesus on her wrist, also described her parents' fondness for speaking in a heavenly language, a common occurrence in Pentecostal Christian circles: "Speaking in tongues is as normal to me as 'Pass the salt.' . . . It's a secret, direct prayer language to God."[9]

Perry's debut album produced three hit singles, including the ubiquitous "I Kissed a Girl," but her third album *Teenage Dream*, would prove that she had the staying power to become a true pop sensation. The album produced a record-smashing *five* number one singles and put Perry in the pop pantheon of artists such as Michael Jackson, Mariah Carey, and others. Yet even as her career blossomed, problems at home would continue to trip up the singer—in 2011, it was revealed that her mother was shopping a book proposal that would once again create headlines. *Page Six* magazine noted:

> Katy Perry's "Teenage Dream" is a middle-aged nightmare for her evangelistic mom—who complains in a book proposal that, "no mother wants to see the top of her daughter's boobs." . . . In the full proposal, she describes her horror at Katy's outfits: Backstage at a concert, "Katy stepped out from behind the changing doors in a tiny risqué costume. No mother wants to see the top of her daughter's boobs . . . my first instinct was to order her back behind those doors and demand she put something else on . . . however, I had no problem letting my eyebrows say what I wouldn't allow my mouth to utter."[10]

If Hudson's book *were* ever written, it would surely be a warning shot directed at many modern Christian parents whose parenting skills would also be severely challenged by children like Katy Perry, who seemed to be attempting the impossible: mixing the religious upbringing she had received from her parents with the sensibilities of the modern world. In her proposal, Hudson openly worried about the effects of that modern world on her daughter:

> "Oh, dear God, how can I save her from all this? The money, the fame, the network, the people surrounding her, how can I compete? . . .

"I recognized the psalmist gift in her performance. Yet she sang out, 'I kissed a girl, and I liked it,' while thousands joined her. One part of my heart soared . . . the other part broke for the thousands of hungry souls being fed something that didn't nourish their spirit, but fed their flesh."[11]

At times the couple appeared to be nearly distraught over their inability to keep their daughter on the straight and narrow. During a church service outside of London, Keith Hudson said:

I understand the burden of having a daughter or son that is not serving God. When my daughter came out and sang that song, "I kissed a girl, and I liked it." I said, "my ministry is over."

We get people all the time saying, "How? How, that you're a minister all these years and you raised Katy in the church, how could she come out with a song like that?" I look at them and I say, "I don't know." . . .

We must pray for our family. We all have our crosses to bear. If you have a son or a daughter that is not serving God, just stand up right now. Don't be embarrassed. Don't be ashamed. Listen, we love them. I love Katy. I want everybody to go to heaven, but I want my family most of all. What would heaven be without them? It won't be the same.[12]

At a different church he stated, "I love my daughter and I will always love her. Stop being judgmental and critical. Do not close the doors to your loved ones, especially your children . . .

"Just because they do not like what you do or what you are, they are still praying that you stay in the race. They are counting on you. I believe in God, for every one of my children."[13]

Hudson and his wife have tried to stay positive, believing

that God would use their daughter's celebrity to bring ultimate good. "God has given us a platform to go in and meet people—and they like us because we are cool," he said.[14]

To a British congregation, Hudson said, "Maybe you're sitting here, you saw in the paper that Katy Perry's parents are coming to church and you wanted to come check it out. Let me tell you everything is divinely ordered. There is no coincidence that you're sitting here today. God brought you here."[15]

In Ohio, Katy's mother told worshippers at Church on the Rise (Westlake), "I'm sure Katy is trending on the internet just to get you to church tonight. . . .

"I mean all over the world, who knows how God is bringing them in? The most important thing is you are here and God wants to put the fire in you.[16]

In early 2012, Perry and Russell Brand were granted a divorce as Perry celebrated the phenomenal success of the sixth single from her album, the pensive "The One That Got Away," a song many regarded as Perry's finest. As she prepared for her next album, Perry warned in characteristic fashion that it would be a departure from the sugary pop songs she had come to be known for: "My music is about to get real f---ing dark."[17]

Part Christian girl defending her Savior, Jesus, from blasphemy, part sex bombshell, part pop tart, Katy Perry personified much of what modern critics of both Christianity and rock music detested about the mixing of the two former enemies. In their eyes, Christianity, a vibrant and transformational faith that was to be countercultural, had been compromised. Rock fans, on the other hand, who were used to their art form being an expression of contempt for the establishment, watched incredulously as Perry defended traditional sexual and religious morés against attacks from elder statesmen of the counterculture. Perhaps leaving both sides dissatisfied was Perry's goal, and if that was the case, she had succeeded.

LOSING HER RELIGION

MTV's Video Music Awards had been known for many years as a forum for artists to push the boundaries of artistic expression. In the '90s, shock jock Howard Stern treated fans to his "Fartman" persona, and in 2003, Madonna and Britney Spears kissed onstage, but nothing could have prepared even the most jaded music fans for what pop star Miley Cyrus had in store for viewers. Although outrage came from the predictable quarters of pop culture, Cyrus had so crossed lines of decency that dozens of fellow entertainers, commentators, and public figures tweeted, Facebooked, Instragrammed, and otherwise noted their disapproval.

"'Disgusting!' 'Raunchy!' 'Desperate!' So went the scathing reviews that poured in after once wholesome Disney star Miley Cyrus' recent bizarre performance at the MTV Video Music Awards," noted feminist commentator Camille Paglia.

"Bopping up and down the catwalk in hair-twist devil's horns and a flesh-colored latex bikini, Cyrus lewdly wagged her tongue, tickled her crotch with a foam finger, shook her buttocks in the air and spanked a 6-ft. 7-in. black burlesque queen," the writer continued. "How could American pop have gotten this bad?"[18]

Paglia, who has no problems with pushing sexual boundaries, is hardly the exemplar of a conservative scold. However, while noting rock 'n' roll's comfortable history with sexual expressions of all kinds, she nonetheless found fault with Cyrus's crude and shockingly *non-sexy* display:

Sex has been a crucial component of the entertainment industry since the seductive vamps of silent film and the bawdy big mamas of roadhouse blues. Elvis Presley, James Brown and Mick Jagger brought sizzling heat to rock, soul and funk music, which in turn spawned the controversial raw explicitness of urban hip-hop.

The Cyrus fiasco, however, is symptomatic of the still heavy influence of Madonna, who sprang to world fame in the 1980s with sophisticated videos that were suffused with a daring European art-film eroticism and that were arguably among the best artworks of the decade. Madonna's provocations were smolderingly sexy because she had a good Catholic girl's keen sense of transgression. Subversion requires limits to violate.[19]

Although Paglia may not have detected any moral sensibility in Cyrus, the pop star *did* in fact have just such a moral compass, once upon a time, and the journey she and her family had traveled—from a down-home Christian lifestyle in Tennessee to a hard-charging life in pagan Hollywood—included some hard lessons for the burgeoning movement of Christians in rock.

Cyrus's great-grandfather was a Pentecostal minister, and her grandfather was a member of the gospel quartet the Crownsmen. Her father, Billy Ray Cyrus, who once ruled country music with his mullet and hit song "Achy Breaky Heart," had returned to his Christian upbringing after his own wild ride to stardom, which included fathering Miley and a son, Cody, out of wedlock, around the same time with different mothers. Cyrus would eventually marry Miley's mother, Tish, and have two more children with her, raising his family far away from Hollywood.

However, an opportunity to star in a David Lynch movie called *Mulholland Drive* opened up new opportunities for Cyrus, bringing him—and his daughter Miley—to Hollywood, where she landed the role of Hannah Montana, and Cyrus was cast as her TV father.

In a painfully revealing interview with *GQ* magazine, Cyrus revealed the tragic road his family had taken:

> "Somewhere along this journey," he says, "both mine and Miley's faith has been shaken. That saddens me the most." When they first came to Hollywood for *Hannah Montana*, the two of them would drive down the freeway together to the studio each morning, and every day Miley would point out the sign that said
>
> ADOPT-A-HIGHWAY
>
> ATHEISTS UNITED
>
> Just before moving out to Los Angeles, the whole family had been baptized together by their pastor at the People's Church in Franklin, Tennessee. "It was Tish's idea," he remembers. "She said, 'We're going to be under attack, and we have to be strong in our faith and we're all going to be baptized . . .'" And there, driving to work each day in the City of Angels, was this sign. "A physical sign. It could have easily said 'You will now be attacked by Satan.' 'Entering this industry, you are now on the highway to darkness . . .'"[20]

GQ's Chris Heath somewhat skeptically questioned Cyrus further, perhaps to gauge whether he was speaking literally or metaphorically. The resulting back-and-forth between the journalist and the country music star would serve as a haunting reminder of the dangers for any devout Christian who sought to be in the entertainment industry:

Do you really see it in such clearly spiritual terms—that your family was under attack by Satan?

"I think we are right now. No doubt. There's no doubt about it."

And why is that happening?

"It's the way it is. There has always been a battle between good and evil. Always will be. You think, 'This is a chance to make family entertainment, bring families together . . .' and look what it's turned into."

Hannah Montana probably has brought a lot of families together—just not one . . .

"Yeah. I know. I know. I know."

And do you see the show as a big part of what has made things not work in your family?

"Oh, it's huge—it destroyed my family. I'll tell you right now—the damn show destroyed my family. And I sit there and go, 'Yeah, you know what? Some gave all.' It is my motto, and guess what? I have to eat that one. I some-gave-all'd it all right. I some-gave-all'd it while everybody else was going to the bank. It's all sad."

Do you wish Hannah Montana had never happened?

"I hate to say it, but yes, I do. Yeah. I'd take it back in a second. For my family to be here and just be everybody okay, safe and sound and happy and normal, would have been fantastic. Heck, yeah. I'd erase it all in a second if I could."[21]

Cyrus's outlook hadn't always been so negative. At the outset of the *Hannah Montana* experience, he had recalled with pride the role he had played in Miley's following him into show business when he brought her in to act on a series he was starring in at the time, called *Doc*.

"You know the old joke, the best way to make God laugh is tell Him your plans? God had something else in store for us," he said. "Not only did Doc's 88 episodes give me a wealth of experience as an actor, Miley did several appearances on the show and [being in Toronto] allowed her to take lessons with some great [acting] coaches. What that did was prepare Miley for her big chance."[22]

That big chance would come soon enough, when Disney auditioned for the Hannah Montana role, although they initially concluded that she was too young. Cyrus recalled:

> But as I read the script, I knew it wasn't going to proceed without Miley. It was just one of those inner voice things you feel inside . . . Six or eight months later, Disney calls back and says, "We'd like to take another look at that Cyrus kid," and she flew back out to California. . . .
>
> When the agent called, I said, "This is Miley's thing . . . I don't want Miley ever to look back and say I got the job, or didn't get the job, because of my dad. So the first decision is, is Miley Hannah Montana? Then we can talk about me later." The day they hired Miley, they called me, and I got on a plane that night. Miley and I did a few scenes together, and they hired me. The rest is history.[23]

A part of that history would be, of course, his daughter's onstage spectacle at the VMAs that would cause conservative

Christians and liberal feminists alike to unite in their disgust. While Miley's rebel pose had been hinted at after her gig with Disney ended, in the early years of *Hannah Montana* she had sounded like hundreds of other young Christians who were determined to take their faith to Hollywood for the purpose of impacting the world: "Faith is a big part of my life. I recently read a book titled *Girl Talk with God* about a teen girl's conversations with God, and I feel that I'm here in Hollywood because of faith and God's will," she once told an interviewer.[24]

"Faith is the main thing," she told another. "That's kind of why I'm like here in Hollywood—to be like a light, a testimony, to say God can take someone from Nashville and make me this, but it's his will that made this happen."[25]

As for her father, he had once told a reporter, "I am at peace with my life—past, present and future. I know all things that are good come from Almighty God above. I count my blessings every single day. Every day I pray God will show me the doors He wants me to walk through, the people He wants me to talk to, the songs He wants me to sing. I want to be the light He wants me to be in this world."[26]

An older and wiser Cyrus would have a completely different take—a warning not only to parents of future pop stars but to the movement of Christians in general who sought to reclaim popular culture with their faith and values. If rock 'n' roll was indeed the devil's music, then he was not likely to cede ground easily, and the destruction of the Cyrus family would provide a clear example yet of the perils along that path:

> The business was driving a wedge between us. How many interviews did I give and say, "You know what's important

between me and Miley is I try to be a friend to my kids"? I said it a lot. And sometimes I would even read [what] other parents might say, "You don't need to be a friend, you need to be a parent." Well, I'm the first guy to say to them right now: You were right. I should have been a better parent. I should have said, "Enough is enough—it's getting dangerous and somebody's going to get hurt." I should have, but I didn't. Honestly, I didn't know the ball was out of bounds until it was way up in the stands somewhere.[27]

As the faithful integrated themselves into the mainstream entertainment industry, the body count of those who couldn't handle the process would increase. Although the final chapter in the Miley-Cyrus-goes-to-Hollywood story hadn't yet been written, it already had much in common with a '70s rock star, Mylon Lefevre, who simply found the pressure impossible to deal with and had dropped out of rock 'n' roll altogether. His words would be a warning to all the up-and-coming God-rockers that what they were attempting to do was nearly impossible without a special dispensation of grace from above, and that, perhaps, some of them weren't equipped for—and therefore shouldn't attempt—a life of faith in the pop music culture. Lefevre, who, like Cyrus, was raised in a Christian home before going on to write hit songs for Elvis, observed:

> We were a rock 'n' roll band who believed that Jesus was the son of God. We didn't know the Word very well; we prayed before we went on stage, but we also smoked marijuana. Naturally it was just a matter of time until the Gospel was taken over by the rock 'n' roll. I got away from my family and I got away from the church. If anybody had come backstage and

talked to me he would have decided that he didn't want any part of the life I was leading. I could not live for Jesus and be around rock 'n' roll. I didn't have the faith or guts to do that.[28]

THE SIMPSONS

In 1999, when singer Jessica Simpson burst onto the pop music scene, providing new competition for superstars such as Britney Spears and Christina Aguilera, few knew just how much of a splash the singer would make later on through her MTV reality series. But the Simpson family was more than just Jessica. Her success was quickly followed by the debut album of her younger sister, Ashlee, and both careers were engineered and managed by their father, Joe Simpson, a Baptist minister from Texas who suspended his work in the ministry to manage their careers. But the manner in which he guided his daughters, and some of their own choices, would cause some to wonder whether Simpson and his charges had left their Christian values behind in Texas in search of the big time. In a profile of the Simpsons, *ABC News* noted:

> Joe Simpson has made his daughters, Jessica and Ashlee Simpson, [into] two of today's hottest pop superstars. But to do that, he had to dress Jessica in skimpy clothes and turn her marriage into a reality television show. The irony to some people is that he is a Baptist minister. Did he betray the values that he preached? And are his daughters paying a price for living in the spotlight? . . . By opening his daughters' private lives to public scrutiny, even the difficult or awkward moments most parents would zealously protect, the former Baptist minister has redefined how you sell records. And in

just a few years Simpson has transformed Jessica and Ashlee into two of the biggest stars in pop music.[29]

When ABC asked the sisters how much of their success could be attributed to their father's management, Jessica responded, "My dad is 90 percent of the success of my career." Ashlee added, "I'm one of those people that like to take control of things. So I would say 60 percent, 50 percent."[30]

Joe Simpson had first tried his hand at getting his elder daughter, Jessica, signed in the world of Christian music, but according to him had run into a roadblock of sorts: his daughter's chest, which he claimed made her a tough sell to distracted label heads who thought potential fans might also be distracted: "Her chest is ahead of her by 2 or 3 feet so, you know, it gets there before she does," Simpson said of his own daughter.[31]

Jessica did independently record a Christian-themed CD, complete with songs that featured Bible verses in the j-card, but she soon came to the attention of executives at Sony and a pop career was quickly conceived and launched.

"Simpson quit his job at the church in Texas and moved the family out to Los Angeles," observed ABC. "By this time, Jessica's sex appeal was no longer a distraction but part of the marketing and the former pastor was accused of making a deal with the devil in the city of angels."[32]

Jessica Simpson, the innocent wannabe gospel singer, was quickly transformed into a sexy ingénue, and many blamed Joe: "I was accused, [because of] my background in the ministry, you know 'your daughter doesn't love God anymore,' 'you've forsaken the church' and I'm like, 'you don't even know me or know my family,'" he responded.

"Part of this is a learning process," he added. "Early on when we started, we weren't equipped with how to say no."[33]

At least one industry veteran didn't buy Simpson's explanation: "He'll come back and tell you things have been a mistake, but I think he would still have done them, regardless," noted *Billboard* magazine's executive editor, Tamara Coniff.

"Sex sells," she went on to say. "It might not be the best in terms of putting on the dad hat—but as the manager absolutely it was the right thing to do."[34]

When Jessica's second album flopped, Joe Simpson was faced with his first big challenge: "That defeat really shook me, because it was my defeat. . . . I had not really prepared for failure," he said.

The challenge was compounded when Jessica married her boyfriend, Nick Lachey, something not widely considered to be a good career move for a teen heartthrob: "My husband was miserable . . . at the wedding itself he was just miserable," said Joe's wife, Tina, of their daughter's marriage to Lachey.[35]

Billboard's Coniff agreed: "I think at that point, her career was just sliding downhill fast. I mean she was considered B-level talent. She wasn't selling records and [Joe Simpson] rolled the dice and took a risk."[36]

That "risk" was his decision to create a reality TV series for MTV called *The Newlyweds* that would put his daughter and her new husband under the pop culture microscope: "For me, the show gave America the opportunity to see the greatest gift she has, which is her heart," said Joe. "What happened was through the show people forgot about the beauty, they forgot about the voice and they fell in love with her."[37]

The show was an often-hilarious look at the foibles and

challenges of a newlywed couple, but it was also notable for what wasn't portrayed: an active faith element that reflected the lifestyle of a typical Christian couple. Some of Simpson's fans were troubled by a lifestyle that didn't reflect her Christian upbringing, but nothing would bring up the old evangelical fear of their tribe being unable to hang on to their faith in the evil world of Hollywood quite as powerfully as Jessica's sister, Ashlee's, debut record, *Autobiography*, which was severely criticized even as it sold an astonishing three million units in the first six months of release, partly due to her own MTV reality series, which was sold as a spin-off of her sister's show.

While her sister had projected a sexy if somewhat wholesome image, Ashlee had cultivated the image of the black sheep of the family, first dyeing her hair jet black and generally opting for a persona that was in stark contrast to her sister's "sexy but sweet" girl-next-door pose. Still, Ashlee was unapologetic while still considering herself to be a healthy role model for young girls. One who did not agree with that assessment was *Plugged In* magazine writer Bob Waliszewski, whose writings were something of a barometer of Christian attitudes about pop culture. While many devout Christians simply ignored the output of pop culture out of sheer disgust, Waliszewski evaluated albums and analyzed the good, the bad, and the ugly in hopes of educating parents about what their kids were listening to. Waliszewski had been critical of Jessica Simpson in the past, primarily because of her album cover photo, which he refused to even show in the magazine, deeming it too revealing. But when it came to Ashlee's record, Waliszewski was stunned at what the *other* minister's daughter had wrought:

The public image Simpson carves out on the title track is that of a "sexy, nasty, bad-a-- girl in this messed up world" (she uses the s-word in the process). Profanity mars other songs as well. A disturbing blend of sex and violence runs through "Lala," on which a woman invites abuse and talks of rough sex on the kitchen floor. Lines on "Better Off," "Love Me for Me" and "Unreachable" suggest sexual relationships outside of marriage. Breakup tunes display dysfunction and codependency ("Nothing New," "Undiscovered").[38]

For those who had argued for greater Christian engagement in popular culture, the Simpsons' saga would be a troubling one that called into question the very purposes of such cultural involvement. Strange comments about a daughter's breasts, divorce, and childbirth out of wedlock, and racy or misogynistic songs were not what any of these advocates had in mind when they envisioned people of faith impacting the culture. The difficult transition from the Christian subculture to the mainstream would have its casualties, and the Simpsons were an example of the challenges to fully integrating people of faith into the mainstream culture from which their forebears had escaped.

AVRIL LOVE

Avril Lavigne was another in a long series of artists whose Christian background would catch many of her fans by surprise, but also an artist whose background seemed out of sync with the image she projected to the public. The sixteen-year-old burst onto the pop scene with her debut album, *Let Go*, which sold upwards of four million copies in the United States alone and gave her three hit songs and the distinction of making hers the best-selling debut album of 2002. Lavigne's persona may have been that of a rebel, but her songs seemed to reflect a street-smart morality and at least a trace of a Christian upbringing. But when *Rolling Stone* tagged along on one of Lavigne's tours to Japan, it appeared to at least one writer as if she were more Billy *Idol* than Billy *Graham*:

> Avril Lavigne's tiny face is eclipsed by a pitcher of beer that she has set about emptying. After the last swallow, she puts the pitcher back on the table, belches loudly and grabs a microphone in time to sing the opening notes of Creedence Clearwater Revival's version of "Suzie Q . . . For the first time during four days of interviews, press conferences and TV appearances, Lavigne is having a blast—and not simply because no one is stopping this eighteen-year-old from drinking as many pitchers of beer, glasses of wine and shots of tequila as she likes. . . . The more likely reason is that, for the first time in over a year, she's going to have a vacation; in just two days, she will be on a beach in Hawaii.[39]

In her short life, Lavigne had traveled far from her roots—both physical and spiritual. Her talent was first spotted by her devout Christian mother, Judy, who noticed something special about her young daughter at the tender age of two: "One day I started singing 'Jesus Loves Me,' and I couldn't believe it when she sang along," Judy remembered.[40]

Later, Lavigne attended Cornerstone Christian Academy, which was connected with her parents' church, Evangel Temple in Ontario, Canada, and had her heart set on a career in music from a very young age. Lavigne remembered herself as being different from her friends, even at an early age: "I've always kind of wanted to be different and stand out," she said. "And I never really wanted to be, you know, a normal person and have a normal lifestyle. And I've always been a crazy kid. And weird and you know I'd go to school with like twist ties in my hair or little candy wrappers in my hair just to be weird. Always dress different."[41]

Lavigne was also different from many of her peers in her early love for and devotion to making music. Sandwiched between an older brother, Matthew, and a younger sister, Michelle, she was encouraged to get into music by her father, a network technician for Bell Canada: "Her father was pushing to make her fantasy a reality," NBC noted. "He got a drum kit, a keyboard, and several guitars, and turned their basement into a music room."

"That's where I spent all of my time after school," the singer remembered. "You know, I remember my dad saying to me, 'you need to be down there for five hours.' I'd be like, 'Mom, that's too much!' . . . My dad had bought me a microphone and I'd be singing the soundtracks. And I just spent so much time thinking about it. And so much time singing and wanting."[42]

Although she played the occasional country fair, Lavigne, like many artists in the R & B world, got her start at church, where her talent was spotted at an early age by her mother, who reportedly asked if they could start a children's choir. Before long, Lavigne was singing solo at the age of ten. While Judy Lavigne thought it nice that her daughter could carry a tune, she would have no idea the course she and her husband would set their daughter on: "We knew she was talented, but we didn't realize how talented," she would observe years later.[43]

Originally enrolling her in a public school in her hometown of Napanee, Ontario, Lavigne decided to move her daughter to a private Christian school—ironically enough, considering the singer's future tough-gal image—because of bullying. Cornerstone Christian Academy opened the year the diminutive singer enrolled in 1994.

"While at Cornerstone, Lavigne, who was raised in a deeply religious family, toured local churches with her classmates singing, reciting Scripture and spreading the Word," wrote one journalist.[44]

But Lavigne's church singing days were numbered, for a variety of reasons: "I remember singing gospel songs at country fairs," the singer recalled. "I got to a point where I was like, 'Mum, I don't feel comfortable singing these outside of church.' Plus, every time I performed she was like, 'You have to wear a dress and wear your hair nice.' It's funny now."[45]

Lavigne's next professional break was her encounter with a local Christian singer-songwriter-producer named Stephen Medd, with whom she recorded several songs. Wayne Van De Bogart, a guitarist who played on the CD, fondly remembered Lavigne: "Avril was always a perfect pitch, from the time she was young, she was singing right on key. That's the one thing that set her apart from some of the other kids."[46]

What *also* set her apart from her classmates was her drive, apparent at a very young age, which would cause her to seize any opportunities that came her way: "I've known all my life that this is what I was supposed to do," she remembered, "thinking all the time what it would be like to have so many people around. Visualizing what it would be like to be famous with my music. And always just dreaming, always daydreaming."[47]

It was a feeling those around her reinforced on a regular basis: "Everyone knew me as the singer girl around town," she remembered. "People would say 'you're going to go somewhere with your music.' I believed in myself. I have like a huge dream. That's all I ever thought about and I think that I wanted it so much and that's why it happened."[48]

Want it or not, the world is full of wannabe stars who dream of superstardom but never achieve it. While most put their talents to use in venues other than the world's stage, Lavigne's preparation and determination to succeed finally paid off when famed producer L.A. Reid discovered her one night in a recording studio: "I got a call asking me to come to the studio and hear this girl sing," Reid recalled. "I was in a rotten mood. I was in a really, really bad space. And really wasn't in the mood to do it at all. But I said, 'OK, you know what? Don't cancel. Just go and do it. Get it over with.'"[49]

"I basically sat down on a stool and sang three songs for him," said Lavigne of her encounter with Reid.[50]

"Within 30 seconds, my whole mood had changed," said Reid. "I went from being a really aggravated, irritable guy to all of a sudden feeling like, 'Oh my God, I have never heard a voice like this' . . . it was very special. It was very, very special for me."[51]

"I remember after he left, everyone was like, 'He loved you, he loved you,'" recalled Lavigne. "And everyone was like picking me up. I was like this little peanut. Everybody's picking me up, swinging me around and being like 'yeah' and I was just like 'cool, cool.' And they're like, 'you don't understand. It doesn't happen like this. You don't just get a record deal, boom, like that.'"[52]

But that was exactly what was in store for the pint-sized Canadian singer, although there were details that needed to be worked out, including what kind of music she would be making. Lavigne's music had often been compared to the work of artists such as Faith Hill and Shania Twain—in fact, she had once opened for Twain—but when it came time to make her debut record, she resisted efforts to point her in that musical direction, to the dismay of her new handlers.

"I probably would have had her prettied up and you know, maybe the clothes would have been a little tighter, a little more revealing and you know, a little more sparkles going on, a little more bling-bling," Reid told then NBC anchor Jane Pauley. "I'm telling you, I would have messed it all up! Being normal is what's hot today and the simple beat, the simple melody, the catchy hook line. Everything is simple. Less is more."[53]

Instead of going along with the image that Reid and others had in mind for her, Lavigne crafted a new one even as she insisted that the rebel teenager image she was scrambling to acquire was her own: "It's kind of weird to me how like you get famous and then everybody goes all glamorous and glittery," she said. "And it's kinda like—it's weird, it's strange to me. I mean OK, maybe yeah you make a bunch of money and you can afford all that stuff. But it's not something I can really do. I just like to dress down, dress normal and comfortable. And that's my style and that's cool."[54]

But her new, "cool" image was radically different from the image witnessed by those who had known her a few years earlier. Director Tom Picotte, who worked at the Selby Community Theater and had directed Lavigne, remembered the singer resisting his efforts to dress the part of a rebellious teenager in his production of *Godspell*: "It wasn't in her to be rebellious," said Picotte. "She was 13."

"Obviously that has changed within the past few years."[55]

Others, like Stephen Medd, witnessed a rather abrupt

change as his former collaborator became a full-fledged pop star: "The thing I noticed was the dark eye makeup and the 'don't mess with me' pout," he stated.[56] Another observer recalled:

> Gone was the preppy teenager who her old classmates say used to tie sweaters around her shoulders. Her wavy hair had been flat-ironed and she favored chipped black nail polish and lots of black rubber bracelets. . . . Most of those who knew Lavigne in Napanee shrug off the change, chalking it up to both a new image to help market her music and the result of an impressionable teenager searching for style in the playgrounds of New York City and Los Angeles.[57]

Her new image, manufactured or not, had helped create a superstar, and Lavigne was soon lighting up the charts with a collection of hit songs that seemed to blend traditional morality, a sprinkling of expletives, and a rebel pose. Her first single off of her debut album was "Don't Tell Me," a song about a girl who was being pressured to have sex with her boyfriend—a regular theme in Lavigne's early music. It was unusual, to the say the least, especially in a pop culture dominated by young female artists such as Britney Spears and Christina Aguilera, who seemed all too ready to give it away to the first interested boy, and L. A. Reid took note: "Look, I think she has a typical way about herself, but I don't think she's typical at all," he said. "I listen to her songs, and I listen to the lyrics and I read the lyrics and I'm so, so impressed that someone could be so prolific, and so special, at such a young age. She's anything but ordinary. She's anything but typical. She just looks like a typical teen."[58]

In the upside-down world of rock music journalism, where artists are peppered with demands for explanations when they make statements or sing songs that advance traditional virtues like self-control or celibacy, Lavigne was often thrown on the defensive and asked to explain the meanings of some of her songs:

> I was brought up in a Christian home. You know, my mom was, like, "have respect for yourself." Very strict . . .
>
> So because of my upbringing, you know, I think that's what caused me to write that song. Just having morals and stuff. It is not a song about abstinence. People ask me that sometimes. It's not. I'm just saying, "have respect for yourself."
>
> And it's about being able to be strong. And not let a guy pressure you into doing something you don't want to do. I think that that's important for young girls. 'Cause I think it's harder when you're younger.[59]

Lavigne's position in pop culture was an unusual one: While music history was littered with the spiritual corpses of hundreds of artists who had been raised in the church and then abandoned their beliefs for a life of rock 'n' roll hedonism, Lavigne seemed unwilling to *completely* leave behind the trappings of her upbringing, and the residue of traditional morality that had survived pop stardom still clung to her. The singer said:

> My mom wouldn't even let me sing [the country song] "Strawberry Wine," because it said "wine" in it and I was this little kid . . . She protected my image. And that's not the only reason why I don't dance around like a ho onstage, but it definitely has something to do with being brought up with tons of morals. And I'm not saying I'll never write a song with a curse word, because there's definitely been times

when it's like, "aww, man, f*** would sound so good there!" But then I think about my mom, and how it would probably hurt her. So I just say "frig" instead.[60]

The morality that stubbornly undergirded Lavigne's songs was clearly there because of the standards her parents had laid down for her, and while the singer seemed to *barely* cling to them, it was altogether unclear which side of her would eventually triumph in the battle that seemed to be raging within her between the world she was refusing to fully embrace and the one she seemed hesitant to completely leave behind. Lavigne recalled her mother's rules:

> I wasn't allowed to have a guy in my room . . . Especially not with the door shut. And she wouldn't let me call guys. They had to call me. I have that attitude now—that if a guy wants to hook up with me, he can come after me. I'm not going running after him. . . . That's a good way to bring up your kid, because if you let your kid do everything—go to parties, get trashed really young and get out of control—she's gonna get taken advantage of, and she won't be taught that having sex with a ton of boys is a bad thing. I do a lot of things that are very rebellious, but it's not like I'm sniffing coke or doing dirty stuff.[61]

Others weren't as sure about Lavigne's studied public pose. Bob Waliszewski, writing in Focus on the Family's sister publication, *Plugged In*, observed of Lavigne's debut album:

> Lavigne cuts loose disrespectful or uncommitted boyfriends on "Losing Grip" and "Complicated." She tells a guy he's lame for

choosing marijuana over her ("Too Much to Ask"), emphasizes the need for trust in relationships ("Tomorrow") and refuses to change who she is to please someone else ("Nobody's Fool"). Tired of a transient lifestyle, a girl longs to settle down and find stability on "Mobile." "Sk8er Boi" is about a young woman who pays a price for letting friends' prejudices sway her decision-making, but . . . a man is deemed a good catch simply because he plays guitar on MTV ("Now he's a superstar . . . See what he's worth"). . . . Mild profanities mar "My World," "Nobody's Fool," "Mobile" and "I'm with You." The latter finds a lonely girl willing to go home with a stranger. . . . This 17-year-old refuses to compromise her sense of self or play the victim. That's good. But Lavigne's pluck also manifests itself in profanity and irresponsible behavior.[62]

In spite of such criticisms from the Christian community, Lavigne wasn't *completely* rebellious, for while it had become commonplace for celebrities to say they didn't want to be thought of as role models, she seemed to welcome that status, hoping to be a good influence on her young listeners:

I never signed up to be one. But I think it's great. I'm just myself. I'm very outspoken, sometimes opinionated, and I think I'm a very strong person. And I think that's great. Some people might look at me and be, like, "Oh, she's not a role model 'cause she swears or whatever."

But that's just me being myself. And not holding back. I'm not afraid when I'm in front of people to let loose and to say things. 'Cause I just believe it's better just to be honest and be myself.[63]

But when it came to the "honest" expressions of other artists, like the often scantily clad Britney Spears, Lavigne was not so accepting: "As far as Britney, I don't have very much respect for her," she said. "I think she's taken it a little too far and she tries a little too hard. And I think it's gross. It's like, 'just do that for your boyfriend in the bedroom.' I don't want to watch it."[64]

Just as music moguls like Clive Davis seemed to push religious artists to leave the trappings of their religion behind, executives also commonly tried to get their female charges to sex up their images. Lavigne had stubbornly resisted such attempts and had made it clear that she would achieve success on her own terms:

> There are these people who say I'm made up by my label . . . It's like, no I'm not. If I was made up by the record label, I'd have bleached-blond hair and I'd probably be wearing a bra for a shirt. . . . . I hate sex-object music. It's not real, and I'd never be able to sit in my room and listen to that kind of stuff. I have moms come up to me all the time and say thank you for wearing clothes, thank you for not being a Britney Spears. I'm like, "Puleeaase, no worries there."[65]

But moms could be excused for beginning to worry a bit when, in 2004, the singer posed for surprisingly sexy photos for the men's magazine *Maxim*.

"I just want to get wasted, dance and hang out! . . ." she once observed. "I don't go looking for fights . . . but if someone comes up to me and pushes me, I'm not going to take it."[66]

Of her fascination with using, if not singing, the f-word, the singer observed, "I don't know why, I just like saying it."[67]

Rolling Stone, tagging along for her Tokyo gig, found her in a similar state of mind: "The first night we hung out, she took us to a bar," said drummer Brann. "Within five minutes she's like, 'We're gonna do body shots. Pour salt on my neck and then lick it.' We were doing tequila, tequila, tequila right away. I was like, 'this girl is insane. This is going to be like Motley Crüe.'"[68]

Fans, traditionalist culture critics, and moms alike could be forgiven for being confused by Avril Lavigne's contradictory persona—it would likely take years to figure out how the singer would affect young fans who were purchasing her records. Unlike pop superstars of years gone by—like Madonna, who had writhed onstage in a wedding gown while singing "Like a Virgin," mocking the notion that sex should be saved for marriage—Lavigne appeared to be upholding at least the *idea* of sex within marriage. But some critics argued that the path that got her to that conclusion was a curiously circular and confusing one that seemed to lose all sense of a worldview that might sustain such a traditionalist moral position. Others argued that part of the problem was that young children without fully formed minds were being thrust into the public debate, and were consequently not ready to be spokespeople for any cause. Lavigne's own mother seemed to echo that sentiment: "I can grasp it, but in the same way I can't. It seems like a dream," she said of her daughter's stardom. "It seems weird for the whole world to be talking about my daughter. She's just Avril to us."[69]

But for millions of teenage girls, she was Avril Lavigne the singer-philosopher, and critics would continue to debate over the messages she was sending, particularly whether young musicians raised in Christian homes who are thrust in the public square helped or hindered the advancement of the gospel message and traditional morality.

THE WRONG PATH

Perhaps no other band on the modern rock scene better embodied the challenges posed by the mixing of rock and religion—and the never-ending battle between the flesh and the spirit—than Kings of Leon. Although their story wasn't the typical crossover tale about a Christian artist moving from CCM to mainstream rock, in some ways it had much in common with that story: its members got their start traveling to churches across the United States, singing and preaching about salvation and repentance with their father, Leon, a United Pentecostal Church minister, and their mother, Betty Ann. And no other artist on the modern rock scene seemed to struggle as mightily with God, Satan, the flesh, and whether or not to sign a record deal: "As soon as I knew we got a record deal, that whole night I never slept because I knew I was going to hell and I wasn't going to be a preacher," said singer Caleb Followill.[70]

"Their childhood was characterized by all-night church meetings, healings and the Holy Spirit," noted *Relevant* magazine. "It wasn't an easy childhood. The brothers were on the road 325 to 330 days each year. There was no place they could call home, and very few friends outside of their family."[71]

In a sense, music became a home to the brothers, something noted by Caleb, who once said:

> When I was younger, I would take this little radio everywhere. I was really lonely because we were always in a different place, usually sleeping in a back room at a church. It was always really scary in there, so I would put my little radio under the pillow and just listen to the oldies station, listen to doo wop and Stand By Me, and that finally got me to where I'd fall asleep. It just lifted the blanket of fear. I heard stuff that made

me forget about all the things I would hear in church every day, things that made me feel as if everything was wrong. Music gave me my own little world.[72]

The entire Followill family was on a heavenly mission to save souls for God, but that mission came tumbling down to earth when their father's alcoholism caused him to leave the ministry and divorce his wife, choices that left the couple's young sons reeling: "When my parents separated, the little glass castles of the world we thought were perfect came crashing down," said Nathan Followill,[73] later revealing, "Our parents' divorce shattered the whole mirage of this perfect little existence the outside world couldn't touch and couldn't pollute . . .We realized that our dad, the greatest man we ever knew, in our eyes, was only human. And so are we . . . This whole new world was open to us."[74]

His brother Caleb, who would one day front Kings of Leon and play guitar, added, "I'd put my faith in my dad and I wanted to follow in his footsteps. I'd always look up to ministers, but at about fifteen I started to see that they were just normal men and it broke my heart. I closed myself off to pretty much everyone and dropped out of school."[75]

In 1997 brothers Caleb and Nathan moved to Nashville with hopes of breaking into the music business, and convinced their youngest brother, Jared, and cousin Matthew to join them in 1999, forming Kings of Leon, named in honor of their father and grandfather. Eventually the group came to the attention of one of Nashville's top managers, Ken Levitan, who signed them to a publishing deal.

"We met guys who got paid to write horrible lousy country

songs, and we were like, 'We could write lousy country songs,'" said Nathan, of their desire to move to Nashville and make music.[76]

Levitan, who spotted the brothers' talent early on, knew otherwise: "They had this amazing sound just singing a cappella," he recalled.[77]

Levitan signed on to manage the band and auditioned them for a number of labels in New York, eventually signing them to RCA. Although Levitan was familiar with the CCM industry, having once managed Sixpence None the Richer, he clearly had no designs on that market for the brothers' music and kept his and the band's eyes focused on the mainstream rock scene. Although their music would continually reference the brothers' belief—or at least the beliefs of their upbringing—there was never any doubt that the songs would never work in the difficult-to-crack Christian music market, so they focused on Europe: "We felt that it was a story the U.K. press and people would really love," said Levitan. "So, we brought them over there first and hired a publicist. It was while we were starting to tour here as well, but really went for the full press there, and it worked."[78]

Famed British writer Neil McCormick was one of the first to champion the American band and, writing in the *Telegraph*, poured praise on the band's work in 2008:

> The Kings of Leon have something of a reputation . . .
> as hard-drinking, drug-taking, straight-talking rock-and-
> roll stars. Although still only a cult success in their home
> country, they may be Britain's favorite American rock band.
> Their arena gigs sell out in record time. They headlined
> Glastonbury. Last year, their fourth album, *Because of the*

Times, went straight to number one. The follow up, *Only By the Night*, looks set to take them global.

> [They] possess the charisma, swagger, intensity, pop hooklines and dirty rock sensibility to make them all-time greats. And with the new album they have added an epic sweep and spacious, ringing production reminiscent of classic U2—who the Followill's adore.[79]

Still, vestiges of their faith would remain. Asked early on about the brothers' beliefs, Nathan replied, "Yeah, we all believe in God, for sure. I think we all still have a lot of the morals that were instilled in us growing up."[80]

Caleb added:

> I think there's always two sides to your personality, be it when you're drunk or sober, or at home or away, or whatever. Our song "On Call" is about the grounded part of you. It says, "And when I fall to pieces, Lord you know I'll be there waiting." You could take that in a Biblical sense. The Bible says that David, or Daniel, or one of those guys, was a man after God's own heart. But he was quite a messed-up person. So if he's the man after God's own heart, well, maybe when you're at your roughest moment, that's when He's watching over you and smiling.[81]

"We realize now looking back on it that the way we were raised definitely shaped us into the guys that we are. There are definitely things from that time of life that I want to keep, especially being a good person and being thankful for everything that you have," Nathan said.[82]

"We're no saints, by no means," he told another interviewer.

"[But] I like to think we're good people and have good hearts."[83]

Nearly every article and interview with the band featured the brothers' Christian upbringing. Yet awareness of the band among devout Christians in the United States was slim at best. Still, conservative outlets, including Focus on the Family's popular *Plugged In*, were noticing the band and offered this mixed assessment:

> At times, Kings of Leon exhibits a maturing perspective, especially compared to the unabashed and unbridled hedonism found in some of the band's previous efforts. But just when you think the Followill clan might be growing up, these would-be arena rock Kings ramble into yet another debauched tale of getting drunk, shooting up drugs or knocking someone's teeth out. Maybe we should hold off a bit on the rock-savior coronation ceremony.[84]

And in interviews like the one the band gave to *Entertainment Weekly*, it became clear that the debauchery bled into the band members' lifestyle as well. When asked by a reporter about the meaning of a song called "Arizona," Caleb replied:

> I hold that place close to my heart. I love the desert and always have. But the story behind that song is kind of bad. I can't really get into it. It's about when Nathan and I went to Arizona, and . . . well, we had quite a few different substances in us, and we decided to go to this brothel. I guess I am telling you now, aren't I? This really is a heartbreaker. We walked in and I looked around and there was this one girl who was so beautiful that all I could think was, "What happened in her life that could bring her here?" as opposed to me thinking, "Yeah! I'll take that one!"

"So you left?" the interviewer then asked.

"No," Caleb admitted. "I took an ugly one. I knew why she was there.[85]

It was a shocking story for a band composed of professing Christians, but it was another indication of the hard road that the Followill brothers and their cousin had chosen for themselves. In some ways it was similar to the road traveled by Elvis Presley, another son of the South from a religious upbringing who struggled to reconcile his faith with his chosen profession. Presley had reportedly approached his minister, James Hamill, and told him, "Pastor, I'm the most miserable young man you've ever seen. I've got all the money I'll ever need to spend. I've got millions of fans. I've got friends. But I'm doing what you taught me not to do, and I'm not doing the things you taught me to do."[86]

Elvis had always had a difficult relationship with the church, and the members of U2 had once been counseled by their pastor not to go into rock 'n' roll. The members of Kings of Leon also wrestled with the idea that going down the road of rock 'n' roll stardom would mean having to leave the church and the values they were raised around and seemed eternally conflicted about it. Caleb remembered:

> When things were starting to happen, I can recall every night trying to go to bed and something was saying, "If you leave, you can never come back." It was like being a kid again, sleepless nights, over and over, and I would have to turn on the TV to drown it out. And then one day I looked at myself and said, "You know, this is what you wanna do," and it was like a weight was lifted. It was almost as if God was smiling down on

me, saying, "Finally, you made a decision, you quit struggling with yourself." And the voices went away. For a little while.[87]

Perhaps the most interesting and accurate assessment of the predicament that the members of Kings of Leon faced was offered by a blogger named Christian Scharen, who connected their issues directly to their association with the Pentecostal church:

> The Pentecostal tradition they come out of has an element of purity-lust, a peculiar kind of sinful desire to leave the world into a "perfect little existence," as Nathan put it. And when this breaks apart, then it can seem a farce. They seemed to think so, running away from God and their past into a life of sex, drugs, and rock 'n' roll. Their songs, and their reputation, through their first years as a band were fairly wild. Fast songs about drinking and sex and life on the road fill their first albums. They aren't without a kind of reflective honesty, however.[88]

The rough ride that was the Kings of Leon story could be, by all accounts, traced back to the fall of their preacher father, Ivan Leon Followill, whose fall from grace had taken place around the same time as that of prominent TV preachers such as Jim Bakker and Jimmy Swaggart. Leon's sons, along with millions of other sons and daughters, would emerge bloodied from the shards of glass that had been left behind by those explosions. Reportedly getting by as a house painter and still struggling against the demon rum, Followill was still worried about his sons' souls: "I don't want to say my kids are going to hell, you know, nothing like that, but as far as what I envisioned, it's a little different."[89]

"Bono said that the most beautiful music, the only relevant music to him, is either someone who is running towards God or running away from it," Caleb Followill once told a reporter. "I think that's kind of right. All that passion and guilt and all that stuff . . . I don't consider myself to be a good person. I know I'm on the wrong path, brother. But at least I know, y'know?"[90]

GOING WEST

In 2004 an up-and-coming hip-hop star named Kanye West was nominated for a Stellar award, a prestigious honor in the gospel music community that recognized the nation's foremost gospel artists. But the decision to include West provoked immediate outrage from many in the community: "It just seems that it shouldn't have gotten through," said Jadda Gunn, a member of the Gospel Music Academy. "For this to be the Stellar Awards they should have known. Kanye West, Roc-A-Fella records— that's not [a] gospel album."[91]

Moving quickly to contain the damage, the Stellar Awards quickly withdrew West's name from consideration for his song "Jesus Walks," which had been nominated in the Rap/Hip Hop Gospel CD of the Year category. It was just the latest in a long-simmering battle that had raged in the African-American community for decades between some traditionalists who preferred that gospel music stay in the church, and artists who often saw the church as a stepping-stone to success in the R & B world. Caught in the middle were those artists like Kirk Franklin, Mary Mary, and others who didn't want to leave their faith behind but sought to have their music heard outside of the church. At the outset, anyway, it wasn't clear which camp Kanye West was in. His record *College Dropout* had sold millions of copies in the United States, and he had become a sought-after producer, but critics wondered: could his expressions of religious faith and devotion be taken seriously when they were coupled with vulgarities and a worldview that seemed to be out of sync with such expressions of faith? West's biggest splash came when "Jesus Walks" became a bona fide hit across multiple formats and on music television. While many Christian and inspirational outlets merely ignored West's declarations of faith as not worthy of attention, *Christianity Today* seemed curious about what West was bringing to pop culture:

> In the impressive "Jesus Walks" . . . West is a soldier of God who wants to break racial barriers and bring peace to all despite the hurdles: "God show me the way because the devil try to break me down/The only thing that I pray is that my feet don't fail me now." And: "I don't think there's nothing I can do to right my wrong/I wanna talk to God but I'm afraid 'cause we ain't spoke in so long." He concludes with a dig at mainstream radio: "Radio needs this/They said you can rap about anything except for Jesus/That means guns, sex, lies, and videotape/But if I talk about God, my record won't get played?"[92]

But the magazine was clearly confused by other songs on West's record that seemed miles away from such devout expressions of faith:

> Despite these overtones, be forewarned: "College Dropout" is far from pious, with an array of expletives and lyrical undesirables. One wonders why West so adamantly makes a case for Christ in "Jesus Walks," yet quickly dismisses him

via duplicitous party rhymes. The answer is probably in the album's liner notes, where West openly declares that he's not where he needs to be, despite still being on God's side. "Matter of fact, [I'm] far from it," he says. Referring to Bible prophets, he then says that when somebody is given a word to preach, one will always have an excuse. "I don't got no excuse," he reaffirms, then adding, "You spared my life, but somehow I'm still on [stuff]. Amen. You're the Executive Producer of my life."[93]

In 2002 West was discovered and signed by Roc-A-Fella Records and experienced immediate success and notoriety with his debut album. Like his record, in interviews West freely mixed God-talk with profanities and talk of marijuana. It was a strange juxtaposition, even for a pop culture in which the lines that separated God and popular music had become increasingly blurred: "It's not so much me behind the success. I think it's God; I'm just in his service," the rapper told a reporter. "I look at what I do as administering his blessings. So if I'm in the studio with an artist and we make a hit record that's what God wanted them to have."[94]

Asked whether he regretted making his debut with "Jesus Walks," West waxed philosophical, remembering his father, who had inspired his faith:

> It would have been riskier for me not to do that song. Some rappers are tough, but Jesus is all-powerful; he has more juice than the record label, than the media and all the gangstas together. He's the one who's in control. . . .
>
> It's not religion; it's spirituality. I say it on my album: religion is something you say over and over; it has nothing to do with spirituality. I was raised in the church. My father

would take me to church three times a week, but he also explained social issues to me. . . .

The things he taught me in those long car rides to church are in my music now, and there's so much more for me to talk about that I haven't had a chance to get to yet.[95]

Yet, to another interviewer, West spoke of his fondness for pot: "I also love the weed. This state got the best herb," he said of California. "Honestly I don't blaze up constantly but when I do, I'm [definitely] going to use the vape kit you guys gave me. The ---- is pimp looking and it knocks me on my ass. Good looking out for getting me high."[96]

Plugged In was feeling anything but good about West's music. In a scathing review of his debut record, reviewer Loren Eaton Bob Smithouser first allowed that "the artist credits God with helping him survive a serious car crash ('Through the Wire'). He expresses a love and need for Christ on 'Jesus Walks.' Lines take issue with absentee fathers ('We Don't Care'), materialism ('All Falls Down') and the racism that sparked the civil rights movement ('Never Let Me Down.')"[97]

But, Smithouser noted, the good was far outweighed by the bad:

Obscene language includes numerous f-words. Drug dealing and tax fraud are acceptable ways for the urban poor to earn cash on "We Don't Care." Angry threats against authority figures include, "F--- the police, that's how I treat 'em" ("All Falls Down") and "If my manager insults me again/I will be assaulting him" ("Spaceship"). The latter also endorses employee theft. "Get 'Em High" is an ode to marijuana that includes crude sexual slang and considers dropping out of college a bold, positive step. West's disdain for education pops up again on "School Spirit" and *three* skits. Hennessy, blunts and oral sex from anonymous women is "The New Workout Plan." As if sex, drugs and alcohol alone aren't salacious enough, "Breathe In Breathe Out" adds guns and a girl eager to videotape her illicit encounter with the artist. "Last Call" emphasizes booze and bragging.

"Despite moments of social and spiritual conscience, 'College Dropout' should be expelled," the reviewer concluded.[98]

While accepting a Grammy award, U2 front man Bono once famously joked that God might have cringed when certain artists thanked Him upon winning their award, and there were undoubtedly some Christian fans who thought the same was true of Bono *and* West. While some would make the case that any time Jesus came up as a topic in popular entertainment, it was a victory, others would argue that when such statements were made by people living a lifestyle that clearly contradicted Christ's teachings, the damage done was greater than any good that might come of it. The discussion would likely continue, and Kanye West and the way his story would ultimately play out would influence the debate and sharpen the arguments.

In 2006 West posed for the cover of *Rolling Stone* with a crown of thorns on his head, re-creating the pose made famous by actor Jim Caviezel in *The Passion of the Christ*, and controversy ensued. The African-American church community was especially sensitive to artists who sprang from their tradition using the church as a stepping-stone to stardom, and Kanye West reminded them of a long history of artists who had used them and the things they held sacred to achieve selfish ambitions. The *Rolling Stone* cover was, for them, just another reminder of that dynamic. Gospel music star Micah Stampley spoke for many in their community when he observed of West:

> I am totally thrown off at his attempt to portray himself as my Lord and Savior Jesus Christ, I am also outraged by the failure and refusal of those Christians of influence to take a stand on a matter that is offensive to our faith. In my opinion, this young man feels that he is superior to his peers and surroundings and to depict himself as Jesus Christ is proof of that. Kanye has a level of pride that is so unique, it's frightening! It reminds me of when Lucifer tried to exalt himself above the throne of God as we read about in the scripture. As a result, God cast him down along with all the angels that agreed and followed him. After he [Satan] was kicked out of heaven, the Bible described him as the fallen star. Here is what I mean by this reference; Kanye West may be a shining star right now but when you try to exalt yourself as Jesus, you open up to being the next falling star and all those that follow and support are in position to be cast down as well. Let this be a lesson learned just because someone uses the name of Jesus Christ it does not mean they stand for what His name represents.[99]

THE EVANESCENCE EXPLOSION

Shortly after a band from Arkansas named Evanescence exploded onto the American music scene, I received a call from a longtime friend and colleague named Chris Willman, then of the magazine *Entertainment Weekly*. Chris was on his way to Little Rock to interview the band's coleaders, Amy Lee and Ben Moody, and he was wondering if I knew anything about their religious orientation. I directed Chris to a website that featured a 2002 interview with Moody and Lee. Armed with that interview, Willman headed to Little Rock, and the conversation caused shock waves across the music business, resulting in the band's CDs being banned from Christian-owned retail outlets.

Moody and Lee were very young Christians who had written and recorded a dark but deeply spiritual record—the kind of record that, in any previous generation, might have gotten them kicked out of mainstream rock and left them stuck in the CCM world. But by the time Willman showed up in Little Rock, the duo had decided to distance themselves not only from their spiritual background but also from their association with the CCM scene. Or, they may have simply been caught off guard by Willman, not realizing that an interview given to an obscure faith-based website would, through the wonders of the Internet, be picked up by a respected reporter at a prominent national entertainment publication. But Willman was no ordinary reporter. A longtime fixture on the entertainment media scene and one of rock's wittiest and most informed, Willman was a man of faith himself who understood the complicated issues and sticky situations that often resulted when the worlds of rock and religion collided. Speaking to the website Strangerthings.com, Moody had once upon a time unflinchingly declared his faith and purpose as an artist:

> I am a Christian. I still have fears, I still have pain, I still have sorrow, I wouldn't be alive if I didn't. The beautiful thing about my relationship with God is that he understands all that and he has shown me what life is really for. . . . The message

we as a band want to convey more than anything is simple—
God is Love. He is a just God, but a gracious God. . . .
The #1 cause of atheism is Christians. We only hope to offset
that as much as we can. God gave human beings amazing
amounts of understanding, but they are still flawed and they
make mistakes. God understands.[100]

He had also spoken to another music site, called *Enclave*,
four years earlier, describing in great detail his first encounter
with the young lady with whom he would one day form a band:

Several years ago Amy and myself were attending a youth
camp. I was playing with the praise and worship group and
Amy was a camper. During some kind of break/recreation
time I was sitting in the gym watching a basketball game. On
the other side of the court was a stage for plays and a piano.
I was just sitting there bored to tears when all of the sudden
I was given a quick jolt as my ears were filled with the sound
of the piano intro to Meatloaf's "I Would Do Anything
For Love." I looked over at the piano and there was this
girl effortlessly displaying immense amounts of talent. After
my initial envious rage subsided I hopped to my feet and
ran right through the basketball game straight to the piano
and introduced myself. She then impressed me further with
songs that she had written. I thought I was in heaven. But
then she sang. I nearly died. Coming from this tiny little
youth camp reject was one of the most powerful, beautiful
voices I'd ever heard. So I somehow convinced her to never
play with anyone else again and she's been mine ever since.
We've had the same dream from the beginning; to write with
everything in us and totally do the music we love while at

the same time using that as a tool to share with others what Christ has done in our lives.[101]

When the interviewer asked Moody how he felt about being a "Christian musician" and his association with the CCM scene, Moody downplayed it, but affirmed his faith:

It's not like it was a conscious choice, actually. We're musicians who write about things that affect our life. If I was taking the trash out and was suddenly struck with the inspiration to write a song about it, I'd probably do it. Our relationship with Christ is one of the biggest parts of our lives so of course we tend to be heavily lyrically influenced by that. We didn't just decide to become "Christian musicians," it just happened that way.[102]

The conversation then turned to the band's Arkansas roots, its association with one of the CCM scene's pioneering metal bands, and Moody's decision to attend Bible college: "The majority of my inspiration to use the style of music you love to glorify God comes from Living Sacrifice," Moody noted. "I've loved them for years and so has Amy. They have one of the most incredible ministries I've ever seen. At the moment I happen to be going to Bible college with the bass player from Living Sacrifice."[103]

Though on the fringes of the CCM scene, Moody affirmed his faith in clear terms, but at the same time was clearly not impressed with much of the music he heard emanating from fellow believers:

There's nothing more irritating than turning on the radio right after you've just been hurt or betrayed and hearing some stupid pop song about standing by you or sunny days or some crap like that. When you're sad, you wanna hear from someone who's been there and understands. And you certainly can't turn to Christian music. We want people to know that your salvation is not going to keep people from hurting you and it's not going to stop you from feeling pain. But you are not alone. God made you the way you are for a reason. There are other people who think, feel, and dream the same way you do and Christ will never abandon you whether you go through trials or not. I think that's why we fell into the "Goth" category. We're just emotional and we find that embracing your "dark emotions" and not denying them brings you one step closer to happiness. You'll never be able to love other people and share the love of Christ with others until you look at yourself through Christ's eyes and accept yourself the way He accepts you.[104]

Evanescence's explosion onto the rock charts, as a result of their work on the *Daredevil* soundtrack, had made them the hottest thing in rock, and Willman could be forgiven for thinking he was interviewing just another artist in a long series of devout Christians who were making their impact felt in mainstream music with their faith. What he encountered instead would also be a blow to Evanescence's label, which had carefully marketed them to both the mainstream and Christian marketplaces. Titling his piece "Southern Discomfort," Willman painted a portrait of two young people who, if not explicitly denying their earlier statements of faith, were at the very least trying hard to put distance between those statements and how they wanted to be perceived after their sudden surge of success:

"There are people that are hell-bent on the idea that we're a

Christian band in disguise, and that we have some secret message," said Lee. "We have no spiritual affiliation with this music. It's simply about life experience."

"I'm not ashamed of my spiritual beliefs, but I in no way incorporate them into this band," added Moody. "We're actually high on the Christian charts, and I'm like, what the f*** are we even doing there?"[105]

While Moody was essentially begging Christian radio stations to take his band off their playlists, Lee upped the ante, doing the same to Christian retail outlets where the band's record was a hot commodity: "I guarantee that if the Christian bookstore owners listened to some of those songs, they wouldn't sell the CD," she teased.[106]

"I suggest that, after this interview, that may no longer be a problem," Willman wrote, tongue firmly in cheek.

"Thank you," Lee told Willman.

Willman painted a portrait of Moody and Lee that was sure to not go over well with their Christian fans, capturing them drinking at a sushi bar, exchanging middle finger salutes over dinner, dropping the f-word, and taking the Lord's name in vain in order to deny the charge that they were romantically involved.

The fallout from Moody's and Lee's statements was immediate: responding quickly to contain the damage, the band's label, Wind-Up Records, issued a statement of clarification, quickly recalled all of the band's product from Christian retail stores, and asked that Christian radio stations drop the band from their playlists. Christian-owned retail and radio outlets happily obliged and the band quickly disappeared from the Christian media world, but mainstream success continued unabated. After several years together, Moody and Lee would go their separate ways, with Lee continuing the band after adding new players. Evanescence's quick rise and subsequent fall from grace was yet another reminder of the challenges facing a new generation of rockers who were attempting to sanctify rock. While some artists learned to deftly navigate between the two worlds—secular and sacred—and sing for both, for others the challenge was too great.

THE RAPPER, CHANCELOR

"When I was younger, my grandma said a prayer over me that damn near sounded like a curse," said a young hip-hop artist named Chancelor Bennett, better known by his stage name, Chance the Rapper.

> I was just doing a lot of drugs, just hanging out. I was gone all the time. . . .
>
> She looked me in the eyes and she said, "I don't like what's going on . . . I can see it in your eyes. I don't like this . . . We're gonna pray." And she prayed for me all the time. Like, very positive things. But this time, she said, "Lord, I pray that all things that are not like You, You take away from Chance. Make sure that he fails at everything that is not like You. Take it away. Turn it into dust."
>
> I'm thinking, like, damn, I don't even know if God likes rap! You know what I'm saying? Is she praying that I fail at everything I'm trying to do?"[107]

If Chance the Rapper's grandmother's prayer was answered, it may very well have meant that the Deity was indeed pleased with the budding rap star, for he exploded onto the charts and, significantly, never seemed to forget to honor his God as the source of his inspiration. For many Americans who don't follow the ins and outs of the music business, 2017 may have been the first time they heard of Chance, and what a year it would be for him. Nominated for an amazing seven Grammy awards, he walked away with three: best new artist, best rap performance, and best rap album. Interspersed between those presentations were dynamic performances in which Chance teamed with an artist who had successfully modeled bringing the gospel message into the mainstream music culture, Kirk Franklin. It was an electrifying performance that was significant not just because it was bringing Chance's unique brand of gospel hip-hop to the masses on a mainstream television event, but because of the significance of the song he chose to cover. Years earlier, an obscure musician named Chris Tomlin, known widely in Christian circles as a "worship leader," had popularized the song "How Great Is Our God," and the anthem had been sung hundreds of thousands, perhaps millions of times in churches around the world. Yet, for the average American music fan, it was likely that Chance's rendition of the song was the first time it had been heard. Once again, Christian themes were bursting out of the religious music subculture and were now front and center, thanks to young and devout artists like Chance the Rapper.

Chance's father, Ken Bennett, was a top aide to Chicago's mayor, Rahm Emanuel, and at least one critic saw significance in Chance's Chicago connection, noting the city's association with a founding legend of gospel music.

"It's not a coincidence that Chance leans so heavily on gospel music," noted Buzzfeed:

The genre as we know it today was born in Chicago. Georgia native Thomas A. Dorsey spearheaded the art form in the historic neighborhood of Bronzeville, the Harlem of the Midwest, in the 1930s. Dorsey penned such classics as "Peace in the Valley" (covered by Elvis Presley, Johnny Cash, and Dolly Parton among others) and "Precious Lord, Take My Hand," which Mahalia Jackson, also a Chicago transplant by way of Louisiana, famously sang at civil rights rallies throughout the country. The Staple Singers, most famous for "I'll Take You There" (perhaps the most orgasmic ode to the wonders that await in heaven), merged Roebuck "Pops" Staples's Mississippi blues guitar and Mavis's growling, grunting contralto with traditional spirituals. As a result of the Great Migration, Chicago became, for a time, an epicenter of gospel's golden era. To this day, the city of Chicago celebrates its gospel heritage with a giant festival every summer. Gospel is in the city's lifeblood, and it's against this backdrop that Chance made his music.

Gospel grew out of faith, and so much of the faith we acquire or disinherit is hereditary, passed down from generations.[108]

Intentionally or not, however, what Dorsey and thousands of other gospel artists had done was retreat from popular culture, making overtly religious music that was for fellow believers. But Chance was part of a new generation of artists, intent on making their presence felt in the public square.

"I never really set out to make anything that could pretend to be new gospel or pretend to be the gospel," he said. "It's just music from me as a Christian man because I think before

I was making music as a Christian child. And in both cases I have imperfections, but there was a declaration that can be made going through all the [stuff] I've been through the last few years."[109]

From Johnny Cash to Elvis, from Al Green to Sam Cooke, musical icons had often wanted to express their spiritual beliefs in their music only to be told by record executives that they should either leave those ideas behind or else express them only on one-off albums that would be explicitly labeled as gospel records. Rarely were they afforded the opportunity to integrate their explicitly spiritual material into their "normal" records, and the practice reached its most absurd zenith when Earth, Wind & Fire front man Philip Bailey, at the height of his fame in the 1980s, was guided by record executives to release two records around the same time, *Chinese Wall*, which contained his mega hit "Easy Lover," and *The Wonders of His Love*, which was released exclusively into the Christian marketplace. Chance the Rapper would not be releasing two records, one secular and one Christian, anytime soon, however, and guided by mentors like Kirk Franklin, he was developing a strong sense of what it meant to be a fully integrated Christian in the middle of popular culture.

"I still think that God means everything to everyone whether they understand it or not or can really see it for themselves or they find God," he said. "I know for a fact we're not pushed or promoted to speak about God with fervor. I don't think there's anything that really allows us to do it as so. But I think the new generation and the forward is all about freedom and all about the ability to do what we want. We're not free unless we can talk about God."[110]

Chance first came on the music scene in 2013 when he released his mix tape *Acid Rap* and in 2015 collaborated with Donnie Trumpet and the Social Experiment on *Surf,* before releasing *Coloring Book.* He had also worked closely with Kanye West on West's album *The Life of Pablo,* and credited West with causing him to be interested in music to begin with. Religion had of course also famously infused West's work, causing the nascent hip-hop star to rap on his track "Jesus Walks," "They say you can rap about anything except for Jesus." Whether through West or his grandmother or other influences in his life, Chance seemed to experience a change in his life.

"If there's any identity that might compete with Chance's South Side status, it's his newfound Christianity, which the rapper has repeatedly referenced on social media and incorporated into the album," noted *Christianity Today* in a profile of the rapper. "One repeated theme: being a Christian has made Chance far more aware of his own flaws, even as he recognizes God's love for him and his desire for redemption in the midst of the complexities of his own life. In *Coloring Book,* Chance assumes this posture toward Chicago's South Side, which suffers from disproportionate poverty and violence. On the album, Chance names his community's flaws while underscoring his undying love, loyalty, and hope for it."[111]

Chicago would play a large role in Chance's music, not just for the shout-outs he would give to the city in his songs and in interviews, but in his determined desire to improve it for his brothers and sisters who called it home. Although he tried to avoid taking overt political stands or endorse one party or another, he too understood his position as a role model and sought to bring positive change.

"Chance's passion for Chicago doesn't keep him from seeing the complicated realities of our childhoods," wrote *Christianity Today*'s Watson Jones III. He continued:

> Although I'm nine years older [than Chance], his lyrics still resonate. In 'Summertime Friends," he takes me back to walking with "socks on concrete," eating "jolly ranchers," and "catching lightening bugs." Listening, I envision kids running as the ice cream truck slowly makes it way down the street. The girls are outside jumping double-dutch.
>
> The song takes a sharp turn: "When the plague hit backyard, had to come in at dark cause big shawtys act hard." I remember my parents discussing the spike of violence in Chicago as if it was a shift in the weather. I think of being 12, walking home from the corner store with my cousins and eating Flamin' Hot Cheetos, when shots ring out at the end of the block, sending us scattering in all directions. I think of walking home from high school, when I was almost shot on two separate occasions.
>
> That Chance's lyrics articulate both the carefree spirit *and* violence of Chicago's summers indicate his hopeful and honest approach in engaging the city.[112]

But whereas many artists, and hip-hop stars in particular, were adept at cataloging the problems of American society and the inner city, Chance's faith compelled him to go the next mile: to articulate a hope and a reason for change.

"Chance believes that God can change the city—and sees himself as a part of this work," *CT* noted.

"I got my city doing front flips, when every father, mayor, rapper jump ship. . . . Clean up the streets, so my daughter can have somewhere to play. I'm the blueprint of a real man," he sings in "Angels." Rather than dodge influence, Chance embraces the opportunity to be a role model. At 21 years old, he partnered with his father, the deputy chief of staff for Rahm Emmanuel [sic], to lead a city-wide effort to stop gun violence for 42 hours in Chicago over Memorial Day weekend. (No one was shot in those 42 hours; in 2016, 69 people were shot over the holiday weekend.) On Twitter, Chance has recently announced his intentions to swear less and quit smoking.[113]

Not everyone was thrilled by his efforts, however, and *New York Post* columnist Phil Mushnick unloaded on Chance's appointment as the Chicago White Sox "ambassador," noting, "He's 22, unmarried with a child, grew up in suburban Chicago. His father had been a political operative for Chicago Mayor Harold Washington, then for Illinois Senator Barack Obama and now for Chicago Mayor Rahm Emanuel."[114]

Mushnick focused his ire on some of the rapper's lyrics:

Chance records and sells pro forma, no-upside, can't-expect-better-from-us, women-denigrating, blood-on-the-breeze rap.

It was suggested that I choose from random any of Chance's songs. . . .

I spun the Google wheel and landed on "Smoke Again," which begins, "I don't even talk to them on the phone again. Leave in the a.m., on the road again. So, b—h, let's f–k so I can smoke again. I gotta smoke again, I got s–t to do."

From there it "grows" more vulgar and, as per the genre,

more boastful. Standard dehumanizing gangsta rap—young black men are N—s, he's especially fond of dope and regards young women as a sub-species in over-and-out service to his immediate libidinous whims, especially oral sex. . . .

Would Mayor Emanuel, MLB Commissioner Rob Manfred and Chicago Rev. Jesse Jackson recite his lyrics in public? For crying out loud, how much faster can we run backwards? How much lower can we fall? And, for what it's worth, Chance, in September, became the father of a daughter.[115]

Not unlike his mentor Kanye West, Chance the Rapper was a work in progress. For American pop culture Christianity, clean heroes who never stumbled were far easier to market. Failures were allowed, of course, but only if they were in the past. While Kirk Franklin had been open about the challenges he faced in the area of sexuality, others, like West, had blatantly flouted the rules when it came to a Christian understanding of the proper role of sexuality in a Christian's life. Chance was no saint, but he seemed to have a sense of knowing when things weren't right in his life and sensing the need for change. Christians might call it the stirrings of conscience or the working of the Holy Spirit in a life, but whatever the label, Chance sometimes took to Twitter to broadcast to his fans the changes he felt he needed to see in his life: "Realizing how profane my speech can be via this interview, gonna work on that," he once shared with his 3 million–plus followers.[116] "I'm leaving cigarettes in January," he shared on another occasion.[117]

PIMPING A BUTTERFLY

Few artists had managed to capture the power of a grandmother's Christian influence on an African-American young man as Doug Pinnick had done in the song and video for his band King's X's track "Over My Head." As Pinnick sang, "Grandma used to sing, every night while she was praying, over my head," the video for the song featured an African-American grandmother with lightning coming from her hands as she prayed over her grandson.[118] It was a powerful visual to showcase the power and import of grandmothers in the lives of young African-American boys for whom dads and grandfathers were sometimes hard to find. As had been the case with Chance the Rapper, for another hip-hop star, named Kendrick Lamar, a grandmother, though not his own, would play a pivotal role in his salvation.

"Mr. Lamar, who grew up in Compton, Calif., had previously been saved as a teenager in the parking lot of a Food 4 Less, he said, when the grandmother of a friend approached him after a tragedy, asking if he had accepted God," observed the *New York Times.* "'One of my homeboys got smoked,' Mr. Lamar recalled. 'She had seen that we weren't right in the head. That was her being an angel for us.' Nearly a decade later, having found that fame and riches did not offer additional salvation, or happiness, he 'wanted to take it to the next level—being underwater,' he said. 'I felt like it was something I had to do.'"[119]

Lamar's run-in with his friend's grandmother had produced an obvious change, causing the *Times*' reporter to observe of the artist that "in addition to being religious, he rarely drinks or smokes, eschews fancy clothes and jewelry and has reportedly been in a quiet, decade-long relationship with his high school sweetheart."[120]

That change seemed to have a lasting impact on Lamar as well as his music, something that would be evident years later when he began his album *Good Kid m.A.A.d City*, with this: "Lord God, I come to you a sinner, and I humbly repent for my sins. I believe that Jesus is Lord. I believe that you raised Him from the dead. I will ask that Jesus will come into my life and be my Lord and Savior. I receive Jesus to take control of my life that I may live for Him from this day forth. Thank you, Lord Jesus, for saving me with your precious blood. In Jesus' name, Amen."[121]

Looking back on those life-changing decisions, which included his quitting drinking and smoking marijuana at an age when many kids were just getting started, Lamar recalled life lessons learned early:

"Teenagers don't get it—we selfish. Go drink, go smoke, go get f---ed up," he said. "Why did I do these things? Because I was brought up around it? It damn sure was in the household. I said, 'I know what happens to my family and certain friends when they get drunk and they smoke. They get out of their minds, they get violent. And that's in my blood.' I have little sips on special occasions, but getting all the way out of my mind may not be a good idea."[122]

In 2009 Lamar released an EP that included the song "Faith," which brought him to the attention of perhaps the most successful Christian hip-hop artist who operated in the mainstream of the music scene, LeCrae. "Faith," was described by one critic as having "a classic, modular narrative structure—like Eminem's 'Guilty Conscience,' or TLC's 'Waterfalls'—with three interlocking verses about people whose belief in God falters under life's cruel gravity. The first verse is rapped in the first person, and resolves with Lamar devastated by the real-life murder of a friend. 'Life is too much, I'm just through,' BJ The Chicago Kid sighs on the hook. It's heavy stuff."[123]

LeCrae, amazed by what he heard, got in touch with the up-and-coming rapper.

"It touched me and I reached out to him like, 'Hey, can I talk to you about it?'" he recalled. "We started talking and that's really how our relationship began . . . In this industry, a lot of people shake hands and high-five each other, but there's not a lot of genuine conversation about the deeper things in life. When you're struggling with your girl or your mom is sick, it's rare that you find someone that actually wants to talk with you on a real level. So being able to connect with him on spiritual matters is definitely something that I value and appreciate."[124]

After several of young Lamar's mix tapes caught the attention of various leaders of the hip-hop industry, his major label debut album, *good kid, m.A.A.d city*, was released and became an instant smash, lauded by *Rolling Stone* as one of the top one hundred debut albums of all time, and he followed that success with the release of his second album. *To Pimp a Butterfly*, in 2015. Fans and critics alike were taking notice of Lamar.

"Unlike most Christian artists who come from a traditional gospel background, like Kirk Franklin or Steven Curtis Chapman, Lamar has never restricted his purview to a discussion of things that are holy," noted BuzzFeed's Reggie Ugwu. He continued:

> For an incredibly famous rapper, his personal life may border on the ascetic: He doesn't go to strip clubs like Drake, or smoke like Lil Wayne; he rarely drinks and has been in a monogamous relationship since before he became famous. But rather than preach about living a moral lifestyle, he gives

full voice to his internal struggles and those of the people he grew up around, deliberately speaking in the language of transgressors.

In the Bible, there is some precedent for this approach. Jesus famously broke from thousands of years of religious dogma by breaking bread with those thought to be morally and spiritually compromised, extending the gifts of God to prostitutes and the unclean. In Mark 2:17, he makes the case for the church to be more accommodating. "It is not the healthy who need a doctor, but the sick," he says. "I have not come to call the righteous, but sinners."

Yet the level at which Christians are to engage with non-Christians is disputed. In a later passage, John 15:19, Jesus says that his followers are not "of the world" but chosen out of it, a distinction that makes them hated.[125]

One of the founding principles of the formation of the Christian music genre—unwritten, of course—was that physical separation from the world, in this case the "secular" music industry, was needed to produce spiritual separation, and these would have many examples to point to of the inability of Christians in the public square to keep the faith in the midst of secular Babylon. To these, many aspects of Lamar's life would be commendable, but they were still likely to be troubled by his unmarried "monogamy" as well as his rough language. Lamar had an answer for those critics as well as others from the more secular side who wished he'd leave his religion behind:

> I wouldn't say I'm the most religious person, neither were both of my parents. I always do quote-unquote religious songs or whatever you want to call them from the standpoint where I'm

trying to find answers. That's the space I speak from and a lot of people can relate because they feel the same way. [I'm] not a person that's putting it in your head—"believe this, believe this, believe this." I'm going through something, I'm a sinner and I'm trying to figure myself out. It never sounds preachy. It sounds like a person who's really confused by what the world has put upon him. [quoted from MTV] . . .

Whether we was inside a church or not, my mother always kept that faith inside of us. The more I started going through my own things in life, my faith got put to the test, and I had to believe that God is real in my heart, my lord and savior Jesus Christ, and I can't run from that. I'll always put that in my music or it just wouldn't be right. People can take it or leave it, I really don't care, because it's for me to put it on records. And I will continue to put more of a spiritual nature in my music. [quoted from *Ebony*][126]

"His ease at moving in the secular world, affinity for profanity, and evolving attitude toward faith are what originally defined Lamar as a mainstream hip-hop star, and not a Christian one," noted BuzzFeed. "And within the Christian community, his overtures toward Jesus have so far been regarded with some skepticism."[127]

It was a common predicament, of course, to be too sacred for the secular and too secular for the sacred, but such was the difficult space that artists like Lamar often found themselves in. Fellow hip-hop star LeCrae was in similar territory and believed that there was a path forward.

"A lot of it is trust," he said. "It's a question of whether or not you're heralding sacred things in your music, and what your motive is. To mainline Christians, there are certain cultural nuances that are acceptable and not acceptable. And I think for them, Kendrick doesn't fall in line with that."[128]

"Some Christians might hear Kendrick rapping about God or Jesus and still reject it," noted Chad Horton, editor of *Rapzilla*, a publication devoted to hip-hop and religion, "because even though he says he's Christian, they listen to his other songs and look at his lifestyle and might not feel like they reflect what a Christian is."[129]

Mainstream music publications, on the other hand, didn't always know how to handle expressions of faith in popular music. Quick to mock much of the output of the Christian rock industry (in some cases at least, justifiably) they were often forced to give grudging respect to artists like Lamar, who combined street smarts with religious fervor.

"It takes you back to 'Faith,' the juxtaposition of feeling near heaven but reality reminds you of the hell that awaits back at home," noted Yoh, senior writer for the website DJBooth. "You can see how these events sparked the survivor's guilt that would be a huge topic on *To Pimp a Butterfly*:

His life had changed, he was facing new pressures from inching closer to super-stardom, but bad news was never far, it could've easily pushed him toward a darker solution, but these trials likely brought him closer to God. Which is why his faith plays such a crucial role in *TPAB*. Kendrick reached a mindset through his beliefs that are soaked into his music but unlike Kanye, he doesn't have a "Jesus Walks" single that commercially and openly displays his beliefs. Kanye was worried about God taking away from his spins, Kendrick doesn't seem to have that kind of doubt, God is the one who brings the spins. Instead of centering his faith into one single, he spread it across the album, wrapped in metaphors and allegories, even without a prayer it's obvious that *TPAB* was made by a Christian man."[130]

By the time Lamar released his next album, *untitled, unmastered*, spotting the religious influence in his music had become something of a parlor game, causing *Billboard* to publish an article that listed the seventeen biblical references that could be found on the record. "The first song is Kendrick's illustration of judgment day, the Book of Revelation in rap form," noted the DJBooth writer. "He even walks us through what he's prepared to reply when God asks, "What have you done for me?" "I made *To Pimp a Butterfly* for you, told me to use my vocals to save mankind for you, say I didn't try for you, say I didn't ride for you, I tithed for you, I pushed the club to the side for you, who love you like I love you?'"[131]

Seemingly unperturbed by his critics, Lamar continued to spread the Word through his music and in his daily life. Dressing up as his hero, Jesus Christ, one Halloween, Lamar explained to fans: "If I want to idolize somebody, I'm not going to do a scary monster, I'm not gonna do another artist or a human being—I'm gonna idolize the Master, who I feel is the Master, and try to walk in his light. It's hard, it's something I probably could never do, but I'm gonna try. Not just with the outfit but with everyday life. The outfit is just the imagery, but what's inside me will display longer."[132]

Kendrick Lamar was yet another who faced the ongoing challenge of integrating religion into popular music. Although the African-American musical subculture was much more open to that integration than, say, elements of the rock music industry had been, there were still many challenges for artists like Lamar, who nonetheless seemed grateful for the opportunity.

"This is truly a blessing from a higher power," he said, "and as long as I understand that there's really no limitations to what I can do. Everything is forward with me. When I'm in the studio I'm looking for creativity I haven't matched yet, a feeling I haven't felt. It's a high. When you look at people like Jay Z, Nas, Dr. Dre, these people are established, but they love music and they love that high. You always want that feeling of creativity."[133]

Not unlike the circuit-riding preachers who once dotted the American landscape, going town to town, warning of impending doom for those who rejected the message of God's salvation and His demands that people turn from their sin and live righteous lives, Kendrick Lamar was bringing the Good Word to a town and a streaming device near you, with the same message of sin, redemption, and salvation.

"We're in the last days, man—I truly in my heart believe that . . . It's written," he said.[134]

4

A CROSS AND A SONG
WHERE I DON'T BELONG

OH, MERCY!

One of the most stunning examples of Christian pop crossing over into mainstream music was the story of the unbelievable journey of a little song titled "I Can Only Imagine." The song was written by a young Texan named Bart Millard, who managed to get his song heard by the devout pop singer Amy Grant, who liked "Imagine" so much that she recorded it as an addition to what was otherwise a record chock-full of hymns, called *Legacy . . . Hymns & Faith*.

Grant, who had just divorced first husband Gary Chapman and married country singer Vince Gill—who had recently divorced his own wife—needed to reconnect with her audience and prove that while she had left her marriage, she hadn't left her faith. Her savvy manager, Mike Blanton, suggested that she hold off on a pop record and record hymns as a way of reconnecting with her Christian audience and reaffirming her faith. Grant did possess that rare ability to breathe new life into old hymns—she had turned in a stunning performance of " 'Tis So Sweet to Trust in Jesus" on the inspirational *Our Hymns* compilation in 1991, miles beyond the other offerings from other artists who contributed to the record.

Legacy was no exception, with Grant masterfully delivering on such classic hymns as "This Is My Father's World," and "Come, Thou Fount of Every Blessing," but the album managed to please no one—alienating her pop fans, who had little interest in hymns, and failing to connect with her Christians fans, who were still smarting over what seemed to be an unwillingness to stay in her marriage, difficult as it had appeared to be. Selling a modest 250,000 copies, *Legacy*'s failure likely contributed to Millard's song "I Can Only Imagine" not getting much of a hearing.

However, by that point Millard and his band, MercyMe, had taken their version to the top of the contemporary Christian pop charts, which measured activity at hundreds of stations across the United States that only played offerings by artists who were signed to Christian-oriented music companies. MercyMe's version of "Imagine" even won a Dove award, the Christian music industry's version of a Grammy, for song of the year. However, the song's greatest days were still ahead.

For decades radical secularists and Christian fundamentalists had worked under a sort of gentleman's agreement when it came to entertainment products with strong Christian content.

For different reasons, both agreed to keep such content off the mainstream pop culture map and ensure that it was, for the most part, only marketed to true believers. For the secularists, who loathed public displays of religious affection, shuffling the religious off into a section of pop culture labeled "inspirational" or "gospel" meant religious devotion would stay out of mainstream circulation. For the Christians, taught for decades that separation was the only way to preserve true faith, and that the public square was not suitable for expressions of devotion to God, having their own industry was an easy solution. There would be no mainstream scrutiny of their messages so long as they stayed in their world. To convince young Christian artists that they must stay in their corner of pop culture, where few nonbelievers would ever hear their work, the leaders of their industry fed them a constant diet of martyrdom, making it clear at every opportunity that songs that clearly addressed their beliefs would never be allowed on the mainstream airwaves.

"Certain spiritual concepts can't cross over," said the late Dana Key, who was once one of the industry's biggest stars before later starting his own label, Ardent. "Talk about God, talk about love—no problem. Talk about Jesus, his death, sin . . . those concepts are very offensive. The cross is still a stumbling block. The mainstream rejects music that is straightforward Christian."[1]

For years this woe-is-me propaganda served as the glue that held the CCM industry together. To be sure, beginning in the late 1960s, when rockers first got the notion to sing about their faith in God, there had indeed been resistance from the mainstream rock business to that type of music. Once, when Capitol Records recording artist Larry Norman had sought to title his record *We Need a Whole Lot More Jesus, and a Lot Less*

Rock & Roll and place a portrait of Christ on the cover, the label had demurred, instead titling it *I Love You* and using a photo of Norman and his band of hippies on the cover.

But as such stories circulated among the early Christian rockers, they began to believe that their only recourse was to create their own culture-within-a-culture, which essentially became a parallel universe of radio stations, record companies, and publications that were removed from mainstream music. What they apparently didn't realize was that any market pressures that might have given them a chance at mainstream exposure—particularly Christians who might have listened to mainstream radio and requested faith-filled songs—simply evaporated as Christians tuned out "secular" pop radio and changed the dial to their local Christian music station. But the success of MercyMe's "Imagine" vividly illustrated just how much pop culture influence Christians had forfeited by withdrawing from the primary music culture, as well as the influence they could exert once again when they decided to reengage.

The song "may be the most overtly religious song to hit the Top 40 since 1974," observed Steve Carney of the *Los Angeles Times*. "That year an Australian nun, Sister Janet Mead, sang the Lord's Prayer and sold 2 million copies worldwide, peaking at No. 4 on the U.S. pop charts."[2]

"Here's how it happened," remembered MercyMe front man Millard:

> I live in Dallas, and there's a station in Dallas called Wild 100 FM. The morning show DJs are Fitz and Big Gay Steven. And as you'd guess, Steven is just over-the-top, flamboyantly gay, kind of the Will & Grace vibe. Somebody called in and

asked them to play "Imagine" and they were like, "Yeah, okay, we'll play it. We'll play it once." And this station plays J. Lo, Eminem, Timberlake, all that stuff. Well, they played the song once and the phone rang off the hook. So they said they'd play it again the next morning. Their whole count-down show is based on Internet and call-in votes. The next day, they played it twice, and it became the number one song in Dallas. It stayed there for like three months, until finally they retired it and put it in heavy rotation.[3]

What Millard's story vividly illustrated was the impor-tance—indeed, the necessity—of engagement on the part of his fellow believers in order to have the kind of profound effect that "Imagine" had on pop culture. Had that one (presumably) Christian listener been listening to Christian radio instead of a mainstream pop station, and not taken the time to contact his or her local station, the song might never have gained a hearing in the mainstream. But as an increasing number of Christian listeners began to turn to mainstream radio and demand equal time for their favorite artists, the stations proved responsive. Before long, help came in the form of a Curb Records radio promotions veteran who saw an opportunity, as Millard recalled:

Some independent radio guy heard about what happened and called this guy in L.A. who's not a Christian, who works for Curb and he got the record and fell in love with it. He called Mike Curb and said, "These guys are your market, what's going on?" So Curb worked out a deal with [our label] INO Records, not really to try to run it up the charts or anything, but just to try to see if the Dallas thing was a fluke. So they took it and tested it in 20 different markets,

and from my understanding, it's been number one in all or
almost all of them. One guy wrote to us and said, "The first
time we played it, we got over 600 emails that day. We can't
answer them all." Another guy said all of his phone lines
were jammed for two or three hours so people were actually
driving to the station to ask what that song was.[4]

Bob Catania, the Curb executive who saw the potential
of the song and worked it to mainstream radio, understood
the challenges he faced in going to market with such a strong
Christian message:

> Any record that has a Jesus reference in it is going to be
> problematic for some people, especially in a major market
> like New York or L.A., especially where there's a diverse
> population . . . What we've been telling is it's really a song
> about loss, one day I can only imagine what it will be like in
> heaven. . . . Since this record has come out, we have never
> received one call from a radio station asking for the 'Jesus-
> less' version. No one seems to be having an issue with that.[5]

As Catania and his staff worked the phones, encouraging
pop radio stations to play the song, listener response was explosive and immediate:

> "'I Can Only Imagine' had the largest response ever in a record
> that I have tested," said Steve Matthews, programming director
> at WZNY in Augusta, GA. "I played the song one time and
> my phones were solid for the next 20 minutes. The calls were
> not asking me who the artist was, but to thank me for playing
> the song. I received calls from surrounding markets begging
> me to call other markets to tell them to play it." . . .

"I have received the most email about this song than any I can remember," said Wendy Gatlin, music director at WKZL in Greensboro, N.C. "The studio lines are jammin.'"[6]

For Catania, the response to "Imagine" was a reminder that listeners were open to a variety of messages:

Top 40 traditionally has been a format of extremes and reaction records . . . There are so many records with so many extremes in one direction. I think a lot of the messages are uncomfortable to a lot of listeners. A lot of these songs are very reactive to a certain constituency. What we're trying to sell is an extreme message with a different message. We know it will elicit a response. . . . people are anxious for a positive message. . . . I think the challenge for radio is not to skew too far to one side. A lot of the hip hop records are just so explosive from a sales and reaction standpoint. You cannot ignore what's going on with 50 Cent (a relatively new hip hop act with top record sales and radio hits). The challenge is to find that balance.[7]

Of course, the "I Can Only Imagine" phenomenon was not the first time a song that was, for all intents and purposes, created for and marketed to Christians had broken through the barrier that separated music with a Christian bent from the pop mainstream. Other songs had made the leap, but few were as clear in their statements of devotion to God as "Imagine." But for too many artists who achieved such success, a particularly grating habit was the tendency to attribute the success solely to God, often ignoring the efforts of those who had helped engineer the song's success. In the case of MercyMe and its label, INO, the song had played its course, and taking it to the mainstream was the furthest thing from their minds. But when success came, rather than crediting those who helped make it happen—like the listener who requested it, the Dallas DJs who broke it, or the canny radio promotions man who worked it—guitarist Mike Scheuchzer had only One in mind: "To me the biggest part of it all is that our record label could have put a million dollar budget behind this song and this wouldn't have happened. It's something that obviously has God's hand in it and something that He's promoting."[8]

While only the most ardent atheist would fail to credit God with having a hand in the matter, the habit on the part of a number of Christian crossover artists to ignore the work of those who actually made their songs hits seemed to bespeak a certain passivity that kept their music from being made and marketed strategically, with a plan to bring it into the great center of popular culture, where most Americans heard their music. Translation: If God was in charge of creating pop hits, why strategize to try to engineer future ones?

The success that accompanied "I Can Only Imagine" also seemed to catch the band off guard, since its members saw themselves not as a rock band but as a "worship band," a common term used to identify artists who intended for their music to be used by fellow Christians to worship God rather than to be enjoyed by nonbelievers. But MercyMe's music had become popular outside of their comfort zone, and the band seemed nonplussed as to what to do next with the amazing and unexpected platform that they'd been given. According to lead singer Millard:

> The biggest, most unexpected and mind-boggling thing that we're going through right now is the whole mainstream thing.

This stuff has left me feeling like, "God, I am completely helpless. I have no clue." I think we're scared more than we're excited about it. I'm petrified about where it's going to take us. . . . As a ministry, we're totally worship leaders, that's what we try to do. I don't know how we got into this whole situation in the mainstream industry. But we're called to be worship leaders.[9]

Some critics argued that far too many young Christians seemed to sense a calling to minister to fellow believers in proportions that were completely out of sync with the number of believers and unbelievers in the world, perhaps forgetting that no Christian was exempt from the Great Commission—Christ's parting command for His followers to enter the world and tell others about Him. In the battle for the hearts, minds, and ears of nonbelievers, far too many Christians in the music world seemed to want kitchen duty rather than service on the front lines. Whether or not MercyMe was among these, of course, nobody could be sure. However, the band amazingly decided not to capitalize on their hard-earned position as a pop/rock band, choosing to make a record of hymns instead of a record that could connect with mainstream fans they had won over thanks to the success of "I Can Only Imagine."

"I really want to do a hymns album, bad. I mean, bad," said Millard. "Our label is always talking about how, 'when it's time to zig we want to zag, and do something different.' So I'm thinking, with all of this quote-unquote mainstream momentum—if it even happens—what better time to do a hymns album? So I'm going to hold them to that and see what happens."[10]

For secularists who loathed the idea of Christian ideas

floating across the nation's airwaves, MercyMe's apparent step back from the pop music market was likely a welcome one; for those who liked the idea of vocal Christians finding their place in mainstream music, the band's decision to retreat back into the confines of the religious music subculture would be a sore disappointment. But finding a place in mainstream music was a goal that the members of MercyMe didn't seem to share as they prepared their hymns record and went on tour with Michael W. Smith, who also seemed to have abandoned the idea of playing for a mainstream audience after his own succession of "worship" records made no discernible impact outside of the cloistered world of contemporary Christian music.

Still, it was difficult to fault Millard and MercyMe for their fear of the unknown. The doctrine of separatism had, in many cases, left young evangelicals woefully unprepared for interaction with nonbelievers, and Millard was getting a crash course in attempting to keep the faith while he occasionally traveled in circles that included those who disagreed with his spiritual beliefs:

> Here we are. And I am scared to death. The whole band is . . . a lot of this we can handle and can kind of see coming, but when you go into an interview and Big Gay Steven is the one doing it, and you're on the air in an "A" market . . . what I learned is, we went in petrified. But when they came to meet us in the waiting room at the station, they were more scared than we were. Because they expected us to be shoving stuff down their throats. So we just tried to kill them with kindness. But they were nervous because they expected us to be in their faces.[11]

For nearly a century the retreat of millions of devout Christians from the primary culture had caused the separation of believers from unbelievers, resulting not only in the creation of parallel subcultures but a lack of dialogue between the two groups. Secular Americans living in big cities like New York, Los Angeles, and Seattle often had no meaningful interaction with the devout, and conversely the devout often had no meaningful interaction with their less-religious counterparts. This arguably led directly to increased polarization between the two groups and a serious lack of mutual understanding. MercyMe's unexpected success caused its members to reevaluate the way they viewed the world, and while it was unlikely they would change their views or give up their faith, they were coming to a better understanding of and appreciation for those who disagreed with them.

STACIE'S RIDE

Stacie Orrico followed the well-worn path to pop stardom charted by artists such as Britney Spears, Jessica Simpson, and Christina Aguilera, except she took a slightly more circuitous one—she started in the Christian music industry as a preteen and achieved a degree of notoriety there before finding widespread success in the pop industry. Her CCM label home, Forefront, had been purchased by EMI, which also owned Virgin Records, and Forefront and Virgin worked closely to develop Orrico's next record, which catapulted her onto the pop charts and gave her unprecedented success on pop radio, MTV, and VH1.

There was one problem with the otherwise flawlessly executed plan: the hectic pace of a career at the top of the pop charts proved to be too much for Orrico. A manic travel schedule, which included multiple trips to Japan, where her record reached the top of the pop charts, left Orrico on the verge of a meltdown, and the singer informed Virgin that she would be suspending her career. Orrico's experience pointed out another problem with the idea of devout Christians going into the mainstream: the music business—and the touring necessary to sustain a career—was often not conducive to maintaining physical, mental, or spiritual balance. While initial reports indicated that the singer was going to retire, it later became apparent that she was simply taking a break. Nevertheless, her experience would at least raise the question of whether or not Virgin would want to invest in artists like Orrico in the future, if the pace of a pop star was too hectic for such an artist. How the Stacie Orrico story played out would prove to be an important factor that influenced future attempts at crossover careers.

Orrico got her start at an early age, and actually signed her first record deal when she was twelve. When most kids her age were first discovering what kind of music they enjoyed listening to, Orrico had the added pressure of trying to figure out what her sound was going to be. After a solid debut album and a bit of notoriety in the Christian music market, Orrico was ready for her leap into the musical mainstream. And her first opportunity came when she was asked to open for Destiny's Child, before her eventual signing to Virgin Records. Winning the opening slot on the Destiny's Child tour was just the beginning of the path to pop stardom that would soon open up for the young singer who seemed ready for whatever lay ahead. However, developing an artist jointly between a CCM and "secular" label was easier said than done. The very fact that it had to be done was something of an admission of failure by the CCM labels, an acknowledgment that, on their own, they were simply unable to take their artists outside of their subculture. But for artists like Orrico it was preferable to continuing to sing only for fellow believers. So began dozens of trips to L.A. for the head of Orrico's label, Greg Ham, who met regularly with Virgin Records' staff to help Orrico craft a record that could withstand the scrutiny of both the mainstream and CCM markets. Virgin, Forefront, and Orrico decided that the song "Stuck" would be her first introduction to mainstream pop fans. Orrico had cowritten the song with a songwriter named Kevin Kadish, who had first asked the singer what the biggest problems young girls like her faced:

> I just said teenage girls end up in these relationships where they're not treated very well and they end up on this emotional roller coaster . . . On one hand, they know they should get out because it's not really good for me. But on the other side of it, they are afraid of being alone, they like the security of having a boyfriend. . . . They are stuck. It's kind of sad; most teenagers don't have a healthy relationship to look to to go, 'that's how I'm supposed to treat a guy,' so it ends up being a mess.[12]

Kadish kept asking questions, and the more Orrico talked, the more an idea for a song was fleshed out:

> Kevin said to me, "Stacie, when girls are dealing in a hard relationship, where do you think it comes from? Why do you think it's hard? Why do you think they feel hurt? Why do you think they make bad decisions?" And I just said I think that a lot of young girls end up in relationships where they are not being treated very well. And they haven't had a

healthy relationship in their life to look to know how they are supposed to do it. They don't know exactly how they are supposed to be treated, or how they are supposed to do it to make it all work out right and to feel good in a relationship. And so they end up on this emotional roller coaster. . . . On one side it's like "I know this relationship isn't good for me, I know it's not healthy, I know I need something more." But on the other hand "I don't know what I'm going to do if I don't have him in my life.[13]

Joint efforts between CCM and mainstream labels to develop artists had often failed in the past, with few notable exceptions, when the mainstream label hadn't been sufficiently motivated. Perhaps the most successful attempt had been the joint development of Amy Grant by A&M and Word Records, which climaxed in the success of her record *Unguarded*. More often they had failed, however, often due to the sheer embarrassment felt by publicists, marketing managers, and others at mainstream labels over having to "work" Christian product to their communities.

But when it came to the positioning and selling of Stacie Orrico, Virgin was completely on target. The label's new head, Matt Serletic, appeared to be 100 percent behind Orrico, and the rest of the label apparently picked up on that and worked hard to make it a success. Before long, "Stuck" was a major pop smash, and the singer was turning up everywhere from MTV's TRL to radio stations around the country. But her success was only beginning—for her all-important follow-up single, which would either confirm Orrico's talent or merely cement her status as a one-hit wonder, Orrico and her team selected the song "There's Gotta Be

(More to Life)," a song that, unlike "Stuck," presented Orrico's Christian worldview relatively clearly and it too became a pop hit.

Generally speaking, those artists—such as Amy Grant, Switchfoot, Sixpence None the Richer, and others—who had successfully crossed over from being exclusively CCM artists to being heard in mainstream circles had, over time, developed a philosophy of cultural engagement. But these had all been at least in their twenties when they made their move and were seasoned veterans by the time they were thrust into the spotlight. Orrico, on the other hand, was still barely seventeen when she became a pop phenomenon but had already developed a worldview that caused her to seek to impact the wider world. She once told an interviewer:

> There's not Christian doctors and non-Christian doctors. You do what you do, and some are better than others . . . It [shouldn't be] so much about "the mainstream," "the Christian," whatever. I feel like music is music. I am an artist and yes, I am an artist who is Christian, but I make music about all the things I deal with in life, not only my faith. I sing about my faith, my relationships, the good things I do, the mistakes I make. All those things.[14]

Orrico also seemed to have little use for the separatism that had caused many a Christian artist to go unheard by the wider culture:

> You know it's difficult for me because I grew up listening to all types of music. I grew up listening to Christian music and mainstream music, and I remember always thinking, "Why do we put artists in all these different categories? She's a Christian

artist, and she's a Christian woman, but her music could be really cool on this station. And maybe by putting a title on herself, maybe it's keeping her from going here." I remember even when I was 6 and 7 thinking about this trying to figure out why there were all these little titles. I am a Christian, I have been raised in a Christian home, when I was 4 years old I prayed in my own little innocent heart and prayed to ask Christ to come into my life, and I cannot do anything without Him. He is the base of everything that I do every single day. I would love it if we could take off all the titles. I wish I could be just an artist. I am an artist who is a Christian, who sings R&B music, who sings honestly about the things I'm dealing with in my life—whether it's my faith or the mistakes that I've made or the things that I'm questioning or the things that I'm discovering for the first time. And, yes, I am a Christian—I have not deserted that. Yes, I would love to take all the titles off of every type of genre of music. I would love to hear all types of Christian artists played all over the world. I'd love to hear good, positive mainstream music played all over the place. I'd love to be able to bring music together. But I have not deserted Christ. I have not deserted my faith.[15]

What would set Stacie Orrico apart from at least some of her contemporaries would be, not only her ability to maintain her beliefs in the world of popular music, but also her determination to stay grounded in her community. Orrico's parents and family members traveled with her constantly and seemed to keep at bay many of the destructive influences that tend to follow young pop stars. At a young age, Stacie Orrico had already discovered for herself the practical reasons behind Christ's admonition to go into the world and impact it. She had spent years performing almost exclusively for fellow believers, thereby limiting her social interactions to people who agreed with her beliefs. But making the jump to pop music brought new ways to take her music and her faith to a wider audience:

> I've had so many cool opportunities in the last year, especially of just getting to spend time with people who have experienced things in their lives that I would have never imagined—people who have grown up in such different family situations from mine, and different cultural backgrounds, people who have literally never been around or had somebody in their life who told them anything about God. And I think I just think that since we're living in America that everybody's been to church a few times, everybody knows somebody who is Christian. [But] there are some people who just don't. They weren't raised with any of that around them.[16]

Despite her generally sunny outlook, by 2004 the singer had burned out and was ready for a break—a very long break. When her manager informed Virgin that Orrico wanted out of the rat race of touring and promotional work, the label was none too happy, according to published reports. They had not invested millions of dollars into the young star anticipating that she would then want to get out. But success came quickly—perhaps too quickly—and a look at Orrico's daily schedule might give even the most energetic person pause. In an interview the singer outlined a typical day in her life at the height of her career:

> You start with the radio station in the early morning, and you usually do the morning drive, so you're there by 6:30 or 7:00.

And between get ready time, and meet in the lobby fifteen minutes early, and drive to the station—you're usually up at 4:30 that morning. And then you do the radio station, and then you hang out and have breakfast, you drive to two or three random little meetings that you have with publications or something media, and then you drop by a couple bookstores to say hey to everybody and check in—we meet them . . . then we go and we do the in-store, so you sound check for the in-store or you get ready, sign a bunch of stuff, sing for a little bit, do a signing, and then you're done. Then you have a dinner. And right now for me, I'll visit three or four different stations in each city we'll go to, because we'll go to the AC Christian station, the CHR Christian station, and then usually two Top 40 pop stations. So then we go to dinner with a couple of the stations, and then after that we'll go have dessert or coffee with the other pop station, and we'll sign all their stuff. So usually the night ends between 11:30 and 12:00. And you get back to the hotel and get 3 or 4 hours of sleep, and then you keep going. It involves a lot of coffee, a lot of candy.[17]

Eventually Orrico would get out of her recording contracts and return to Seattle, where she was reported to be working as a waitress. Her rise to fame and sudden departure raised all sorts of questions about the appropriateness of teen fame, especially the perils of entrusting such a deep and profound message to such a young vessel whose life experiences, merely by virtue of age, were so severely limited. Still, Orrico clearly understood the youth culture in which she was operating and seemed to intuitively sense that somebody would be setting the moral tone for a new generation of girls.

"A couple of years down the road, I would love it if people are on MTV or wherever and instead of saying, like they would for Britney Spears, 'this is the artist who single-handedly convinced young girls to run around in midriffs,' they would say, 'this is an artist who was able to challenge me and made it great for little girls to be ladies, and to respect themselves, respect others, make wise decisions in their relationships, and think twice about what life is about.'"[18]

THE GREAT BATTLE

In 2012, a "new" duo known as the Civil Wars was given the highest accolade the music business has to offer when it garnered two Grammys for its debut album, *Barton Hollow*. Critical acclaim mostly echoed the comments of a reviewer for *Paste*, who noted that "'Barton Hollow' may be a fictional location, but The Civil Wars' music gives it a voice and identity—one of mystery, mystique and beauty. War has never been so pleasant."[19]

The band's lead singer, Joy Williams, said:

I came up with the name. It has nothing to do with the historical meaning. There is a great quote that I believe is Plato, who said, "Be kind, for everyone you meet is fighting a great battle." As I was thinking about the music we make, that sense of battle seemed applicable. That sense of yin and yang, of male and female, of our differing backgrounds, all that seemed to allude to the battles that we all face with faith or addictions or jobs or relationships. Every single person walking down the street is fighting a great battle, whether or not you can see it.[20]

For fans of contemporary Christian music, there was nothing new about Williams or her talent—she had won nearly a dozen Dove awards in her previous incarnation as a solo artist signed to the Reunion label. And the civil war she described in choosing her band's name could easily have illustrated the one that had gone on inside her own mind as Williams the Christian singer battled Williams the recording artist who wanted to sing for the world. After selling more than a quarter of a million records in the Christian music industry, she had grown tired of the confines that walled her off from the mainstream world, so she begged out of her recording contract, moved to Los Angeles, and eventually began work on a solo EP aimed at the mainstream market and released it independently on her and her husband, Nate Yetton's, label, Sensibility Music. Williams then met an unexpected new friend named John Paul White, who would take her career in an equally unexpected direction. Williams remembered:

> We met in 2008 at what, in Nashville, is known as a "writing camp," a gathering of songwriters for the purpose of writing radio singles for a band that didn't even have a name at that point. . . . I was like, "OK, I'm going into this room with somebody named John Paul White." I had no idea what I was walking in to. . . . In Nashville, it's not uncommon to harmonize with someone but what was strange was that when he started singing it was like I knew where he was going to go before he went there—it tightened my stomach and made me pay attention. . . . meeting John Paul brought this weird feeling of falling in love with music again.[21]

"Joy and I have definitely talked about the moment a million times between us," recalled White.

White, a family man from Alabama, was looking for a big break, and his connection with Williams was unexpected:

> I was in this room with the other person who was in our group, Greg Becker. I'd written some songs with him before, so I was sitting there thinking, "At least I'm not in a room with two strangers." Then Joy walked in; we both peppered her with questions and it soon became clear she had the same kind of story and that none of us really wanted to be there.
>
> When we started singing together, there was this weird click; it was like there was a dance going where I knew I could lead her but she could lead me, too.
>
> We immediately made another appointment to write at her house. That day it was just the two of us and we wrote "Falling," which is on our album. We were both like, "Who cares what or who this song is for; this is really cool." So we went into the studio to record it. I played the result to a close friend and she said: "She's the female you, vocally," and I totally understood what she meant. I still wasn't sure what was going to happen but I thought to myself, "From now on, she's going to sing everything that I write."[22]

The Civil Wars' debut record, *Barton Hollow*, was a stunning success that exceeded the band members' wildest expectations, debuting as the best-selling digital album in the country and quickly becoming the darling of music critics. Although the parallels between Williams and Katy Perry were evident—both had achieved success in the CCM world before "crossing over"—it was also clear that Williams had wrestled mightily with her heritage as a Christian singer, and she wanted to carefully leave behind the things that weren't helpful while holding on to the good. Asked about her past by a reporter, she replied:

> I started so young in CCM, and as I look back at who I was at 17, I realize I was willing to be more of a mouthpiece than necessarily an artist. As the years went by, I started recognizing that the music that I connected with the most was honest and open and broken and mostly written by the artists themselves. So the journey of trying to find my voice amidst a marketing team, a radio team, a budget, a bottom line, and a message I felt could be so much deeper, was difficult for me. I had a hard time trying to express myself without being met with some serious opposition. I kind of had to fight my way through my last few projects to get my songs out there, and to me that seemed a little bit odd.[23]

After three hit records, Williams had, in her own understated way, come to question the organizational paradigm of CCM:

> I understand that the mantra for a lot of Christian music is that it's "safe for the whole family," but I don't believe that faith is always meant to be safe. I started really wrestling with the fact that I was only allowed to talk about certain things. I felt like the label was asking me to become two separate people in order to get the job done. My name is Joy and I smile a lot, but I've gotten older and been married almost five years and I've lived a little bit more of life. I know now that so much of life is really broken, and there is beauty and strength in that acknowledgement. All in all, I just felt like I needed to take a break, step back, and reevaluate why I was doing what I was

doing. I'm really proud of the last label record I made, and I was able to talk a little more about some of the brokenness and shadows we all face. And I'm so thankful for the people who had been so supportive all those years, and I can look back and be grateful. But I still just felt that it was time for a new chapter, and I don't necessarily think I'll ever return.[24]

Signed as a teenager to one of Christian music's top labels, Williams, like many other young God-rockers, was determined to set the world on fire with her faith despite being young, naïve, and relatively unaware of the pitfalls of life. Her awakening came to be a warning to young artists about the challenges of impacting the world with faith at such a young age, as well as the importance of giving artists the freedom to reach the entire culture, even those outside of their natural philosophical and religious spheres. She remembered:

At 17, I was so excited about changing the world, telling people about the Lord, and rubbing shoulders with people and hearing their stories. The more I heard stories of some of the things that people were going through, it made me realize that faith was not some sort of religious high. It's a lot less performance-based than I thought it was. For so long, I felt like if I wasn't doing things perfectly, then I was just getting in the way, and that God couldn't use somebody who was getting in the way.

I'm so thankful that when I was 19 and 20, I got counseling from some amazing women who told me, "God doesn't need you to change the world; he needs you to be who you are." There is glory in acknowledging the cracked, stubborn, scabbed places of who you are, and there is beauty in the nuances of your femininity that is both fragile and strong. It has been a deepening processes to be outside of the context of conservative church language, even though the heart of it still very much rings true, and discover a faith that is more my own.[25]

The saga of Joy Williams and the Civil Wars was watched closely by their fans, many of whom had no idea that Williams had been involved in CCM. The duo had attained massive success in a very short amount of time, culminating in their winning a Grammy in 2013, but by the following year creative tensions between them caused them to call it quits, although Williams would continue her solo work. But her story was also a part of a larger story about people of faith reentering the primary culture, facing the challenges that inevitably arise when deeply religious people develop shared communities with more secular Americans. Williams's experience in Christian music would serve as a guide for the journey ahead:

> I enjoyed what I learned in the process of being in CCM for about six or seven years, but I think, too, on top of that, I started feeling a little bit boxed in. I think within that genre of music, it's very important to overtly express the worldview that you have versus what you see actually through that worldview. So I've been really enjoying the freedom of being able to write what I see through my worldview. And I think writing about truth and beauty in a way that plays with dark and light is really fascinating to me and something that I really enjoy.[26]

CARS, GOD, AND ROCK 'N' ROLL

Around the time Evanescence was turning the rock world and the Christian community upside down with its on-again, off-again faith stance, another band with deep roots in the Christian community, Chevelle, was quietly but steadily making inroads into the mainstream rock world. Picked out of obscurity by Squint Entertainment founder Steve Taylor, a longtime veteran of the CCM scene, the band made its entry into the musical big time—and it caught many by surprise, including the three brothers who made up the band, Sam, Pete and Joe Loeffler.

The band had taken its name from one of their favorite cars—which they thought described them as well. And an encounter with producer Steve Taylor would open up a career path for the band. Taylor had attained iconic status in the Christian community with his well-received solo albums, which took him to the top of that world in the mid- and late 1980s. In the '90s he made his first attempt at mainstream success when he formed a band called Chagall Guevara and released two critically acclaimed rock albums via MCA. By the late '90s Taylor had launched his own label, Squint, and was looking for an act to follow the success that his first band, Sixpence None the Richer, had experienced. In Chevelle, Taylor found what he was looking for. Squint quickly had Chevelle record what would become their debut album, *Point #1*.

"We did the album in 17 days, which was a little rushed," said Sam, shortly after completing it. "I'm happy with the CD, but there are things we could have done better if we'd taken more time recording."[27]

Taylor, because of his background as an artist, was usually spoken highly of by his bands for his ability to guide their careers without overstepping his bounds. That meant personally producing some of the artists, like Sixpence None the Richer, while allowing others, like Chevelle, to work with outside producers, and before long the band was making waves in the fickle world of hard rock. Despite the fact that they were on an unknown indie label with no track record, Chevelle was added to regular rotation on MTV's *120 Minutes* program, and was nominated for two *Billboard* Music video awards. Two singles, "Mia" and "Point #1," charted on both the rock and alternative charts. Later, when Squint folded and was subsumed into the label that had funded it, the CCM label Word, things threatened to get ugly as the band sought to get out of its contract: "The company we had signed with folded, and we couldn't get out of the deal in order to put out another record, because they had a parent company," Sam recalled. "The case was in court for eleven months and settled out of court the day before the trial date."[28]

With the case settled, Chevelle was quickly picked up by Epic and released a second record, *Wonder What's Next*, which surprised many by opening at number fourteen on the album sales chart. While casual listeners could be forgiven for not picking up immediately on the brothers' faith as expressed through their music, for those who listened carefully, faith was an undergirding force and generally served as a subtext to the band's songs.

For a long time, many Christians had been arguing for the creation of music that went beyond certain buzzwords, and instead consistently reflected the presence of what they described as a "Christian worldview." Chevelle's music was the answer to their prayers. One case in point was the band's hit single "Send the Pain Below," which generally reflected a Christian understanding of pain as not being random or purposeless, but something allowed by God in an individual's life that one could learn important lessons from.

"Despite its grimace-inducing title, 'Send the Pain Below' isn't a directive to deliver a low blow," noted one reviewer. "Rather, it serves as a self-help guide that teaches one to suck it up, no matter the gravity of the situation."[29]

Pete Loeffler observed:

The amazing thing about pain in someone's life is that it's not always something that someone should avoid, because pain can, if you let it, make you grow. And you can honestly use pain to create art, and that's honestly what we try to do with music. A lot of people in this day and age are always trying to get away from situations that cause them grief, and if you do that you're not really going to be a well-rounded person, because you're not going to know how to deal with the ups and downs of life.[30]

Other songs on the band's second record were even more direct, such as the simple yet inspirational "Grab Thy Hand," which was built around the chorus "God, how I long to grab Thy hand and walk."

Perhaps because the members of Chevelle were more grounded in their faith, or more experienced in the difficulties that lay at the intersection of religion and rock 'n' roll, they handled the same pitfalls that had tripped up the young members of Evanescence with ease and class, never dissing their Christian fans who had given them their start and who still admired them and still considered them one of their own. While some artists overreacted during the difficult maneuver of separating themselves from the "Christian rock" moniker without alienating those who populated it or separating themselves from their faith, the members of Chevelle were unruffled when listeners associated them with the Christian rock movement: "I think there are certain people out there that need that confidence that what they are listening to is not motivated by something evil," Sam said. And in order to listen to music, they have to be assured of that. It's not like it bothers us either. It's certainly not a bad thing to be called. It's better than being a satanic band, I suppose."[31]

The rock world was filled with some of the gatekeepers, from journalists to disc jockeys to record executives, who sometimes failed to hide their contempt for the Christian faith. For many rock bands composed of Christians, the trick was to tiptoe around those gatekeepers who could barely stomach the very notion of Christians in rock. Sam Loeffler was accustomed to such "inquiry." With respect to Chevelle's "Christian band" label, he told one journalist, "It's something that's probably going to follow us around forever and that's fine . . . It's pretty simple. We originally signed with a record company that was backed by Word [Records], so the record was in Christian bookstores. It was really an accidental thing."[32]

The critic seemed relieved, assuming (incorrectly) that a Christian worldview would not be wafting over the nation's airwaves:

> Assuring me that the band had nothing to do with the Christian rock industry, Sam states that they are "recovering Catholics" who are still Christians, but that any religious attitudes on the part of Chevelle's members are distinctly separate from the band and their music. With repeated listens to WWN, I feel qualified to state that there are no sermons

detected on the album. Now I can enjoy Chevelle's music without fear of subliminal Christian messages intruding my subconscious. Thank God, no pun intended.[33]

But the subliminal and sometimes overt Christian themes would continue to pulsate through Chevelle's brand of hard, grinding music. By the time its third record, *This Type of Thinking (Could Do Us In)*, was released, fans and critics alike were beginning to understand Chevelle as a group for which faith was not incidental but rather something that permeated their work. *Christianity Today* noted:

> Whereas previous tracks like "Point #1" and "Grab Thy Hand" hinted at their Christian connection, *Thinking* is more elusive and enigmatic. Frontman and principal songwriter Pete Loeffler is a cryptic songsmith, his choppy rhyme schemes and fragmented sentences being quite a task to untangle. Closer inspection, however, reveals that *Thinking* is an interesting, somewhat conceptual look at the twisted, misinformed mentality of our culture, which places emphasis on silence, guilt, and cheap substitutes to help it along.[34]

The magazine's reviewer zeroed in on two songs in particular that raised troubling questions about the assumptions of American society and addressed the underbelly of suburban American culture, the penchant to look for cures to deep problems with drugs and the inability to shake an attraction to sin:

> First single "Vitamin R" for example, looks at the increased abuse of ADHD drug Ritalin (code-named vitamin R in street lingo) among people in America: "It's typical/Create world/A special place of my design/To never cope or never care/Just

use the key 'cause he's alone/Over and over a slave became." "Panic Prone" is directed at people who dabble in shame and sinful practices, always hiding them but never addressing them: "Gave in again . . . /Can't keep refusing rights/So he'll loan the cash/But the sin is on the hands of you/So to care or plead silence, weak hands are calling/ . . . To end this catastrophic scene, awake and breathe in . . . face all that's shameful.'[35]

Whereas Evanescence's overreaction to being branded "Christian rock" had caused a backlash that alienated them from their core fan base, Chevelle charted a path through the difficult world of rock music that did not compromise their artistry, their faith, or their position in the Christian media industry that had effectively given them their start. That level of maturity would be a model for up-and-coming artists who also sought to walk a similar path. The members of Chevelle had once said that their goal was to be rock stars without acting like rock stars, an apt description of the difficult work Christ had given His followers—to simultaneously be in the world, but not of it (see John 17:15)—and Chevelle appeared to be trying to follow that command:

"We don't want to be rock stars," noted Sam Loeffler. "We work really hard not to be. I mean, we're 'rock stars' by definition, but not in rock star mentality. We really don't want to be a part of that. Just by being normal people. It's good because people will approach us like normal people. No screaming little girls."[36]

BEST FOOT FORWARD
If Chevelle had positioned itself as the anti–rock star, San Diego, California-based rockers Switchfoot would take that position

to a whole new level with its brand of thinking man's pop/ rock. While Chevelle's music often came out in choppy, half sentences filled with angst, Switchfoot presented fans (and the pop music culture) with a winsome group of surf rockers whose smiles, floppy hairstyles, and comforting personae masked a deep message—one that was, in some ways, far more troubling than anything that Marilyn Manson, Eminem, or Insane Clown Posse had managed to shock the public with. As those artists regaled pop culture with songs about drugs, meaningless sex, and spousal murder, Switchfoot was busy filling its records with profoundly disturbing and troubling questions that challenged many of the basic assumptions of modern American life. With a sound that mixed the rock stylings of King's X with shades of Depeche Mode and the Police, along with a touch of sun-soaked pop for good measure, Switchfoot politely but relentlessly questioned nearly everything that suburban America treasured.

"Maybe we've been living with our eyes half open, maybe we're bent and broken," began the band's sonic assault on its major-league debut "The Beautiful Letdown." "We were meant to live for so much more. Have we lost ourselves?"[37]

When asked how the band members, which included siblings Jon and Tim Foreman, had met, Tim joked:

Jon and I met through mutual parents when we were zero years old and two years old. Jon and [percussionist] Chad met in High School; they were on the same water polo team at Carlsbad High School. Chad was the big senior, and Jon was the little freshman that kept getting dunked by Chad. . . .

We were in two different bands, local bands playing around town. We would open up for Chad's band; he would open up for our band. That was way back in the early days. Then when those bands went their separate ways we, being good friends, just thought as a natural progression to form what has become Switchfoot.[38]

Drummer Chad Butler added:

We grew up banging on pots and pans. It's just in our blood. I think we are all so satisfied. And we learned that music and worship can be so satisfying in a context of church, or just a couple of friends in your house, in your room by yourself, just sitting on your bed playing guitar or whatever. That's complete and fulfilling in and of itself. And so to add numbers to your audience is just a blessing and also a stretch of responsibility. I think as God's been teaching us the last few years, He's also increased our audience. We've had to respond to that and had to grow up in the face of that responsibility. I think it's been exciting and challenging.[39]

Butler is the son of two stalwarts from the Jesus music era, both of whom had played with different bands on the Jesus music circuit, most notably the pioneering band Parable. While Butler's parents and their Jesus music cohorts had successfully integrated Christian spirituality into the popular music of the 1970s, they had also failed at presenting the resulting music to the wider popular culture. That would be left to the next generation, who would make sure that their music was not just made but heard by everyone as well. In that quest to be heard, the band soon got the attention of producer Charlie Peacock, a veteran of both the mainstream and CCM industries.

"He's a producer who wrote songs for Amy Grant, he's won

many awards, he's been nominated for Grammys and things like that," explained lead vocalist Jon Foreman. "And so it's pretty much a miracle that he heard [our demo tape] at all. . . . Somehow a friend of a friend gave it to him. But the songs on the first album were very much just songs that had been written in our bedroom, just us having fun."[40]

In 1997, Peacock was starting his own label, Re:think, to which he hoped to sign artists who intended to have their music heard both in the mainstream and CCM markets. The band's first album, *The Legend of Chin*, went largely unheard in mainstream rock circles, but the band got its big break when the producers of the hit movie *A Walk to Remember* used several of its songs in the film's soundtrack. After two albums with Peacock and Re:think, the CCM label that had funded Peacock's venture, Sparrow Records, grew impatient and closed the label down, leaving Switchfoot in a quandary. They had signed with Peacock because of his desire—which they shared—to be more than just a band that would be serviced exclusively to Christian America. With Peacock's venture shut down, Switchfoot members realized that the label would no longer be hospitable to their goals.

"When Charlie Peacock signed us to his label, Re:think, in '97, the label's goal was to release albums both in and outside the church, which definitely resonated with what we were doing playing a campus pub one night and a church the next," Jon told an interviewer. "Then, when Sparrow bought out Re:think, half of who we were was lost. Sparrow is amazing at what they do, but they're not in the same market as we're in now."[41]

Jon Foreman's faint praise for Sparrow aside, the fact that a popular band composed of devout Christians couldn't find a group of people within the largest Christian music label in the world who would share their mission pointed out the major problem that had always haunted the God-rock industry: its executives too often wanted to sell product, like soap, to their targeted demographic, even as the artists sought to reach fans outside of that target demographic. In the case of Switchfoot, losing their powerful ally, Peacock, meant that they would have to go to the mainstream market to find a label that would take their music to the masses. Smartly, the band gave Sparrow the right to distribute their record to the Christian retail market and then began the hunt for a label that would sign them for the mainstream. The band eventually found the right company in Columbia Records; Although the move to Columbia was a result of Re:think's collapse, the band had already been questioning the label's effectiveness at reaching beyond the walls of their natural community, as a result of a message from one of the group's fans. According to Jon Foreman:

> It all started when we got this email on our . . . discussion board. This guy was like, "I totally respect your music. I really relate to what you're singing about and the searching lyrics that you have about spirituality, but I went to a show, and the atmosphere was so . . . heavily Christian that I couldn't get into it. I don't think I'll come to another Switchfoot show." And that was pretty heavy because, for someone to say that, they thought it through and they were totally offended. I think it wasn't so much what we said or what we did on stage but people in the audience and the atmosphere and the other people that got up on stage before and after us. And this really challenged us because other people wrote in saying they felt that way at our shows and it was like, "Wow, are

we so inside our little bubble that we are completely unable to see how irrelevant we're being?"

So we thought about it for a long time and prayed and went over who we are. We talked and argued and really just fought it out. We came up with two essential things that we want to be. We want to be represented by two catch phrases, one being a revolution of being and two that we want to be salt and light. And so the revolution of being entitles . . . the idea of transformation, regeneration, abundant life, truly living out what Christ was talking about. And then the second aspect doing it in context, in culture, in darkness, where it's needed. Not high up on a hill, unaffected, ineffective.[42]

Jon Foreman would prove himself to be one of the most articulate and effective spokesmen for the emerging movement of Christians in rock music. As a pastor's son, he had thought long and hard about what it meant to be taken seriously by the primary culture and at the same time be true to his beliefs. He had watched his parents' generation of God-rockers make interesting music that was almost never head by the mainstream culture and was determined to avoid death by labeling for his band. Foreman also saw lessons to be learned beyond the world of rock music, principles that could be applied by all believers as they sought to live out the most difficult and challenging Christian doctrine of being *in* the world but not *of* it:

I think that the more we can try and figure out who we are in the body of Christ and not come up with our cultural world of "I only eat Christian cereal and buy Christian products and use Christian shampoo," pretty soon, you've surrounded yourself with this Christian ghetto. You're completely free from the chains of Christ. Buying Christian products doesn't make you a Christian any more than going to church. It's easy to get sucked into that thinking of "I went to a Christian festival. That means I'm Christ-like." No. Actually, those people make money, too, and maybe they don't do it in the most ethical way. Is that Christian?[43]

Rock's potential to inspire social change and personal transformation was quietly being realized by a most unlikely cast of characters, of which Switchfoot proved to be an important leader. Serious Christians like these were marching into mainstream rock, making innovative and challenging music that seemed miles away from the comfortable and safe American brand of Christianity that had once caused pundit Franky Schaeffer to refer to its adherents as "jellyfish."[44] That spirit was clearly evident in Switchfoot's second record, a stunner called *The Beautiful Letdown*, which pounded the listener with grinding power pop/rock and more disturbing questions about human mortality.

"The songs on this album are the most forthright about our spiritual lives as any we've written," said Jon Foreman at the time of its release. "It's interesting that Columbia is signing us, because I feel like this album is so spiritually driven."[45]

"This is your life. Are you who you want to be?" asked the singer on track 2 of *Letdown*. "Is it everything you dreamed that it would be when you were younger and you had everything to lose?"[46] The theme continues throughout the album to track 9 with the line "Everything inside you knows there's more than what you've heard."[47] When asked about the album's themes, Foreman responded:

It's the idea that, okay, the beautiful letdown. Everything in our lives will fail us. Everything is moving towards disorder. That's the second law of thermodynamics, the idea that if I fool around with this plate long enough, it's going to break. In the same way, the more I am involved with various aspects of this world they're going to fail me. People will forget to call me back. I might accidentally step on your toe. I might make the food a little too hot. Things will happen. But all those letdowns are redemptive and beautiful when they show us the fact that that is not where our hope is to be. When we realize that all these things fail us, then we are forced to seek a truth that will not fail us. And that's what the beautiful letdown is about . . . We want to be coming to the very bottom of human existence and the pain and the suffering and the things that all of us go through, hopefully only from time to time. We want to come to the very bottom and see that even there, there is a light that's shining, one that the darkness has not understood. That's what I hope this album is.[48]

The album's central theme, similar in many ways to the ones running through Chevelle's music, was the notion that difficulties encountered in life could be redemptive if seen through the prism of a God who allowed all things to happen for a good purpose. In Switchfoot's case, it was expressed as the concept of a divine letdown, or God-ordained difficulties. Foreman said:

The letdown is the idea that your hands are ripped away from all the things that the earth has established. Sometimes, your fingers are torn off in the process. When all those things are stripped away and all that remains is who you truly are, that's where the kingdom of heaven lives. [Christ] didn't come for the people who have their hands on the money. He didn't come for the people who didn't need a doctor. He came for the sick, the poor, the broken, the losers, and the ugly jerks. He came for you and me, and that act is basically the beautiful letdown.[49]

Occasionally Foreman and Switchfoot hinted at answers, but they mostly stuck with questions, modeling the technique first perfected by One who both inspired and annoyed the masses by offering up at least as many questions as He did answers. Foreman seemed to work at asking provocative and disturbing questions that, if not scaring people into the kingdom of God, perhaps caused them to think about spiritual issues in a way that would force them to consider the possibility of the divine. But Foreman also saw the ultimate hope that the band offered as a key difference separating his group from others:

So many bands around today have incredible music and incredible songs, very thought provoking, but they lack a hope. I think our generation in general is seeking for hope, and everyone admires and respects people who are real, who are genuine, and that's something we hold very dear to us. We are ourselves, on and off stage. We don't say something and do something else. A lot of times I think that we don't have a belief in a God who is big enough to provide a genuine hope. We kind of put on a face and go to church on Sunday. That's great, but he can't touch me in my real life and my real problems. We believe in a God who's bigger than any question that we can ask, who's bigger than any problem we can face. And that's an incredible hope—that we can be genuine and truly who we are—and God accepts us for that. That's a hope that's bigger than anything on the earth.[50]

What the members of Switchfoot also had in common with their master, Jesus, was a steady stream of complaints from fellow believers about associating with the nonreligious and venturing a bit too far outside of their natural community of Christians. While Christ took His lumps for dining with tax collectors and other sinners, Switchfoot was sometimes attacked for its members' decision to play in mainstream venues. Jon Foreman noted:

> As we venture into clubs and other areas, it has been evident to us that a lot of people are not completely on board with what we are doing. Several people misunderstand our desire to play in a club instead of in a church, for example. When we have a chance to talk to those people face to face and say, "Hey listen, here is what we are about and this is why we are doing what we are doing," then it is a lot easier to make people understand where you are coming from. But when it comes to people just hearing one thing and making an assumption that you are doing something else, it's hard.[51]

Faced with similar accusations two thousand years ago, Jesus had said that His message was for "those who have ears to hear,"[52] and Switchfoot seemed similarly inclined. Of course, the genius of Jesus' own storytelling technique was that it allowed people to examine their own lives without feeling assaulted, seeing their own sin in the stories of others, and thus being motivated to change from within, with divine help from without. Switchfoot's music seemed to have a similar effect, as song after song hammered the listener with disturbing questions and only hints of answers. When they did come, those answers found their voice in lines that could easily be missed by those without "ears to hear."

By late 2004, the era of Switchfoot was in full swing, as the band landed a song on the *Spiderman 2* soundtrack, and continued its steady march toward integrating themselves into pop culture. Whereas rock stars of the past seemed to spend an inordinate amount of time singing about one-night stands and drug trips, Jon Foreman represented a new era of socially conscious rockers who saw rock's role in the lives of listeners as a nurturing one, able to inspire spiritual growth in fans:

> The way I see it, rock and roll always stands in the face of what's going on in the world. I think of myself as a farmer who waters, plants, and writes songs every day. None of the songs are my own, they just pop up and grow. And then I get to talk about them. Since they aren't really mine to take credit for, I just say, 'Aren't they great? Look at them! A great crop this year!" . . .
>
> All of the songs are very personal and deal with issues I struggle with, but for the most part, they're about trying to understand the world around me.[53]

American fundamentalism had long preached separatism— that spiritual purity could only be maintained by physically and spiritually separating from the "secular" world that could infect people of faith. Savvy beyond their years, the members of Switchfoot had managed to carefully walk the line between the mainstream and faith-based communities, and have effectively modeled how to be a part of the world physically while remaining separate spiritually for an entire generation of artists with similar spiritual inclinations.

It was a difficult task to pull off, but one for which Foreman and company, with their background in the church, seemed uniquely suited. Asked if there was intentionality behind their decisions to position their band in certain ways, Foreman was clear in his assessment: "If there's any intentionality, it's honesty. That's something we've always tried to be. If you come to one of our shows, you'll find the same people on and off the stage. What we do on stage is fairly important, but the way we live our lives off stage is immensely more so."

"What's the biggest challenge balancing that platform and your new-found connections in the mainstream industry?" the interviewer asked.

"We haven't figured it out yet," Foreman responded. "We have spirituality, commerce, and the arts all colliding. At first I used to see things that cause tension as something to run from or something to solve. I think the thing that causes the most tension is that we're supposed to be light in darkness. That's a tense place to be with so many conflicting elements. But we're trying to be that light in the darkness and trying to live within that tension.[54]

Meanwhile, Switchfoot continued to speak and sing for many bands emerging from a community that had long been kept on the fringes of American public life when it sang:

I will carry a cross and a song where I don't belong.[55]

5

ROCK IN A HARD PLACE

RETURN TO MEGADETH

The quiet transformation of American popular music from being a relatively hostile environment toward serious expressions of faith to an atmosphere in which the presence of faith-friendly bands was commonplace also included established artists who experienced religious conversions but refused to disappear into Christian America. Among these was the founder and front man of the legendary metal band Megadeth, Dave Mustaine. In metal culture terms, Mustaine's change of heart was no less dramatic than that of the apostle Paul two thousand years earlier—by his own account, Mustaine had been through drug rehab more than a dozen times. Though the Jehovah's Witness–reared singer had long been exposed to the trappings of religion, his wife's conversion played a significant role in Mustaine's decision to kick drugs and turn his life around.

Mustaine was born in La Mesa, California, in 1961, and lived with various relatives after his parents divorced when he was seven. Twenty years later he formed Metallica with James Hetfield and Lars Ulrich, but soon left because of various conflicts and quickly founded a second band, Megadeth. Over the next decade and a half, his new band sold 15 million records, and Mustaine developed a reputation among metal fans as one of the genre's guitar legends. Although his transformation was not unprecedented, most conversions didn't include such a high-profile artist with such an in-your-face attitude as Mustaine's, as famous for his snarl as he was for his riffs.

But what made his change of heart significant was the philosophical underpinnings of the church culture in which it had occurred. Beginning with Elvis's pastor, who had begged his charge to quit the ugly world of rock 'n' roll, and U2's church, which had urged the Irish rockers to disband, for years religious leaders had been urging converted rock stars, especially those with Mustaine's kind of background, to leave their bands behind and "sing for the Lord." This usually meant recording hymns for the faithful or touring the church circuit. But Mustaine's pastors had no such thoughts, and neither did Mustaine. Although some conversions happen instantaneously, Mustaine's was more gradual, with a slowly growing understanding of his need for God. Part of that journey to faith included an injury that threatened to end his career.

I had fallen asleep on my arm. It is just that simple. I wish I could tell you that I was sword fighting, or saving a baby from a burning building or something. You know, sometimes you are wearing shoes that are too tight or you are sitting the wrong way and your leg will fall asleep a little bit. That is what happened to my hand. The circulation was cut off to the nerve on the inside of my left bicep. When the nerve lost circulation, it shrunk like a crunched up straw. The nerve didn't talk to the muscle and the muscle didn't talk to the hand, and the muscle died. I couldn't move my hand anymore. It took me four months to get the feeling back and another year of weight training just to get my hands operating properly. . . .

The doctors said that I wasn't going to play again. They said I would get 80% use of my arm back, but not 100%, and I was told that I was certainly never going to play the way I played before again, if ever.[1]

But Mustaine was quickly back in the game, crediting his miraculous recovery to God and physical therapy, ready to record his first solo record. Informed by his publishing company, however, that Megadeth still owed it some records, he set to work on what would become his first post-conversion record using the Megadeth band name, *The System Has Failed*. The record was released in late 2004 and debuted at number eighteen on the American music charts, a stunning opening for a band that many had assumed was washed up. Mustaine had cleverly sprinkled his Christian faith into the record but had been careful not to let it dominate in a manner that would have alienated longtime fans of the band with a sudden departure from the themes that had always threaded through the band's work.

Mustaine sprinkled *System* with biblical allusions, most notably in the song "Truth Be Told," which recounted, as only Dave Mustaine could, the story of Cain and Abel. Even the hard-rocking online journal *KNAC.com* took notice, although Mustaine's credibility as a rock legend appeared to mollify any objections the publication might have had against such an overt mixing of religion and rock:

> "Truth Be Told" has a Biblical theme that is conveyed along with instrumentation that leaves the listener actually wishing the Bible was longer so there might be more axe-grinding pleasure. If telling a story as epic in scope as the Holy Bible isn't enough, Mustaine has also taken on the task of relating his own story in the doubtlessly autobiographical "Of Mice and Men." No, there isn't any retarded Lenny guy in this one. You probably aren't interested anymore, right? Well, too bad if you're not because this is one of the top two or three selections on this disc even though . . . gasp, Dave discloses that he used to "abuse alcohol" and the possibility exists that he maybe even "ingested illegal substances" on occasion. I realize this is really groundbreaking lyrical territory, yet at the same time, it completely works here on a surface level.[2]

KNAC.com also gave props to Mustaine's most audacious move, a spoken-word rendition of the Twenty-Third Psalm that he titled "Shadow of Deth":

> "Shadow of Deth" is actually another Biblical song which essentially consists of the 23rd Psalm being chanted as Mustaine's guitar creates a different kind of atmosphere. The rendition

of Biblical lyric can at times be a bit disconcerting, but by this time Dave has continuously proven willing to splice all types of audio quotes and effects into this work, so it's [*sic*] presence at this point of the disc shouldn't come as any surprise.[3]

From Wings drummer Joe English to Outlaws bassist Rick Cua and Grand Funk Railroad singer Mark Farner, the '70s and '80s saw numerous successful entertainers convert to Christianity and leave pop culture for the comfortable world of CCM. But Dave Mustaine was a different type of artist living in a different era. He would stay put as lead singer of Megadeth and allow his old fans to get a glimpse of his continuing spiritual journey, refusing to exit cultural stage right and continuing his work with the band that made him a household name, all the while changing the nature of the band and its message in a manner that reflected his newfound faith. In 2017, that hard work paid off as Mustaine and Megadeth won their first ever Grammy award, in the category of Best Metal Performance for its album "Dystopia."

A PASSION FOR THE CHRIST

"I am a Christian," declared the lead singer of one of the nation's biggest-selling rock bands of the new century, in an interview in *Christianity Today*.[4] Scott Stapp, who had dodged questions about his faith for years in an attempt to avoid being pigeonholed, was finally ready to own his faith, emboldened by Mel Gibson's film *The Passion of the Christ* and his agreement to contribute a song to the film's official "inspired by" soundtrack, an album of songs inspired by the film, which I produced. Stapp joined a variety of artists on *The Passion of the Christ: Songs*—including Lauryn Hill,

Brad Paisley, Mark Hoppus of Blink-182, MxPx, and others—
and the album was released six months after the theatrical release
of Mel Gibson's epic film, on the same day the DVD hit store
shelves. Gibson's film had somehow given Stapp the courage to
be more forthright about his faith.

"In Creed's almost ten years together—including a few where
they were one of the hottest rock bands on the planet—nobody
ever asked lead singer Scott Stapp if he was a Christian," observed
Christianity Today. "Many asked if Creed was a Christian band,
and their reply was always no—even though some of their lyrics
included a message of faith. But no one ever directly asked Stapp
about his beliefs. Well, we asked him the other day, and Stapp
says he's glad no one asked him about it until now."[5]

Stapp was asked directly whether he was a Christian by Bill
Maher, host of the then popular TV show *Politically Incorrect*:
"I was really nervous when I went on that show; and when Bill
asked me if I was a Christian, it sort of caught me offguard,"
Stapp recalled, adding that he had said, "I'm not sure" in
response to Maher's question. "That's where I was at the time;
that was as honest an answer as I could give."[6]

In 2004, Stapp told *Christianity Today*:

> I'm glad nobody asked [if I was a Christian], because my life
> wasn't right with God. The Christian community latched
> onto a lot of my music, because there were a lot of things
> about my struggle they related to. But I didn't really want to
> come out and be identified as a Christian, because I didn't
> want to be a hypocrite, because my life wasn't right. I didn't
> want to make any kind of public profession until I felt like
> my heart was right. I've since learned that my life's never
> gonna be right, and I'm always going to be scrutinized and

looked at under a microscope. And it took me since I was 17 and left home, running from God, to now, as a 30-year-old man, when I honestly feel like I've come full circle and my heart's finally in the right place. I'm still going to make mistakes, but I don't have any problems with publicly professing my faith now. It just took me a long time to get to the right place in my relationship with Christ.[7]

"There was a point when my life really was sex, drugs and rock & roll," Stapp admitted. The last thing I wanted was for someone to think I was in a Christian band. The constant questions about whether Creed was a Christian band only made me more angry and intent on proving otherwise.[8]

Asked how he would have defined himself at the time if not as a Christian, Stapp replied:

I'd have called myself a struggling Christian who was trying to find holes in everything he had been raised to believe. I was a doubting Thomas. I was raised in a climate where I believed in God because I was afraid of going to hell—and I didn't think that was the right way to fall in love with somebody. I always believed in God and Christ, but I was in rebellion—trying to make my relationship with God fit into my life instead of making my life fit in with him. I was stubborn.[9]

Recalling the harsh words of his father, which had obviously haunted him but nevertheless proved true, Stapp painted a pre-*Passion* picture of a young man sorely in need of hope and inspiration: "My dad always said I was hard-headed, that it would take something like that to wake me up spiritually, and I guess it did," he said of the film. He continued:

My heart had gotten so beat up that I didn't have anything left to give. I was emotionally and spiritually dried up, so I was just searching for God. I reached out to my pastor and my father for some guidance. I was really soul searching and, I guess, on my path to coming home spiritually. And once that process began—and I'm still going through that process, and probably will for the rest of my life—that's when things started changing in my life. I started making some proper decisions, getting things in order. It's kind of like cleaning up your house. I was looking for direction for what God wanted me to do—and that's when I got a call about *The Passion*.[10]

Stapp's encounter with Gibson and the actor/director's epic film was a catalyst in his personal transformation. I had invited Stapp to see the film and he had traveled to Los Angeles from his home in Florida with his manager. After arriving early at Sony's Culver City studio lot, the pair retired to a Starbucks across the street from the lot with us to discuss the plans for the CD. Stapp had already been working on a song even before he saw the film, and let us listen to a rough demo. As we huddled around the CD player of his rented SUV, we heard the first sounds of what was to become Stapp's contribution, a power balled he called "Relearn Love." At Starbucks, Stapp gave no hint of the upcoming breakup of Creed but talked about his desire to be more up front about his spiritual beliefs.

"For 8 years I've been asking questions," he said. "Now I want to start offering answers."[11]

After moving across the street and back onto the Sony lot, we soon sat in a hushed theater as the film's showing began. Five seats down from Stapp, in the same row, was the lead singer of

Nine Inch Nails, Trent Reznor, who sat next to producer Rick Rubin. Across the aisle was ABC News anchor Diane Sawyer, who was in town to interview Gibson, and further back was one of Mel Gibson's brothers and the singer Brian Setzer. These were among the chosen few—dozens of Hollywood A-listers had been clamoring to see an early cut of the film, but Gibson had severely restricted those he allowed to screen the film, turning down the likes of Madonna, the Weinsteins, and other Hollywood heavyweights. Stapp recalled:

> There was already a song percolating inside of me, so to speak, concerning a renewal in my heart. Interestingly, my personal life and my spiritual walk were kind of coming full circle around the same time I was asked to be involved in the project. I had been shedding all the callousness and the weathered state that I had been in, personally and spiritually, even prior to seeing the film. Seeing the film just kind of closed the door and allowed that song to be born.[12]

As the lights went up on the screening room, there was no reaction from the audience—only silence. Some audience members stayed in their seats while others headed for the restrooms or began milling around in the lobby, while others, like actor Chris Tucker and Sawyer headed out. Rocker Trent Reznor's reaction in particular spoke volumes about what Gibson and the film had accomplished. Known as something of a shock rocker for his provocative imagery early in his career, as he retreated to the restroom and headed for a urinal, his face was ashen, as if he had just seen a ghost—Gibson's epic—depicting a brutal Jesus story that was light-years away from the Precious Moments Jesus that seemed to dominate the often-kitschy world of Christian pop culture—had shocked the shock rocker. For Stapp, the entire exercise was far more than just a film, and he saw the hand of Providence in his being asked to participate:

> When I was called to write for the film, it was a final confirmation I was on the right path. With going solo, it's just ironic that Creed had to handle all the Christian connotations and questions, then [after] that I would launch my solo career on the heels of the *Passion of the Christ* movie. It's really weird to me that as I'm going solo and as I'm getting my life right with God, when I step back into the public eye, that I'm doing it stamped right on the cover of the *Passion* CD. It's like my spiritual life and professional life are now finally going hand in hand.[13]

But it wasn't just Stapp's professional life that had brought him to the end of himself. Personal problems, including the breakup of his marriage and his use of prescription medication, which had some nasty side effects, including bloating and depression, had taken their toll on him:

> The *Passion of the Christ* opportunity came along at a time when I was dealing with a lot of things in my personal life. I had no other way to look but up. I have been broken down as a human being. So many various painful things. An unfortunate divorce. I've had friendships and relationships that went astray. I was just hurt as a human being. I don't think I'd ever dealt with my divorce, or with my other struggles, because I was so busy with Creed, always going forward, going forward, going forward. When all that shut down, it forced me to deal with the struggles, and my spiritual life was always over in

the corner calling out to me. When Creed broke up, I finally didn't have anything else to distract me. I had nothing else to do but cry out to God for help. For me, it had to get to the point where there was nowhere else to turn but to God. Once I did, I started to get some freedom in my life. I started to grow as a Christian and a person.[14]

When he was first asked to be a part of the project, Stapp said yes but initially indicated that he didn't need to see the film since he was familiar with the story, reared in a devout Christian family and having starred in passion plays when he was a child. After the screening though, Stapp recounted his feelings of seeing an old story with a new perspective:

At first, I was saddened and disheartened. I couldn't believe this is what Christ had to go through. I knew the story, but I was seeing it through different eyes. It was not just a Bible story that I had heard since I was four years old. It made sense to my life as a man, and as a father and as a friend and as a son. I was shocked that someone loved me so much that they would do this for me. I also got angry at various times during the film. . . .

I had a whole gamut of emotions—love, peace, anger, humility, sadness. I left the film exhausted; I was drained. But also, I was happy, because it helped me get a visual picture of what I finally understood.[15]

"When I was a kid, and even as a young adult, I was always asking God to prove Himself to me. After seeing *The Passion* it was kind of like God saying to me, 'I'm here, what further proof do you need?' I finally got to that place where I looked up to

God and said, 'You can have me; You can have everything I've got, if You'll just take me back.'"[16]

The day after the showing, Stapp paid a visit to Gibson's fourth floor Santa Monica office and presented the actor with an autographed guitar. Between Creed's 30 million albums and Gibson's megastar status, these two larger than life figures had much in common, including a worldview that was at odds with many in their respective industries. It was a meeting of equals—the rock star at the top of his game and the actor about to release the biggest film of his career—and Stapp remembered the meeting fondly: "He was excited that I was interested in the songs project. He said, 'I don't know much about music, but my kids love your band.' I had a little demo of 'Relearn Love' and I played it for him, and he said, 'Listen, man, I'll leave that stuff up to you.' He was like, 'This is your experience, and I want you to express it however you want.'"[17]

Stapp's experience of the film had clearly surprised him, and the lessons he learned were unexpected—especially unusual since he was reared in a strict Pentecostal home, and the story of Christ's death and resurrection was so familiar.

"It's simple for me," he replied when asked about his take-away from the film: "It's giving without expecting anything in return. Prior to this, the way that I loved people around me, I always expected something—even if that was just expecting them to treat me like I treated them. But now I understand that real love is just giving without expecting anything. That's what love is to me, and that's what I feel that Christ showed us."[18]

Scott Stapp may have thought that he was merely starting a rock band when he formed Creed, but in reality he was embarking on the difficult job of negotiating the difficult terrain that was the intersection of rock 'n' roll and religion. Some of his lifestyle choices had caused fellow Christians to question his beliefs, while his refusal to shy away from expressing his deep religious convictions in his lyrics perturbed many in the rock establishment, including fellow band members. These were the kind of pressures that had caused many artists before him to either leave their faith behind or retreat to the Christian subculture. Stapp recalled:

> The criticism over the lyrics was really a blessing in disguise, especially for the other guys, who had no idea why those questions were being posed. I had run from my faith when I left home and ran right into rock 'n' roll, which was the worst thing my dad could have ever expected me to do. But when you're called to write, you just write what you feel. At the time I was writing those songs, I didn't think about or question why the lyrics had religious or spiritual connotations. I just wrote about what I was feeling, what I was struggling with. It did mess with the dynamics of the band. They were mad at me. They'd say, "We didn't want to be in a Christian band!" They wanted to be in a rock 'n' roll band. They thought [being Christians] was, I guess, a dorky thing to have said about you. And I thought, "Man! I can't get away from this stuff." At the time, we could honestly say we weren't a Christian band. I was rebellious, kind of running from God, struggling in my faith. It was challenging, but it was a blessing in disguise, because it really allowed our music to go places where normal secular music wasn't allowed to go.[19]

Stapp looked back on his experience with Creed as a time of preparation for what he would do next, beginning with his contribution to the *Passion* album. It would be his first foray into the music scene as a solo artist, and as such he felt an increasing freedom to speak his mind, less worried about the opinions of others in the band:

> It's just crazy how things have come full circle for me as a solo artist. I kind of look at everything that happened with Creed as a preparation—me going through things to get my life ready for God's plan. It's been a journey and a learning experience. . . . The nature of my answers are a lot different now that I'm no longer with Creed. I'm a solo artist now, and I don't have a band to hide behind. So when someone asks me if I'm a Christian, I have to say yes, because I am.[20]

"I don't have anything to hide behind anymore," he told *World* magazine. "I don't have a band to hide behind anymore, and say, 'We're not a Christian band.' I was always afraid to speak about my faith publicly. I would always talk to God about it: 'I'm not perfect. I don't want to be a stumbling block.' What's helped me is that people are starting to realize that Christians don't have this holier-than-thou attitude, that we're not perfect."[21]

Stapp's new stance would cause reporters to raise challenging questions regarding his faith and also allow Stapp to be more forthcoming about those beliefs. During his interview with *Christianity Today*, correspondent Mark Moring, in an attempt to better understand Stapp's worldview, raised a question with Stapp that had less to do with rock 'n' roll and more to do with theology.

"On Creed's website, you had answered an FAQ in part by writing, 'Who are we to say that being a Christian is the only way to heaven?'" Moring said, but before he could follow up with his own question Stapp stepped in:

"I can honestly tell you, I didn't write that."

Moring persisted: "But your name was on it."

According to Moring, Stapp then turned to his manager and said, "Tell them there's something on the Creed website that I didn't write . . . again."

Stapp continued:

> I didn't write that. I would *never* answer a question that way. That sounds like something the owner of my record company [Wind-Up Records] would say. . . . I would never say that, dude, because that's not what I believe. We'll be sure to make a note of that. That stuff happens all the time, because my label, you know, they're about making money. They don't want to disenfranchise people. Creed wasn't a Christian band, but I would never insinuate or say anything that would make that kind of a statement. I'm glad you told me about that.[22]

The post-*Passion* Scott Stapp seemed to be a markedly different one from the man who had fronted Creed. He was confident in the beliefs he'd always held, but also seemed to embrace the notion of grace and a separation from the legalism of his upbringing, which had emphasized "works," the notion that one could attain favor with God by doing good deeds.

"When Stapp arrived at a surrendering point, he started getting back in touch with Rick Berlin, his former pastor," noted journalist Tim Adams.[23]

Stapp credited Berlin with helping him make a fresh start in his journey, offering counsel about what was and was not essential as he tries to walk the line between the legalism of his formative years and the grace he was searching for. "Pastor Rick is really liberated from the old ways," Stapp said. 'He's really helped me understand how important joy is, how being human and a Christian are not contradictory ideas."[24]

Perhaps because of Berlin's influence, Stapp was also wrestling with deep philosophical and theological issues, wondering aloud to his interviewer about the differences in outlook among Christ's apostles, and relating it to his own experience:

> I never realized the kind of conflict that Paul had with Peter and James over the issue of the law [of Moses]. Paul was obviously the radical of the three—but not in the sense that he was right and everyone else was wrong. He was the one out in the world coming in contact with people who were pagan and nothing like the rest of the church . . . Paul wasn't out trying to get people to conform to a set of rules about how they looked on the outside so they could join some club. He was preaching love and reaching people's hearts. . . .
>
> I think there has been a maturing among a lot of Christians. In a lot of ways the church seems to be growing into this place where fear is no longer being used as the main way to get people to give their lives to Christ.[25]

Stapp was also beginning the difficult task of trying to synthesize his seemingly conflicting worlds of rock and devout Christian faith. Asked whether he was now a "Christian artist" or a "an artist who happened to be a Christian," Stapp chose the latter and couched his answer in theological language:

> I'm an artist who's a Christian, because I don't write music to be evangelical. Now, if that happens, it happens. My dad's a

dentist, and he's a Christian. Now, does he put in Christian fillings? No, that's just part of his three-dimensional life. Now, there are people that are Christian artists, because they have a purpose to be evangelical for Christ. I don't feel I've been called to that yet. Now, that could change. There's no telling what kind of call God will put on my life.[26]

The Scott Stapp that emerged from the experience of working on the *Passion of the Christ* album seemed more confident of his place in the world, carefully putting together the broken pieces of his childhood and reconciling the angry God he grew up hearing about with the God of love that he had seen in Mel Gibson's epic movie. It had clearly been a cathartic experience and had caused him to both question and affirm aspects of his faith:

> Over the last two years I've come full circle, spiritually. Unfortunately, it took a lot of heartache to get to that point; but I've always been a little hardheaded. I had to finally get to the place where I wasn't being influenced by how I was brought up. . . . I had to finally stand alone as a man and see Christ from my own perspective and choose Him for myself. When you grow up in church, especially the kind of church I did, it's sort of like, "Your name is Scott, and your faith is Christianity." I didn't get to choose my faith any more than I did my name; so it was time to come to terms with where I stood, what my commitment would be . . .
>
> My dad used to always say, "It's a matter of 12 inches. There's 12 inches between your head and your heart." There have been plenty of times when I've cried out to God in the past; but it was almost always when I was in a jam, when

I wanted to make a deal with God. In my head I knew it was right to call on the Lord in a time of need; but I wasn't ready to give Him my whole heart, to recommit my entire life to Him . . . That's what's different this time around. I've stepped back into the arena of faith, of faith in Christ. I'm not just looking at God as a way out of a jam; I've embraced being a Christian as what shapes my values, my worldview, my morals. My commitment to Christ is what establishes my priorities, how I will raise my son, my whole person.[27]

A new and matured Scott Stapp was coming to terms with his own rebellion against the faith of his upbringing and reaching some surprising conclusions:

I have to admit . . . that a lot of my rebellion was just an excuse to live the way I wanted to. But you can only make excuses for so long. What I've learned as an artist is that I can be a Christian human being and have a relationship with God through Christ, but I don't have to be a full-blown evangelical Christian artist. I'm a three-dimensional human being. Yes, I'll talk about my faith; and I'm sure that'll come out in my music because I've always had a tendency to wear my heart on my sleeve. . . .

The important thing for me now is that I want my heart to be renewed, which is what I was trying to express when I wrote the song "Relearn Love." I saw the movie . . . while I was going through all of this, and it really brought home the idea of how I needed a new heart, that I needed to relearn what it means to love. For me, that's what salvation is—asking God for your heart to be reborn.[28]

With *The Passion of The Christ: Songs*, Scott Stapp embarked on a solo career that would take him in new directions, and he looked to the future with a long look over his shoulder, remembering a path that he was convinced had been marked out for him.

In 2009, Creed reunited for a fourth studio album "Full Circle," and Stapp would release two solo albums "The Great Divide" and "Proof of Life," as well as an autobiography, "Sinner's Creed." A highly publicized emotional breakdown followed by a stint at a rehabilitation clinic and a move with this family to Nashville found the singer in a healthier place and in 2016 he became the frontman for the supergroup Art of Anarchy.

"I had a [spiritual] calling on my life from when I was younger, and the way I was raised, and I couldn't run away from it," he said.[29]

ANOTHER COLD WAR

Although the flood of professed Christians into mainstream rock had become ubiquitous, that didn't necessarily mean that all parties in the music business were supportive of it. Perhaps no artist discovered this as readily as a four-piece band from Southern California that called itself Cold War Kids and debuted in 2006 on Downtown Records, a subsidiary of Warner Bros., with its first album, *Robbers & Cowards*. The band quickly became the talk of the music business. The rock industry's bible, *Spin*, noted:

> *Robbers* may be one of the most important debuts to drop this year. The quartet doesn't abscond from a traditional rock setup, making the album all the more impressive. The dozen tracks comprising the album circumvent any notions that the

band is one-dimensional, and make a sturdy argument for the band's pioneering approach—bass lines throb, pianos clink and clank almost at random sometimes, the percussion finds a playground to test out its limitations and curiosities.[30]

It wasn't just the music, however, that *Spin* found deserving of such high praise:

> Lyrically, Cold War Kids' songs are about life, fictional or not, like brief, vaguely detailed glimpses into short stories in the making. What makes it invigorating and vital is the presence of imagery and intimate detail, the slight character development over a track's brevity, the empathy invoked in the listeners
>
> *Robbers & Cowards* is one of those records that will be revered or shat upon, but begs not to be ignored. May its greatness not be lost on the general public [and] reach more deeply into hearts than heads.[31]

Rolling Stone had once famously crowned U2 as the "Band of the '80s,"[32] and while *Spin*'s endorsement didn't quite carry the weight of such a pronouncement, it did offer similar praise for Cold War Kids' debut, proclaiming that the band members were "the ones to lead indie rock into a neoteric age."[33]

But what a difference a college would make—Cold War Kids had left out some important information about themselves that would suddenly dampen the enthusiasm of the all-important gatekeepers who populated rock journalism, a group not typically known for their religious devotion. When one influential media outlet, Pitchfork Media, discovered that the band's members had attended Biola University, a Christian university in suburban Los Angeles, it launched so excessive an assault on the band that it caught the attention of the popular *San Diego CityBeat*. In a piece titled "Down with the Jesus Freaks! Cold War Kids Get Nuked by Agnostics at Large," *CityBeat* dissected the antireligious fervor the band had stirred up among rock critics who were surprised by the band's background:

> The rock press doesn't like to imagine that a middle ground exists when it comes to religion. Having failed to clearly report their religious "baggage" to the customs officers of popular culture, Cold War Kids are almost viewed as missionary spies who've infiltrated the largely agnostic world of rock 'n' roll. Rock writers view them as fakes—hiding their religion in order to "make it" in a secular scene—and think it's their duty to "out" the band.[34]

According to *CityBeat*, it was the mention of Biola, a one-hundred-year-old university known for its adherence to Christian principles, that triggered the nervous breakdown among some rock journalists:

> When the band first casually acknowledged that three members attended Biola University, it seemed harmless enough. But we're talking about "Bible Institute of Los Angeles," a private Christian university whose website features a hand holding a Bible with the caption: "Make this a meaningful part of your college experience."
>
> After revealing their time at Biola, it seemed recognizing Cold War Kids' talent was secondary to having a loud opinion about them. Worse, they were pigeonholed as a "Christian band."[35]

Loved or hated, the Cold War Kids were definitely getting noticed. Started by lead singer Nathan Willett, guitarist Jonnie Russell, bassist Matt Maust, and drummer Matt Aveiro, the group met at Biola, where three of the four attended (and where Russell's father remains a professor). The band formed in 2004 in the Orange County bedroom town of Fullerton, which straddles the OC/LA border, and, after signing to Monarchy Music, released its debut EP, *Mulberry Street*, the next year. Two more EPs followed, and after signing with Downtown Records in '06, Cold War Kids released its debut full-length album, the critically acclaimed *Robbers & Cowards*. The idea for the band's name had first come to Matt Maust as an idea for a website, which eventually morphed into his band's identity. As evidenced by the fact that their very identity as a band grew out of other artistic ventures, the band had little in common with some early Christian rock bands for whom artistic expression seemed to take a backseat to communicating a gospel message. To be sure, there was a gospel message in the band's songs, but it was carefully woven into the storytelling, something mastered by a previous generation of sacred/secular genre-straddlers, like Johnny Cash. Speaking of their songs, Maust said "There are so many people and characters in the songs, and they're really funny and serious at the same time. A lot of the characters in the songs remind me of the Peanuts characters."[36]

The Schulz mention was not lost on one music critic, who astutely perceived that the reference may have been not only to interesting comic-strip characters, but also Schultz's legendary ability to integrate religion into them. He noted:

It's interesting that Maust brings up Peanuts as I'd just come upon a paperback copy of Robert L. Short's 1968 book "The Parables of Peanuts," which goes into great detail to explain how Schulz took great pain to infuse notions of the gospel and religion into his long running comic strip. Many writers have a hard time not suggesting a degree of gospel living inside Willett's songs. . . . Termed "art-parable"—or the strategy of "wounding from behind"—as Danish philosopher Søren Kierkegaard said, it's a method that Willett seems to use in reverse, touching on religion, but craftily using it to make greater gains in art.[37]

A new generation of young Christian men and women were furiously working to integrate their religious beliefs into their rock music, well aware of the pitfalls that had caused many of their forbears, such as Stryper and Petra, to be ridiculed by the rock music establishment. Not only had such bands been accused of being inauthentic and preachy, seeking to use music not for artistic expression but strictly for saving souls, but dozens of musical performers had traveled the road from secular to saved only to disappoint their fans with their subsequent musical offerings, a phenomenon duly noted by at least one critic:

> No matter your generation, you've probably witnessed at least one amazing artist fall off the map in search of some god. Whether it was Cat Stevens finding Allah, Prince discovering Jehovah, or Lauryn Hill worshipping some jackass who claims to be the Messiah—the one thing they have in common is that while they may have saved their souls, they damned their music.[38]

But perhaps the most clear-eyed view of Cold War Kids would come from a most unlikely source: a review of the band's debut record in *Rolling Stone*, which had long been harshly critical of strong Christian messages emanating from what was supposed to the home of hedonism:

> This suburban Los Angeles foursome has some actual holy roller bona fides. . . . and the spirit of an old fashioned tent revival infuses the band's remarkable story songs. . . . And much as Bruce Springsteen feels deep sympathy for the murderers and f---ups who populate Nebraska, *Robbers & Cowards* has a deeply Christian take on its titular anti-heroes: that even the worst among us is capable of redemption.[39]

"Any amount of theology can now be smuggled into people's minds under the cover of romance without their knowing it," wrote C. S. Lewis, the creator of the famed Chronicles of Narnia series.[40] Although two generations removed from Lewis, in many ways Cold War Kids were his philosophical progeny with a harder edge, telling stories that pointed to salvation but with an artistic flair that set them apart from many of their contemporaries.

MUM'S THE WORD

"Rock 'n' roll gave us the Vineyard Church movement; one wonders if Vineyard has given us Mumford & Sons."[41]

So wrote Christian Scharen, assistant professor of worship and theology at Minnesota's Luther Seminary, in an essay on a British rock 'n' roll band that had its roots firmly planted in the soil of American evangelicalism. Indeed, when a middle-aged American preacher named John Wimber began a Christian splinter denomination in Southern California, called the Vineyard, little did he know what a profound impact he would have, not only on the world of religion but also on the rock music scene. No stranger to music himself, Wimber had been one of the cofounders of the Righteous Brothers and played keyboards for the band. It was at one of the offshoots of his denomination where Bob Dylan studied, and, two decades later, the rock band Lifehouse would also emerge from the same church, the Malibu Vineyard. But a decade after Wimber's death in 1997, it was a British export named Mumford & Sons, children of leaders of Wimber's denomination, who would bring the Word to the rock culture of the twenty-first century. And for the platinum-selling rock band, things were about to come full circle; when they were informed that they would be opening for a living legend named Bob Dylan, the band's front man couldn't contain himself:

"When our manager said, 'It's Bob Dylan,' I got out of bed and ran outside and jumped around like a madman! You can imagine the reaction of someone who probably wouldn't be playing music at all if it wasn't for Dylan," said Marcus Mumford, whose mother had first introduced her son to Dylan's music: "She had *Slow Train Coming* on vinyl. It's pretty much the first vinyl I ever listened to."[42]

Eleanor Mumford wasn't just any mother when it came to religion, for she and her husband, John, were leaders of the UK branch of Wimber's movement, which John served as executive director. Scharen noted:

Marcus Mumford, Mumford & Sons' lead singer and songwriter (and drummer if you include his penchant for stomping on a kick drum), was born in Southern California where his parents, John and Eleanor Mumford, were on staff at Anaheim Vineyard. That short stint set them up for planting a Vineyard church in 1987 in southwest London, where young Marcus grew up. The Vineyard movement has its own highly professional music labels, recording artists, and hit records in the Christian music genre. The story of how Marcus Mumford emerged from a scene that pioneered the merger of Jesus and Rock 'n' Roll to later front an indie punk hoedown band that takes faith seriously is as yet untold, but one can hardly understand Mumford & Sons, let alone weigh their significance on the music scene today, without at least gesturing to this background story.[43]

Far from keeping his spiritual beliefs out of his music, Marcus was seemingly unafraid to talk and sing about them, and the world was taking notice.

"Perhaps one of the factors that has made some listeners recoil is the songs' lyrical earnestness and their exploration of the idea of faith, a theme that might sound strange on record, but which takes flight when performed live," noted the *Guardian*.[44]

Mumford described his music as "a deliberately spiritual thing but deliberately not a religious thing. I think faith is something beautiful, and something real, and something universal, or it can be." Gesturing to his bandmates, he told the *Guardian*'s Laura Barton, "We all have our separate views on religion, but I think faith is something to be celebrated. I have my own personal views, they're still real to me, and I want to write about them."[45]

If their fans minded the Christian leanings, however, they didn't seem to let on, and the *Guardian* captured the flavor:

To see this band live is an extraordinary experience: there is something fevered and euphoric, about both the way they play and the audience's response, that puts you more in mind of an evangelical church than a rock'n'roll show. At the Forum in north London last autumn, they appeared first on the bill, coming on at barely seven o'clock, but the venue was rammed with fans there specifically to see them, not the night's headliner, Paloma Faith. The crowd danced and whooped and cheered and sang along, and when the set was over and the night's 'special guest,' the R&B artist Mr. Hudson, appeared, the applause swiftly turned to boos. "I think it's a lot to do with the time—people enjoying rootsier music, reacting to manufactured music," posits Mumford quietly. "But no, you can't really explain it."[46]

Mumford and Sons was formed in 2007, consisting of Mumford, Ben Lovett, Winston Marshall, and Ted Dwane, and their debut album, *Sigh No More*, was released in 2010. Although the four members of the band were unrelated, they settled on the name Mumford & Sons for a variety of reasons:

We chose the name because in the U.K., and I think you get it here as well in the States, but a lot of companies, like anything from undertakers to cobblers—like Marcus and I both worked in an antique shop called "Something & Partners"—we tried to set the band up as like an English family business sort of thing. And it's very hard to name a band, it is very hard to do it, cause it's something you've got to stick with, we've got to really like it. So we thought it best represented us.[47]

The reaction from both within and without Christendom was instantaneous and positive. Christian–leaning *Relevant*, a hip youth-oriented magazine, proclaimed:

> *Sigh No More* . . . not only takes inspiration from the Bible, but near-direct quotes. *Let the dead bury the dead, they will come out in droves*, sings Marcus Mumford in the song "Thistles & Weeds." Even the narrative arc of the album reflects a literary work of art that is ripe with storytelling and (Christian) imagery. And in spite of their focus on God and spirituality, Mumford & Sons has become one of the most popular bands in today's music scene, admired by millions of Christians and non-Christians alike.[48]

But while a helpful review from a fellow Christian was to be expected, it would remain to be seen what mainstream music critics, not typically inclined to praise the musings of the son of the leader of a major evangelical denomination, would think of the album. For these, Ben Schumer, writing for *Pop Matters*, seemed to capture the wonder that was Mumford & Sons:

> When the stunning title track's claim of "Love that will not betray you / Dismay or enslave you / It will set you free" comes barreling at you, there's not a moment to roll your eyes. You simply submit to the rush.
>
> "Awake My Soul" shows that Mumford is also capable of Waitsian lyrical gems: "In these bodies, we will live / In these bodies, we will die / Where you invest your love, you invest your life." . . .
>
> If I had to place a bet on the Mumford song that will fare best with American ears, my money's on "The Cave," a song

that distills Ralph Stanley, the Band, and Arcade Fire into a transcendent anthem with a chorus tailor-made for karaoke: "But I will hold on hope / And I won't let you choke / On the noose around your neck / And I'll find strength in pain / And I will change my ways." Yes, that all looks terribly trite written down, but in the context of song's thrust, it just works (as these things often do). The fact of the matter is that *Sigh No More* is an album meant to be sung along to—loudly and shamelessly.[49]

Rock critics had a long and storied history of being hostile to religious expressions in rock music, especially if they came from artists who appeared to be serious about their beliefs. In 1973, for example, *Rolling Stone* reviewed Mylon Lefevre's album *Over the Influence* this way: "Lefevre is part of the whole Jesus Creep movement. Two thirds of the songs on his album are totally devoid of any relation to the real world. No sex, no drugs, no booze, no cars, no worldly problems, no worldly happiness. Everything revolves around this f------ ghost Jesus."[50]

Although the Cold War Kids had experienced a bit of that same chilly reception when its background at a Christian university was revealed, other artists, such as Switchfoot, had won grudging respect from the likes of *Spin* magazine, which reviewed the band's CD this way: "When singer Jon Foreman cries, 'I don't know that I ever felt so alive' on the band's sixth album, he's probably describing a new peak in his relationship with Jesus. But Foreman could also be referring to the San Diego outfit's sound: *Oh! Gravity* is their liveliest record, full of dive-bombing guitar fuzz, juicy arena-alt choruses, and art-rock ear candy. Your turn, Satan."[51]

And when it came to artists like Mumford & Sons, even *Pop Matters* seemed compelled to acknowledge that Larry Norman, the godfather of Christian rock, had perhaps been right thirty years earlier when he demanded to know, "why should the devil have all the good music?"[52] *Pop Matters'* Schumer noted:

> Sigh No More inspires evangelism through sheer force of will. Between Mumford's gripping wail and the Sons' whirlwind revelries, it's a revival hard to resist. It's not a flawless record, but it does a damn good job of making you look the other way. The more I listen to this album, the more I realize that it's teflon-coated against cynicism. Mumford's platitudes would normally grate on me, but they're surprisingly easy to forgive when they're being howled over the Sons' locomotive folk-rock. Like another celebrated Londoner before him, Mumford obviously realizes the vital importance of being earnest.[53]

Despite Marcus Mumford's deeply religious background and pedigree, the songs that emanated from his band were a bit more literary than most Christian-flavored rock music, relying heavily on influences that many Christian rockers had likely never been exposed to, something noted by *Paste*:

> The Shakespearean title and lead track are echoed throughout the album with imagery that blends royalty and spirituality, in a very Anglican, or Arthurian, move. On "White Blank Page," Mumford queries in a gravelly growl, "Can you kneel before the king, and say I'm clean?" and "Awake My Soul" directly recalls the Thomas Ken hymn, repeated in that church's liturgy for hundreds of years. Meanwhile, "Timshel" is straight-up Steinbeck worship and "Dustbowl Dance" keeps him close at hand as well.[54]

Other critics, including Scharen, noted the literary influences in the band's work and praised its reflectiveness:

His stint reading classics at Edinburgh University goes
some way toward explaining the literary bent of their songs.
Shakespeare makes the most frequent appearances ("Sigh No
More," the name of both their album and the first track on
it, for example, is drawn from the comedy *Much Ado About
Nothing*), but writers as diverse as Pascal and Steinbeck make
appearances. As does, of course, Scripture, but usually in
more subtle ways than the direct quotes taken from literature.
The band's clear yet subtle engagement with Christian faith
allows them to write songs that allow the hearer to make a
kind of sense of one's life without feeling forced to take away
a "message" from the song.[55]

Still, there would remain dangers on the road of integrating
religion into rock, and the band faced one of them head-on, on
its debut album, as noted disapprovingly by some Christian
critics, when the band included the f-word in one track, "Little
Lion Men." It was a word not lost on Marcus's parents, though
he claimed to have won them over on its necessity.

When we were recording it, we weren't going to put it on the
album, actually, but Winston [Marshall, vocals and banjo] was
the real champion: "We've just got to!" I was very reluctant
especially, but he was right, and I'm really glad we put it on.
There were [industry] people asking, "Is there any way you can
write a different word? We'll do anything!" we were like "No,
there's no other word, we tried it and it was just horrible, it
didn't work at all." But I now have my parents agreeing with

me as well. My mum's justifying it to other people—"There's no other word that fits, it has to be that one!" [*Laughs*] We had a guy who mixed our album called Rory who's a genius, brilliant guy, and he did a really good job on the radio edit. But we really didn't pick a single, we just gave them a bunch of songs, and this is the one they went towards.[56]

Others disagreed: "Listening to the rest of *Sigh No More*, however, I better understand those unnamed record company execs' concerns," noted the Christian publication *Plugged In*. "Not only is the profanity in question the only real issue worth noting here, it contrasts starkly with the beautiful and spiritual messages about life and death, grace and forgiveness found in the remainder of Mumford & Sons' otherwise breathtaking debut."[57]

Still, a rock band led by a Christian, the offspring of ministers, quoting the Bible, Steinbeck, and Shakespeare was clearly not what Chuck Berry, Elvis, the Beatles, or the Rolling Stones had in mind when they collectively invented a genre of music. But thanks to a variety of forces, that was now the reality of the twenty-first century rock music scene. Mumford & Sons was leading the way to a more literary and perhaps spiritually enlightened rock music culture, and the Christian gospel was being preached in the unlikeliest of venues, once said to have been dominated by Old Scratch himself. *Plugged In* noted:

The poetic "Roll Away Your Stone" seems a clear allusion to Jesus' parable of the prodigal son. Marcus Mumford tells the story of a man who hasn't found satisfaction in the world ("I have filled this void with things unreal/And all the while my character it steals"). Then he discovers grace amid the apparent loss of everything ("It seems that all my bridges have been burnt/But you say that's exactly how this grace thing works/It's not the long walk home that will change his heart/ But the welcome I receive with the restart").[58]

GOD-RELIENT

After Jonathan Bautts, a contributor to the website Absolute Punk (now chorusfm), saw a YouTube video of Matt Thiessen's punk rock band playing the hymn "Holy, Holy, Holy," he told Thiessen, lead singer of Relient K, that he found the song choice "unexpected." "How did you end up picking that song?" he asked.[59]

Rock 'n' roll may have had its origins in songs that plantation slaves sang to their God, which turned into gospel music and then the blues before becoming modern rock, but the notion that mainstream punk rock bands would feel comfortable singing hymns—not to mention being asked about it at punk rock websites—was just another indication that the times were a-changin' in unexpected ways. If he was embarrassed to be outed, Thiessen showed no trace of it. He told the writer:

Whenever I can't go to church, at my house I'll just sit and play a group of hymns on my piano, and I call it church at home. Especially on Sundays when we're on tour, I love just having church. That's kind of how that came about. But, yeah, it's really good to be able to do that stuff and get out of your artist moment for a little bit and more into a universal, life is bigger than us sort of thing.[60]

Guitarist Matt Hoopes added:

That song's always been really important to me too. I remember we did that when my grandma passed away, and it's a song my family would always sing before dinner on Sunday at my grandparents' house. We were at the funeral and singing that song and it was so meaningful to me.

It was around that same time Matt was like, "Hey, why aren't we singing that song?" We were literally talking about how it was so meaningful. I think that's part of the idea too, so when we play it live and perform it, it's never a forced thing. It's not something we have to do, it's more of something that was personally important to us and something that we wanted to do.[61]

Formed in 1998 by Thiessen, Hoopes, and Brian Pittman in Canton, Ohio, the band quickly got the attention of dc Talk's Toby McKeehan, who signed them to his fledgling label, Gotee. Gotee may have had hopes of becoming a mainstream label, but because of McKeehan's long association with the Christian music scene, the band's music didn't break into the mainstream in a major way until Capitol Records picked up their fourth album, *Mmhmm*. The band would experience its greatest success, however, when the album *Five Score and Seven Years Ago* shocked the rock world by debuting at number six on the album charts, selling sixty thousand records in its debut week. Seamlessly making the transition from the world of Christian music to the mainstream, the band seemed completely comfortable playing mainstream venues, touring with bands that didn't share their faith, and generally being a part of both the punk rock and the Christian scenes. Still, playing the famed Warped tour early in their career, typically an inhospitable venue for

Christian-oriented bands, was a challenge. Thiessen said:

> We were a little apprehensive about that. We didn't know how well things would go over as far as [our sound and what we stand for]. We anticipated that we would be the black sheep on the Warped Tour because of our beliefs. But really we were the black sheep because we were the only band that didn't "scream." No bottles were thrown at us, or anything like that. I feel like a lot of bands—Sixpence None the Richer, Switchfoot, P.O.D. and Dash—have really paved the way for us. So while many of those bands on the Warped Tour didn't share our Christian beliefs, I guess they were just intelligent or open-minded enough to tolerate us and be cool with it.[62]

Navigating both worlds, Christian and secular, would always prove to be a challenge for songwriters, tasked with reaching both worlds without losing either. Thiessen, who wrote most of the band's songs, had developed a philosophy about how to handle the challenge, thanks to a handful of bands that had preceded him:

> I look at some musicians for lyrics, like Paul Simon or Mike Herrera and let them influence me. A lot of it comes from the spirit. I'm a huge fan of Jon Foreman and how he writes, getting the brain and heart to work together. As time goes by, though, you get better at your own skill.[63]

If rock 'n' roll had developed around themes of rebellion against authority and unbridled sexuality, bands like Thiessen's had obviously missed or ignored the memo—the only f-word he was writing and singing about was *forgiveness*. Thiessen observed:

I always write about what I'm going through, and there are a couple things about forgiveness on the record about making sure we're not holding any grudges against people. Writing is the way I vent about how I'm getting over being hurt. Though one person or another did hurtful things, I'm smart enough to know that I can't hold a grudge against them forever. I use growth and grace to push myself there. I also have a good thing going with my girl, and I couldn't really help but write about that too. Forgiveness and girls . . . the songs are potpourri, and sometimes they seem like a thrown-together mess.[64]

What also set Relient K apart from other punk rock bands was their collective sense of humor, sometimes expressed in album titles such as *Two Lefts Don't Make a Right . . . but Three Do* and a most unusual "love song" titled "Marilyn Manson Ate My Girlfriend." The Christian music industry hadn't been noted as a hotbed of humor or satire as it attempted to bring Christian themes into rock 'n' roll, although there had been some notable exceptions. One of the pioneers of the genre, Larry Norman, had riffed off of the Rolling Stones by calling his label Solid Rock, and had made his own version of the famed Stones logo: an open mouth with three crosses inside lodged uncomfortably on a heart-shaped tongue. He had also written songs comparing Jesus to a UFO, and famously penned the song "Why Should the Devil Have All the Good Music?" Another artist, Steve Taylor, mastered the craft of faith-informed satirical songwriting with dozens of songs, such as "I Blew Up the Clinic Real Good," the ironic tale of an ice cream truck driver who spent his evenings blowing up abortion clinics, and managed to take swipes at the likes of Bob Dylan and his religious ambiguity when he declared, in the song "Meltdown," "Dylan may be fillin' the puddle they designed / Is it gonna take a miracle to make up his mind?"[65]

Relient K carried on that tradition with "Marilyn Manson Ate My Girlfriend," this time with the ear of the mainstream audience, which Norman and Taylor lacked. Thiessen noted, "A lot of the silly stuff is very random. We usually think of something fun we want to write about, and it just happens. I have a lot of songs that no one will ever hear because they're really dumb. Then there are the more serious, spiritual songs that come from life experience and our personal relationships with God."[66]

Christianity Today noted:

With the chorus "Marilyn Manson ate my girlfriend / Satan consumed her mind, and he may do it again," the hit single "My Girlfriend" could be considered one of the most unusual "love" songs in Christian music history. Relient K's guitarist/vocalist/chief songwriter Matt Thiessen wrote the song when he was 15 (before the Ohio-based group had even formed), inspired by a female friend who lived eight hours away in Pennsylvania.[67]

Thiessen recalled:

It wasn't a girlfriend/boyfriend relationship, but it was a friend who was a girl. We had a relationship where we would talk a lot on the phone. Sometimes we would talk about things of deeper consequence, of spiritual matter and usually just kind of seeing where God was taking us in the future.

After a while, though, things started to change with her . . . She started getting so into Nine Inch Nails and Marilyn Manson that an obsession grew out of it. And through this she changed her lifestyle [and] what she believed in. . . .

Through it all she had this newborn dislike for me and what I believed in . . . She felt that Christianity was stupid and just this big hypocrisy. Being young and impressionable, I just wrote this little, stupid song, but that was the way I dealt with it—writing this song about how she got so consumed by Marilyn Manson.[68]

The song, which appeared on the band's debut record, brilliantly showcased Thiessen and company's impish humor and made it abundantly clear that they had no desire to stay in a walled-off Christian subculture without referencing what was going on in the mainstream. Predictably, the song caused a small backlash in the Christian music world, which sometimes preferred that their artists avoid referencing such topics or personalities: Thiessen said at the time of its release:

Some moms didn't want their kids listening to our records and stuff, but that's expected. People look for stuff like that sometimes just because they want to be safe all the time. . . .

A lot of kids like it . . . We're a little tired of it, but it's still a fun song . . . You know how a lot of bands have their cliché one song about a girl, the relationship that went wrong or all that stuff? We don't actually have any of those right now. I think we may in the future. You never know how it goes.[69]

The punk rock scene, once home to bands such as the Dead Kennedys and Sid Vicious, was now being led by bands like Relient K whose members had an entirely different kind of rebellion on their minds: a rebellion against the libertine founders of their genre. Though writing songs filled with irony, humor, and pop-punk aggression, at their core were the traditional Christian doctrines of sin, repentance, and forgiveness. Thiessen explained:

> A lot of times we get so engulfed in the sins we've committed that we forget about the concept of grace. We need to realize that it's over and done—ask God for forgiveness, turn around and move on. I struggle with that a lot, thinking that I mess up way too much for God to forgive me. . . .
>
> Lately, I've been reading in the Old Testament about David. He messed up a lot, too—especially with the whole Bathsheba incident. Yet, God forgave him and totally blessed his life. Sometimes I feel like I'm constantly messing up, but for some reason God continues to bless me and this band. He also gives us opportunities to reach people. Even when I'm having the worst day, I'm reminded that someone could buy our album, and it could touch his or her heart. It's amazing how God can use us as vessels.[70]

INTO THE FRAY

After selling more than three million copies of its debut album, *How to Save a Life*, Colorado rockers The Fray decided to do something very few rock bands had ever considered: they crossed over into the Christian music market, allowing their music to be sold at Christian-oriented retail outlets and to be played on Christian-oriented radio. It was a complete turnabout from the days when Christian-oriented bands desperately sought to cross over from gospel to the mainstream, and The Fray was leading the way for a new generation of rockers whose feet were firmly planted in the mainstream and were so comfortable in their own skin that they were willing to reach back across the divide and allow their music to reach the Christian subculture.

But The Fray didn't arrive at the enviable position of being able to cross back over onto their home turf (the members were all raised in Christian homes and even led worship at their churches), but rather, because of a calculated and well-thought-out effort to ensure that their music would be accessible to the broad mainstream of American cultural life. In fact, the band turned an argument often used in the past by strictly "Christian" bands on its head by insisting that their calling from God precluded them from becoming stars on the gospel music circuit.

Composed of Isaac Slade, Joe King, Ben Wysocki, and David Welsh, the foursome hailed from Denver and attended Faith Christian Academy, yet studiously avoided pitching their music to Christian-owned record labels, choosing instead to sign with a mainstream label because, they insisted, they wanted to avoid letting God down:

"I feel he would be disappointed with us if we limited ourselves," Wysocki said.[71]

It was a twist on the standard answer, but Wysocki and The Fray firmly believed in it. They had grown up in the Christian subculture, listening to artists such as Steven Curtis Chapman and dc Talk, who, though talented, hadn't made much of an impact on the mainstream music world. Wysocki was determined to do things differently:

We all grew up listening to Christian music, and once we got old enough, we discovered that there was this whole world of music outside of music that our moms bought for us. . . .

We're all Christians, and we all come from Christian backgrounds. We grew up playing worship music in church. I learned to play drums in church. So we all come from a background of being raised in Christian families.

We got to a point where, as far as making our art, we realized that to make Christian music, as far as the music industry, if we're going to enter the music industry, we can either . . . In some ways it's sad that it's like this, but it's just the way that it is, but there's a pretty sharp distinction between Christian music and secular music. Some of the lines are getting blurred now with some bands lately, but there's still definitely that distinction. There are Christian radio stations, and there's a lot of labeling going on.

Knowing that, we wanted to steer clear of those labels and a lot of that baggage and make art in way that can relate to Christians and non-Christians. Whether that's a ministry opportunity or not, that's great and that's an extra bonus, but as musicians, we didn't want to limit ourselves to just making Christian music.[72]

The members of The Fray had come of age in a post-Christian rock culture in which many had come to question the arrangement that had been in place for at least four decades, and while that may have worked for their parents' generation, it would no longer be tolerated by a new generation of artists who hungered for access to those for whom they were called to sing. The first order of business in the new world was to write songs that could be understood by those outside of the Christian club, and the members of The Fray quickly realized they had work to do. Of the worship-oriented songs that he had been writing for his church, Slade said:

> None of my friends outside the church understood any of my songs; we had a different set of vocabulary . . . So I went home and threw away all those songs . . . If I handed somebody a double grande mocha latte and told them, "Jesus loves you and has a wonderful plan for your life," they might throw it back on me. If we grow up in the church, it's easy to think it's our Christian duty to preach to every single person because God is the most important thing. And he is, but I'm a musician first. This is my job. We're not pastors. We're not preachers. We're not even missionaries. . . . If you're a painter, paint, but you don't have to have Jesus in every picture. Paint well, and if you paint well enough, they might ask you why you do that.[73]

Wysocki echoed the sentiment:

> As Christians, we set out to make really honest art that is relatable and that's understandable for people, regardless of their religious orientation or faith background. Isaac grew up writing Christian songs in a Christian language about Christian themes and Bible verses, and then he started making friend[s] who weren't Christians. They couldn't understand what he was singing about and they didn't know . . . they couldn't relate to it, and they didn't understand it. There are some really great Christian bands out there that we really respect and are really good at making Christian

music for Christians, and that's a really good thing for some people. But for us, we're called to make music for more than just the Church, to make music for the unchurched people and hopefully speak a bit of life into them.[74]

If gospel music was birthed in the fields of suffering, as noted earlier, where African-American slaves toiled and sang to God, Christian rock came from the 1970s Christian subculture that was animated by books such as *The Late Great Planet Earth* and teaching about the "end of days," which held that the return of Christ and the end of the world was imminent. This mentality had ramifications across the board, including in education, art, and politics, and in the case of art, sometimes gave artists an overwrought sense of mission that made their work urgent, dogmatic, and insistent, instead of artistic, understated, and challenging. Slade likened the impulse in the religious community of his day to the religious leaders of Jesus' time:

"The Pharisees just quoted Bible verses," he said. "Jesus related the parables to people's lives. The people were drawn in by the plot development, character and conflict."[75]

That new insight led Slade to write the band's smash hit song "How to Save a Life," about an experience he had had with a troubled teenage friend who lived at a halfway house.

I was a sheltered suburban kid when I met this guy. He was a recovering addict, coming out of a really tough teenage life. Thankfully, he was on his way out of that life, so he was able to really look back with some objectivity. The song is more of a memoir about his slow motion descent and all the relationships he lost along the way. . . . It is the easiest one for me to sing every night. I constantly get emails from people who relate to it.[76]

Slade was now on a roll and employed the same process of honest self-examination in his next hit song, "Over My Head (Cable Car)," a song that explored a strained relationship with his brother.

"We had our ideological differences . . . We were not seeing eye-to-eye on a whole lot of things, and we had to figure out whether or not the relationship was going to continue. . . . I think that's the part that a lot of people can relate to. All real relationships don't just happen. They take so much work, sacrifice, compromise and understanding and determination to keep going."[77]

Those words could just as well have described the relationships between the band members themselves, whose friendships were forged in junior high and high school and were cemented by the common experience of achieving superstardom together, a bond that kept them grounded. But rather than take the easy path to stardom, the one taken by hundreds of artists before them, which would have found them in Nashville, to garner the attention of a Christian music label, the band focused their energies instead on the local Denver music scene, which landed them attention with local press and radio stations. That fan base catapulted them to the attention of scouts for Sony's Epic label and, eventually, gave the band a home for its music, and just like that, the band took off like a rocket, selling millions of singles and albums, and touring the world with some of the biggest acts in rock. But the foursome was also met with criticism, both from inside and outside of the religious community that birthed them, and some of the harshest reviews came from fellow Christians. Critic David Session carped:

The lead single is loaded with enough evangelical code language to ensure approval in all markets. The music is just as calculated, inoffensive, and forgettable. The record shows I have no objection to music that's decidedly mainstream, but the Fray's problem isn't that their name is all over New York City taxis when they've only produced two hits. The issue, I'm afraid, is that they were never terribly talented in the first place, and even a bottomless budget and nationwide promotional blitz can't cover that up.

The opening line of the coyly-titled "You Found Me" forecasts the lukewarm temperatures and tepid rainfall on this boulevard of broken dreams: "I found God on the corner of First and Amistad." It sounds snappy enough, until it dissolves into milk-and-water spirituality that waffles between dejection and redemption. (The chorus is all about the titular event, but later we hear that "the call never came" and "everyone ends up alone." Well, which is it?). . . .

It's a shame that such down-to-earth, earnest guys can't do more to make us feel alive.[78]

Mainstream critics were not far behind their Christian counterparts, and the criticism continued on the band's next release, *Scars and Stories*, in a review in *Rolling Stone*:

"I wanna kiss your scars tonight," Isaac Slade sings on "Heartbeat," a hope-rock anthem inspired by a visit to Rwanda. If it were a Lonely Island parody of an earnest rock band it'd be kind of funny. Unfortunately, the Fray are terrifyingly serious. Six years since their hit "How to Save a Life," they're still pumping American-Coldplay ballads full of sky-groping choruses and symphonic rushes. Producer Brendan O'Brien seems to have pushed them to turn down the Chris Martin piano rock a little. But a song about a boxer losing his last bout while his woman calls out his name ("The Fighter") is a patient beyond song-doctoring.[79]

If the criticism affected the members of The Fray, they didn't let on, continuing to tour the world with their version of earnest rock 'n' roll, informed by their Christian consciences and designed to appeal to the masses both in terms of message and music. Slade confessed, "The reason I started writing songs was because I have a talent for it, and I just love getting an emotion in my head out on paper . . . It helps me make sense of life. It's the same way people write in journals so they can look back in years. I basically just put my journals to music . . . Then we try to tighten them up a bit and make them catchier than the average diary."[80]

Part of the equation with The Fray, as with other, similarly situated Christian-oriented bands, was the importance of keeping its members' faith alive on the road. Rock had a history littered with trashed hotel rooms, drug use, and misogyny that accompanied life on the road for half a century. The Fray's members built in safeguards to keep them out of the kind of trouble that their forebears had often wandered into.

"There's not a wild card in the band," Welsh maintained. "It's a group of four solid guys."

Slade added. "We're pretty boring."[81]

Boring or not, The Fray was the most successful example of what was happening in the wider culture, as more and more Christian-leaning rock 'n' roll bands exited the subculture and came to the attention of the primary one. The pop and rock charts were now filled with such acts, and the pace of cultural penetration was only increasing. Rock 'n' roll, birthed in rebellion against authority, was now being led by bands such as The Fray, earnest young men who were now commonplace in rock and roll.

FINDING GOD'S WILL

Another indication that rock music was entering new territory as the devout invaded it could be found in the Internet musings among fans of another Colorado-based band, OneRepublic. Noting that lead singer Ryan Tedder had two Chinese characters tattooed on his arm, one poster asked if fellow OneRepublic fans could identify the meaning. "God's Will," opined one, while another, based in Hong Kong, said the meaning was closer to "God's Support." Tedder set the record straight with a tweet posted at this account:

"Many ppl have asked what my tattoo is. I got it in Osaka, in traditional/old Japanese means 'God's will'. Yes it hurt."[82]

Tedder later added in another Tweet, "The more literal translation is 'God Gives, God Takes."[83]

Whatever the exact meaning, it was another indication of how the times were changing in the world of rock.

OneRepublic was influenced by the Texas-based pop/rock band Sixpence None the Richer—the band's first incarnation was named after Sixpence's debut album, *This Beautiful Mess*, and led by Tedder and Zach Filkins, classmates at Colorado Springs Christian High School in 1996. After parting ways, the duo reunited in 2002 in Los Angeles, forming OneRepublic, and were quickly signed to Columbia Records. Although later dropped by the label, the band scored major worldwide hits with songs such as "Stop and Stare," "Apologize," and "All the Right Moves," and would quickly become a worldwide phenomenon. In addition to his work as a solo artist, Tedder also gained acclaim as a noted songwriter and producer for a number of artists, including Adele and Beyoncé. In 2012 he won a Grammy for his collaboration with Adele.

Like many devout Christians of his generation, Tedder, a graduate of Oral Roberts University in Tulsa, Oklahoma, had consciously rejected the confines of the Christian rock industry, choosing instead to aim his music at the mainstream. But the decision had come after spending time in the Christian music mecca of Nashville, an experience that left him even more convinced that he needed to take his music to a wider audience:

> I got offered a Christian record deal. I'm Christian, I grew up in the church. But I'm not going to tour churches. I was raised in Oklahoma. Tulsa's like the buckle of the Bible Belt. I grew up in that environment. I was in Nashville for two years, [and] I quickly became friends with probably half a dozen of some of the biggest Christian recording artists. Every single one of them was absolutely miserable with the fact that they were "Christian" recording artists. I saw some stuff in Nashville that turned my stomach. Some of the most pretentious, insecure people I ever met were Christian recording artists.[84]

While it should be no surprise to any fans of Christian music to learn that their heroes are only human, Tedder's insights into the CCM genre were nonetheless trenchant, particularly his realization that many who were in the business were dying to get out, a desire often fueled by the awareness that their evangelical desires were being thwarted by Christian music labels who only saw dollars to be made by selling music to fellow believers. Tedder, grounded in his faith, had a dream to make his music for the wider culture, yet found the dream sorely tested when his band was dropped from its label:

> Our first album came out about three years after we had made it. It was shelved by Columbia. We actually got dropped by Columbia the same day they dropped Katy Perry and the Jonas Brothers. They dropped all three of us."[85]

One of the Christian virtues that Tedder didn't seem to lack was perseverance and setbacks like the one he experienced with Columbia were one of many that preceded his eventual success:

> I lost count how many disappointments (there were) and just things not working out. On the producer side, I started out writing what I thought were these great songs for these big artists and not even getting the time of day because I was a nobody . . . getting a deal, getting dropped, having a lot of label interest and then not getting signed—I kind of looked at it as trial by fire. I just thought, 'If I stick this out long enough, everyone else is going to give up, and I'll be the last one standing . . . I had so many people, since I was in high school, tell me, 'you've got the talent. You've got it.' After awhile, you don't want to hear it. You don't want to hear your parents, your friends giving you any kind of accolades. That's great that you think that, but I can't pay my bills. Your compliments don't turn into currency for me. It was really frustrating. . .[86]

Tedder and his band got the big break they were looking for when they were introduced through mutual friends to music impresario Timbaland:

I connected with him through mutual friends, and we just hit it off. We started collaborating, and he said, "You're a producer. You need to start working on artists." I did that for a couple of years. [But] I thought, if I don't try and pursue this artist thing . . . it's never going to happen. I parted ways with Tim . . . regrouped in Colorado. The rest of it [eventually reuniting with Timbaland and signing to his Mosley Music Group] is pretty much on Wikipedia.[87]

Soon, not only was Tedder's band OneRepublic thriving with a string of hits, but Tedder was winning accolades and becoming a sought-after producer, working with artists like Rihanna and Kelly Clarkson. While Tedder was indeed another example of the phenomenon of Christians in rock, in some ways he was less evangelistic than some, more focused on the art and craft of songwriting, preferring to let his faith flow naturally through his music, and less focused on trying to convince his listeners of what he believed. He had clearly thought about the craft of songwriting quite a bit and spoke extensively on the subject in interviews.

OneRepublic was part of the fabric of the mainstream rock community and unlike their brothers and sisters of yesteryear, who were cut off from being a part of a mainstream community of musicians, they were comfortable being in the center of the musical culture of their time. If Christianity was influencing pop culture through the likes of Ryan Tedder, it was doing so in subtle ways, involving broad themes of redemption and forgiveness instead of more obvious messages with specific Christian dogma. Asked why listeners around the world had connected with one of his biggest hits, Tedder responded:

Lyrically, I think that so many people can connect with it. Anybody who's been wronged one too many times and felt taken advantage of, taken for granted. The moment I wrote the chorus, I had goose bumps for days. I think there are certain chord changes, certain things that happen musically and melodically, that are almost spiritual in a sense.

Sincerity is the single most important thing with music. The whole album was written that way. If it's not something that moves me, no one else is going to be moved by it.[88]

GOD'S PARAMORE

Legend has it that a young African-American man named Robert Johnson was told to go to a certain crossroads in rural Mississippi near where he lived, and that the Devil would meet him there and give him great musical talent with the guitar in exchange for his soul. Johnson would later sing about the alleged event in the song "Me and the Devil," and it would be one of many accounts that led some to think that rock music was inextricably linked to the enemy of men's souls. Decades later, John Lennon famously remarked, "Christianity will go, it will vanish and shrink. I needn't argue about that. I'm right and will be proved right. We're [the Beatles] more popular than Jesus now."[89] And in the '70s and '80s a cottage industry grew around Christian evangelists cataloging allegedly blasphemous statements made by rock stars. Whether sincere or a mere pose to outrage Christian America and bring attention to their music, blaspheming God was not an unusual component of the rock 'n' roll experience. But in the brave new world of the post-secular rock era, rock was now populated with not just socially conscious rockers—like Bono of U2—but rockers with consciences, who were sensitive to the charge of blasphemy and were doing their best to be faithful to both God and rock.

When a rock band named Paramore, led by a female singer named Hayley Williams, released a song called "Misery Business," which included the phrase "but God does it feel good," most rock fans would likely not have noticed.[90] But for Williams, it was a line she would later come to deeply regret, and one that would cause her to issue a public statement disavowing it. She wrote to her fans:

> "Misery Business," like we've explained before in interviews . . . is a true story [of a girl who used sex to manipulate one of Williams's friends]. . . .
>
> I forced myself to relive some of the very vivid memories that I have of the times he dated her. . . . to finally explain my side of the story and feel freed of it all. . . . Every word I wrote was like a thousand weights lifted off my shoulders. No more burden. What I didn't realize, as I wrote some of those lines, was that while I was escaping one burden, I was also giving myself another.[91]

Quoting the lyric in question, Williams continued:

> "But god does it feel so good . . . to steal it all away from you now, and if you could then you know you would, cause god it just feels so . . . it just feels so good."
>
> I'm ashamed to say that, although I'm a believer in Jesus Christ and I claim him as my God, when I wrote those lyrics I wasn't addressing him. I was using his name casually. In vain, to be blunt. If you know much about the Christian religion (which I'm not too fond of addressing my faith as),

you'll probably know that one of the ten commandments is "Thou shalt not take the name of the Lord your God in vain". . . . it goes on to say, ". . .for the Lord will not hold him guiltless who takes his name in vain." As a believer in Christ, that last part scares the hell out of me. I don't want to be held accountable for being the cause of so many people using his name in vain. You don't have to believe in what I believe and no one in Paramore is ever going to go around forcing our faith into people's lives . . . but believer or not, I might have led some of ya'll to believe that I take my saviour lightly. And I don't."[92]

An unusual posting for a rock star, to be sure, but for a new generation of Christ-embracing rockers, whose devotion to God was often paramount, it was just another day at the office and a small misstep in a difficult new world in which the mixing of rock and religion sometimes created unexpected problems. Rock stars were used to pushing the boundaries of culture, including the occasional bad word, but religion had long been about avoiding such adventures. Williams was trying to navigate both worlds and risked angering both sides in the process. And more challenges were to come; in 2010 Paramore went on tour with the lesbian duo Tegan and Sara, and Williams was asked by a gay website, "As a Christian in a band that has openly identified as Christian were you worried that your audience might not accept Tegan and Sara as they are lesbians and not a part of the Christian rock scene?" Williams replied:

Fortunately, we've never really been associated with the Christian rock scene. I wouldn't want to be a part of something so easily pigeonholed. It's an understandable misconception though—we've never preached but if someone asks us about our faith, we're not scared to talk about it. The biggest fault I find within the Christian community is that there are too many judges in the courthouse. What I know is that I'm not going to let myself be one of those. Not to sound selfish, but I've got my own life to figure out and faith is constantly surprising me. Hopefully, we're surprising people too. I mean, who would've thought that Christians can actually hang out with lesbians without bursting into flames?![93]

Williams got her start at the age of fourteen, when she was discovered by two managers who noticed the young woman's voice after she moved to Franklin, Tennessee, home to artists such as Amy Grant, dc Talk, and Jars of Clay. She was quickly signed to a production deal. Williams later formed the band with three friends, Josh and Zac Farro and Jeremy Davis, and its debut record was released on the Atlantic subsidiary label, Fueled by Ramen.

"I met Zac and Josh when I moved to Nashville and started going to a private school and it was cool to meet people that liked music as much as I did," recalled Williams. "As soon as we started writing together, it was pretty obvious."[94]

"I totally agree," added Josh Farro. "Our music was okay; it was a lot of fun writing, but as soon as we had Hayley come and sing, then we knew—and everyone was telling us, 'You guys can make it.' And now we're here."[95]

In a later interview Farro added:

Zac and I had a garage band in high school with the intentions of just making music for the love of it. We met Taylor and our friend Jason Clark at our school and found out that we shared the same musical tastes. So, we asked them to join our band. It was some of the greatest times of our lives playing music in Taylor's basement with them. We obviously needed a lead singer and one day Zac met Hayley. We asked her to come try out and eventually to join the band.[96]

From the outset the band was vocal about its members' shared religious beliefs. Farro said:

Our faith is very important to us. It's obviously going to come out in our music because if someone believes something then their worldview is going to come out in anything they do. But we're not out here to preach to kids, we're out here because we love music.

We do believe that God has blessed us with an opportunity to be in a band and tour the world and we're going to use this gift to the full potential.[97]

Asked about her upbringing and whether she listened to Christian music growing up, Williams admitted, "Yeah. There was definitely some of that. My mom remarried, and my stepdad was a super Southern Baptist Nazi, I guess you'd call it. So I definitely got a good bit of, you know, dc Talk. What's weird is we actually know some of those dc Talk dudes now because we all live in Franklin, Tennessee, which is like the mecca of Christian music."[98]

Farro told the *Houston Chronicle*:

We don't want our fans to feel like we're preaching to them or that we're out there to tell them how to live their lives or what they should believe. But at the same time, it is really important for us to let people know that we do believe in

Jesus Christ, and we are Christians.

It's not easy, because not everyone agrees with you. But I think for the most part, our fans are really cool about respecting what we believe, whether they're Christians or not.[99]

Although success for the band had been building slowly, Paramore would stun the music world in 2009 when its album *Brand New Eyes* was barely edged out by Barbra Streisand's *Love Is the Answer*, selling 175,000 units to her 180,000 and finishing in the number two slot that week, just ahead of Mariah Carey's *Imperfect Angel*, which sold 168,000. It was a clear indication that the band would be around to stay, and that Hayley Williams and company were no flash in the pan.

But a year later, the rise of Paramore—if not Hayley Williams—came to an abrupt halt when the band imploded. Williams and two of her bandmates wrote on the group's website (now defunct):

> A couple of months ago, Josh and Zac let us know they would be leaving the band after our show in Orlando last Sunday. None of us were really shocked. For the last year it hasn't seemed as if they wanted to be around anymore. We want Josh and Zac to do something that makes them happy and if that isn't here with us, then we support them finding happiness elsewhere. But we never for a second thought about leaving any of this behind. We really hope that you can be encouraged by the fact that the three of us who are still here are ready to take on another chapter of our journey together. You have always been what keeps us going so why would we stop now? We want to stick by you. Knowing that we have a unified passion and a clear vision makes us feel stronger than ever."[100]

Williams's post produced a quick rejoinder from the Farro brothers, one that placed the blame for the breakup on Hayley's shoulders and hinted at religious reasons. Farro wrote:

Hayley and Jeremy's views started changing from what we all once believed in. The band almost split after cancelling a tour in Europe, but we managed to keep it together somehow. This is when Zac and I started to consider quitting the band.

Once we finished touring on Riot, we came home for a break and started writing for Brand New Eyes. Hayley presented lyrics to us that were really negative and we didn't agree with. For example, "the truth never set me free," which contradicts what the Bible says in John 8:32 ("and you shall know the truth, and the truth shall sat [sic] you free"). We fought her about how her lyrics misrepresented our band and what we stood for, but in the end she got her way. Instead of fighting her any longer, we decided to just roll over and let it go.

Hayley claimed that this record reunited us as band and made us grow closer together, when in reality we were all growing further apart. Suddenly the band had spilt into two sides. Touring became more difficult since we couldn't agree on anything. The friendships our band once had were no longer existent. Amos 3:3 says, "Can two people walk together without agreeing on the direction."[101]

"You feel every single type of emotion possible when something like this happens with someone that either was—or is—very close to you," Hayley said in an article on EW.com. "You just feel everything, all at once. . . . I've never felt so . . . I don't know, I couldn't even figure out how I felt. But after realizing, like Taylor said, that it was kind of going to happen this way, you've just got to know that what's important is the three of us are still here, and that we want to do this, and that's the positive part about this."[102]

From the Beach Boys to the Beatles, the breakup of rock bands was as old as the genre itself, and the new world of Christian-oriented rock bands wouldn't be immune to the same challenges their forefathers had faced. Paramore would continue on without two of its founders, and a bright new talent named Hayley Williams, an outspoken yet spiritually sensitive young woman, would continue to speak and sing for millions, continuing the difficult and sometimes dangerous task of mixing God and rock 'n' roll.

IN THE FLYLEAF

When a band named Flyleaf's eponymous debut record sold a million copies, the music world immediately took notice of the female-led rock band from Texas. Accolades including winning a popularity poll at Yahoo.com, being named MTV's artist of the week, and the band's lead singer being nominated for the "Hottest Chick in Metal" award quickly confirmed the band's budding superstar status. But it was apparent from the beginning that Flyleaf wasn't your father's "hottest chick in metal." Led by Lacey Mosley, Flyleaf was signed to a mainstream label called Octone, but was up front about its members' devotion to God from the beginning and incorporated that faith into the music without the slightest hesitation. The band's debut record even included an ode to Cassie Bernall, the equally devout Christian high school student who was reportedly asked whether she believed in God before being gunned down in the Columbine High School massacre.

Mosley's devotion to God, shared by her fellow band members, seemed especially unlikely because of her background. Unlike many devout rockers, who usually emerged from equally devout Christian families, Mosley took a more circuitous path to God that involved a stint as an atheist and a near-suicide attempt. She recalled:

> When I was 10 I remember I stopped believing in God because I had a three-year-old cousin who was beaten to death by her stepfather and I . . . started getting depressed and first started doing drugs. . . . I planned to commit suicide that next morning—I don't think I went to sleep that night—but I went through the next day and did some stuff that I had planned out. Like to go to school and see a couple people and then I left school and came home and my grandmother wasn't supposed to be home, but she was home. . . . She kind of knew something was wrong and she told me to go to church. And that was like the last place on earth I wanted to be because I hated Christians and I thought they were all naïve and hypocritical and fake and that everybody acted all happy all the time—I just hated them . . . I didn't want to go.[103]

But Mosley reluctantly went to church, and what happened next would change the course of her life. Stories of religious conversion are as diverse as the people that have them, and Mosley's was nothing short of dramatic.[104]

Scriptures records that when faced with a woman who poured perfume on His feet and wiped them with her hair, Jesus Christ remarked, "Her many sins are forgiven; for she loved much; but he to whom little is forgiven loves little" (Luke 7:47 DARBY). Flyleaf's lead singer would come to God through a very dark tunnel, and her subsequent devotion seemed to be directly linked to the gratefulness she felt at having come out the other side of that tunnel into a life of faith. Mosley made a direct connection between the success in the rock world that was awaiting her and her emergence from drugs, depression, despair, and suicidal thoughts:

> I went in the back and tried to suffer through it until it was over. Then the preacher started talking about . . . well, he pretty much described my life in a series of stories he told about people he had worked with over the years and families he'd helped through different situations. And it was just pretty crazy that he said all these things that just described my life and the reason that I just hated life in general. . . . And he stopped in the middle of the sermon and . . . said, "There's a suicidal spirit in this room." And like all the hairs stood up on my arms and I was like, 'I gotta get out of here; this is kind of weird.'"[105]

Mosley didn't instantly turn to God, but took in all that had happened and tried to make sense of it. With the passage of time, the steps she had begun to take in her journey of faith began to make more and more sense, confirmed by what she saw as divine signals that she was on the right path:

> I remember going home and being real turned around. I was like, "Is there a God," you know? And "What does that mean?" I was like, if there is a God then I have to think about all of this. And I remember waking up the next day and going, "OK, God, if you're real, then why did you wake me up today because I wasn't supposed to? And what do you want me to

do with this life and why is it that important to you?" And ever since then I've been trying to figure out what that is."[106]

Mosley made a direct connection between the success in the rock world that was awaiting her and her emergence from drugs, depression, despair, and suicidal thoughts: "There were a lot of things that came out of me not dyin'," she said. "But Flyleaf is one of those things I guess. . . . We weren't trying to do anything huge, we just wanted to say, "Whatever you want to do God, do it."[107]

After various stints in child care and waitressing, Lacey teamed up with several friends from junior high—Sameer Bhaattacharya, Jared Hartmann, and James Culpepper, as well as Pat Seals in Texas—and formed what would eventually become Flyleaf.

Despite Flyleaf's Christian devotion, one listen to its music clearly showed that its influences were not from the relatively polite world of contemporary Christian music, but from rock's darker underbelly, something Mosley readily admitted:

> I grew up listening to Nirvana and Pantera and '90s grunge bands. I mean I like pop too. I liked pop during the '80s! And when I was younger, . . . I was like 12 or 11 years old and my brother went to a Nirvana concert and he came back with a tape [of Nevermind]. . . .[108]

The notion that the movement of Christians into mainstream rock would be led by a four-foot-ten, twentysomething woman who had cut her teeth on the greatest metal bands of the '90s was ludicrous. However, it was true in the case of Mosley, who had imbibed deeply of the greatest heavy metal, rock, and grunge bands of her era but somehow managed to combine that with a love for God—the same God who had inspired preachers of yesteryear to ban and burn such rock albums. Having her life changed, first by Kurt Cobain and then by Jesus Christ, Mosley and Flyleaf landed like a thud on the rock scene, quickly scoring success with their debut album and connecting with millions of fans. If Mosley's God was indeed real, perhaps it made perfect sense that He would need to recruit a broken vessel like her to reach a generation of broken young people with whom she had many shared experiences. Mosley was, to them, a fellow broken human being who had somehow found hope and peace in the chaos of her life. And despite being in a business filled with narcissism and materialism, Mosley was focused on her mission to connect with her fans and bring them out of the depths of despair, just as a preacher had done with her:

> They usually say that [our music] helped them a lot through really tough times. A lot of people say, "My parents got divorced and it really helped me through the divorce." Or "My friend died in a car wreck and it helped me through that." Or "I was really suicidal and depressed because of all kinds of things and your music helped me through that."
>
> There's a million directions, but it's always something really heavy. I'm just so thankful that something I went through and got over and wrote a song about helped somebody else get through, get over it enough to come there and have a smile on their face and hug me and thank me. I'm so thankful for that because if we can help somebody get through something, then they can also help somebody get through something and it just keeps going and hopefully it'll make the world a better place in the end.[109]

In 2009, Flyleaf released its follow-up album, *Memento Mori*, a title that reflected the band's deep humility at having met such success with its first record. Mosley had gotten the idea for the title from an old story about a conquering Roman general. She said:

> In ancient Rome, when a Roman general or King would come back victorious from battle, the whole kingdom would celebrate and throw him a parade. As they sang praises to welcome him home, a slave travelling behind him shouted, "Memento mori!" which is a Latin phrase meaning "Remember that you're mortal; remember you will die." In other words, the slave was saying to him that we ultimately share the same fate. At this moment, you are on top, but tomorrow is another day and our positions can be reversed. So "Memento mori" really was an amazing phrase to find, and it just sums up what we've learned over the past 7 years of being together.[110]

A rock band at the pinnacle of success titling its follow-up record after a lesson in humility was probably not what rock 'n' roll's founding fathers had in mind when they invented a genre of music that brought them in front of screaming fans in different cities with a license to behave as they pleased. But thanks to unlikely rock stars such as Lacey Mosley, rock was becoming, for many young people, the primary vehicle from which to receive traditional religious and spiritual messages, and the diminutive rock star seemed to clearly understand her role:

> I believe there's a purpose for your life that only you were meant to fulfill. So our prayer, for anyone who listens to the message on the record, is that they would fulfill their purpose and answer the highest calling for their lives.[111]

Committed to seeing transformation in the hearts and minds of her many young fans, the young evangelist in rock-star clothing had a prayer for her fans that she kept close to her heart:

> We . . . pray that the Holy Spirit would come in the same powerful way that He did when I was saved. Jesus said, "If I am lifted up, I will draw all men to me." So as we worship and praise, we pray that the Holy Spirit would fall on the whole room and on the people. And we pray that the Lord will continue to go with them after the concert and that they will recognize that the Lord is pursuing them. And also that He would break off chains and bring healing and do everything the Holy Spirit does.[112]

A decade into the twenty-first century, many Americans seemed to be tuning out televangelists after two decades of fallen leaders began to take their toll on a population weary of hypocrisy. But reinforcements were coming from a most unlikely quarter of popular culture and from the most unlikely of heroines, like the lead singer of Flyleaf, who seemed to see her mission as being not dissimilar to that of the religious leaders of yesteryear:

> Isaiah 61:1 says: "The Spirit of the Lord is upon me, for the Lord has anointed me to bring good news to the poor," and that one Scripture has been the inspiration behind our music. God has written His Word on our hearts. He's anointed us, just as Christ lives in us, to bring good news to the poor, and that's why we go out and do what we do. In fact, it wasn't until after someone once told us the good news that we got saved. So now the purpose of our lives is to go out and share the good news of God's love with others.[113]

6

HIDING IN PLAIN SIGHT

A SWIFT RISE

When the CBS News show *60 Minutes* got around to inter-viewing her, it merely served to validate what millions of teen-agers around the world already knew: Taylor Swift was a major star who was completely comfortable being held up as a role model for young girls everywhere and contrast with other stars, like Miley Cyrus, was evident:

"My job isn't to tell your kids how to act or how not to act, because I'm still figuring that out for myself," Cyrus once told a reporter. "To take that away from me is a bit selfish. Your kids are going to make mistakes whether I do or not. That's just life."[1]

Swift, on the other hand, told *60 Minutes*: "I definitely think about a million people when I'm getting dressed in the morning, and that's just part of my life now. I think it's my responsibility to know it and to be conscious of it. It would be really easy to say, 'I'm twenty-one now, I do what I want. You raise your kids!' But it's not the truth of it. The truth of it is—every singer out there with songs on the radio is raising the next generation."[2]

If parents of teen girls across America were breathing a sigh of relief, it may have been because after a generation of faux rebel poses, a young female pop star was, for once, positioned to help their children reach adulthood in a healthy way. Swift was yet another example of a Christian young person entering the mainstream pop culture and having a positive impact far away from the Christian music world. Not only was she giving girls a positive image of what a girl could be; she was also casting her fan's parents in a positive light by singing about times when her parents knew better than she did:

"All Taylor Swift's songs are autobiographical. 'Love Story' grew out of a teenage argument she had with her parents over a boy. They thought he was a creep," noted *60 Minutes'* Lesley Stahl.

"And he was," Swift admitted, "but I, at the time, just thought he was amazing. And I got this pre-chorus in my head that said, "You were Romeo, you were throwing pebbles and my daddy said stay away from Juliet."[3]

As rock stars began to be culled from well-adjusted, non-rebellious members of the American heartland, artists like Swift would flood mainstream pop. Traditional music outlets, which emerged from the countercultural '60s, were sometimes nonplussed when confronted with a generation that had little interest in its issues. Barely concealing its incredulity, *Rolling Stone* noted:

> On a bright Sunday afternoon in Los Angeles, Taylor Swift is on good behavior, as usual. In high school, she had a 4.0 average; when she was home-schooled during her junior and senior years, she finished both years of course work in 12 months. She has never changed her hair color, won't engage in any remotely dangerous type of physical activity and bites her nails to the quick. At 19 years old, she says she has never had a cigarette. She says she has never had a drop of alcohol. "I have no interest in drinking," she says, her blue eyes focused and intent beneath kohl liner and liberally applied eye shadow. "I always want to be responsible for the things I say and do." Then she adds, "Also, I would have a problem lying to my parents about that." Swift has gotten far playing Little Miss Perfect.[4]

Born in 1989 in Pennsylvania, Taylor Alison Swift grew up on a Christmas tree farm that belonged to her family.

"We had, like, 15 acres," she recalled. "It was really fun as a kid. I also spent my summers at the Jersey Shore, on the bay in Stone Harbor. I walked everywhere barefoot. It was just the most amazing, magical way to grow up."[5]

At an early age Swift had a passion for singing and would often venture to Nashville with her mother. A transfer to Nashville for her stockbroker father allowed the singer to pursue music full-time, and she quickly landed a songwriting deal. With it came a new perspective for the budding singer:

"In Pennsylvania, I was weird. I would play singer-songwriter nights every weekend instead of going to parties. I think it's weird to go to parties and get drunk when you're 13, but whatever. Then I moved to Nashville, and all of the sudden I was a normal kid."[6]

That normalcy was exactly what rock music had fought against, more often than not, and it seemed at the time as though. The whole point of rock celebrity had been to *not* be normal—but to push the boundaries of acceptable behavior. Trashed hotel rooms, drugs and booze, unbridled sexuality, and outsized egos had become a staple of the rock 'n' roll lifestyle. But Swift was part of a new generation of artists who had thought through those excesses—and were determined to be different.

"My biggest pet peeve is people who feel they're entitled to success and fame," she told a reporter. "I haven't reached the point where I'm like, 'Hey, man, I've made it!' And I hope I never do get to that point."[7]

If her refusal to drink and smoke weren't enough for *Rolling Stone*'s editors, Swift also espoused traditional views on sexuality and frowned on wearing skimpy outfits to promote her music. An article in the *Telegraph* noted:

> Her lyrics, which she used to co-write and now writes single-handedly, are wholly unlike the banal sexual come-ons that crowd the music of most of her contemporaries. Her image, too, is about as far away from Rihanna or Lady Gaga as you can get.
>
> I remind her of something she said a couple of years ago: "I don't want people to think of me as sexy."
>
> It wasn't a career decision, she says, pulling on a sandy curl that's got caught in her necklace, "it's just a life decision. I like wearing pretty dresses and I like trying out new styles but I don't feel comfortable taking my clothes off.

"I wouldn't wear tiny amounts of clothing in my real life so I don't think it's necessary to wear that stuff in photo-shoots."

Do people ever try to talk her into it? "Not anymore, no."[8]

Fending off pregnancy rumors with characteristic style, Swift implied that she was a virgin: "I read a very creative rumor this morning saying I'm pregnant, which is the most impossible thing on the planet. Take my word for it. Impossible."[9]

When a reporter mockingly asked about an ex-boyfriend, Joe Jonas of the Jonas Brothers, and whether the Brothers' famous virginity promise rings were a problem for her, Swift swatted back: "I don't ever talk about how I feel about that sort of thing because it makes people look at me sexually, which has never been a goal of mine. So, honestly, deal-breaker? That's actually a plus for me."[10]

Unlike more explicitly evangelistic rock and pop stars who were flooding mainstream music, Swift projected a more mainstream image and didn't fill her music with explicit Christian messages. Raised by Presbyterian parents who homeschooled her through a Tennessee-based Christian homeschool program, Swift studiously avoided political or religious pronouncements that might offend or keep away fans. Although it once had been reported that she noted in social media that Republicans "do it better," she had also expressed satisfaction with the election of Barack Obama. Still, she insisted that she wanted to avoid alienating fans.

"I follow it, and I try to keep myself as educated and informed as possible," she said of the 2012 election. "But I don't talk about politics because it might influence other people. And

I don't think that I know enough yet in life to be telling people who to vote for."[11]

Although she may have coyly denied trying to influence fans politically or religiously, her impact would be felt by another Christian-influenced band, the Civil Wars, which was heavily promoted by Swift when she took to Twitter to declare her love for them: "@CivilWars show. Belcourt Theatre. Caitlin and I bought t-shirts cause we're superfanssss. They RULE live!"[12]

Swift later asked the Civil Wars to sing a duet on a song called "Safe & Sound," which was featured prominently on the soundtrack for the *Hunger Games*. The explosion of popularity for the duo was clearly a result, at least in part, of Swift's enthusiastic cheerleading.

Taylor Swift wasn't out to save souls or shill for a political party. But she was, in many ways, a throwback to an earlier era of civic morality—a time when girls saved themselves for marriage and boys behaved. She was no wallflower, and her steely determination to succeed on her own terms was clearly evident. Nominally Christian, she was yet another example of the pop-culture results of a generation of young American Christians who were steered away from the world of gospel music and whose presence was being felt in the musical mainstream.

"Every singer out there with songs on the radio is raising the next generation," Swift once noted. "So make your words count."[13]

THE REALEST THING YOU'VE EVER SEEN

For those who had cheered for the new approach of artists like Dave Mustaine of Megadeth who had stayed put in his band after his conversion experience, the unexpected announcement by rap star Mase in 1999 might have been viewed as a setback. The rapper, who had been brought to the nation's attention by hip-hop mogul P. Diddy, announced that he was retiring for religious reasons. Mase had "become an icon of bling thanks to the gold foil suit he wore in the 'Feels So Good' video," noted one observer. "His sleepy sounding flow made him an instant success. But then he had a vision of himself leading thousands of people into hell and, on the eve of the release of his second album, announced he was leaving music for the ministry."

A few days later, Mase explained his decision to walk away from a flourishing career in hip-hop.

"It takes a great person to walk away from money," he said. "If you ask any person, 'Would you walk away from that money to do something you felt in your heart?' and nobody agreed. . . . it takes not only a great person. It takes a strong person. It takes a courageous person. It takes a person that you've never encountered. And everybody always questions what's real. 'What's real about Mase?' This is the realest thing you ever seen."[14]

Mase's cryptic comments left many inside and outside of the industry scratching their heads. A few months later, he was still explaining himself. "You can't do gospel and rap," he told MTV. "Either you're of the gospel music, or you're a rapper. You can't put the two together. You can, but is it right? It's questionable."[15]

It was a stunning move for one of rap's brightest up-and-coming stars, although not an unprecedented one for those in the black community, who had long drawn a clear line in the sand between gospel and R & B music, and it was reflective of a widely held view in the gospel community that anybody who sought to mix the two would not be tolerated. Mase felt he had a calling from God to leave music and become a pastor, a decision that was met with skepticism by those closest to him. But the truly amazing part of the Mase story was yet to come—in 2004 he made a surprising comeback, releasing a new record and reclaiming his status as one of hip-hop's brightest superstars. Explaining his reasons for returning, Mase made the case that the most effective way to reach his old fans was to get back to work at the craft he excelled at, and bring his message to bear on the music. In an interview with the industry's top magazine, *Vibe*, he said:

> When I left, it was because of God. And when I came back, it was because of God. If I want to tell somebody something, I don't print it in a newspaper they don't read. I felt like my life would be more effective in hip-hop. And I had to get strong enough to be able to live and maintain my lifestyle right in the midst of everything that made me contrary. . . . a mentor mentioned that it would be good for me to be a part of hip-hop again, and I began to consider it. Then I began to think about what kind of music I would make, what my style would be like, and who would I be able to touch. Because I didn't wanna make music to make music this time, I wanna really touch people.[16]

Mase was indeed back, but he likely knew his audience well enough to know that the transition from his old topics to the interests of the new Mase would need to be made slowly and tactfully if he intended to keep his audience: In so doing he found himself on terrain common to many of the R & B/ gospel stars of yesteryear. Upon his conversion experience, Al Green had first tried to integrate his faith into his R & B songs, then recorded strictly gospel albums, then finally came back to mainstream R & B. But a new generation of artists, like Mase, would resist the temptation to flee the primary culture, and for those who expected a collection of hymns, Mase made it clear that integrating his music and his newfound belief in God meant hip-hop with a clear subtext of faith. He was one devout young Christian who tried hard to avoid the trappings of religion, emphasizing that the Christian life was something that had been sorely misrepresented by Christians in the public sphere. He continued to pastor his El Elyon Church in Atlanta, and speak at churches and colleges across the country:

NOTHING LEFT TO LOSE

Rock critic Jase Luttrell, while reviewing Mat Kearney's sophomore album, *Nothing Left to Lose*, could just as easily have been describing much of the music that was emerging from a new crop of Christian-oriented artists who were planting their flags squarely in the middle of the mainstream music culture.

> The first surprise is "Undeniable," which opens the disc with a muted electric guitar and a subdued backing vocal loop. It then breaks into a steady stream of rap lyrics. Most surprisingly, this song is not about his love for a girl, but about his connection to God. This is one of the only songs that is religious, at least overtly, though this song isn't blatant about its religiosity; it is easily accessible to mainstream audiences. . . .
>
> The third track, "Crashing Down," is. . . . a song either about one of the loves in his life or about his relationship with God. The delineation is not clear, which is likely on purpose: Mat, as an innovative newcomer, does not want to alienate any potential listeners by falling into the precipitous genre of Christian rock.[17]

It was no accident that Kearney was in the mainstream music world, and he was in many ways living out the ideal that many devout Christians had hoped could happen when Christians stayed in the mainstream and still made strong statements of faith set to great music. Many artists trapped in the Christian rock industry for decades longed for the kind of platform that artists like Kearney had earned, and one, TobyMac of the groundbreaking group dc Talk, spoke openly about his regrets at not having taken a path similar to Kearney's: "I had an interview with TobyMac late last year," wrote one reporter. "When I asked him if he could start it all over again, what would he do, he said he would make music like Mat Kearney."[18]

Informed of the comment, Kearney responded with characteristic humility:

> Toby is the reason I am in Nashville. He is one of the main reasons I am doing music because he heard a little demo I did and he said, 'Man you need to pursue this!' He has been a huge supporter since day one.[19]

And dc Talk's famed lead singer wasn't the only one. Mac Powell, lead singer of one of Christian rock's biggest-selling bands of all time, Third Day, also heaped praise on Kearney, declaring: "This guy will make it in the mainstream."[20]

"Every artist wants to be appreciated by what they do. So that is nice when people get it," said Kearney. "And it is humbling when people compliment you—people like Mac. That was a very nice compliment he gave me. I actually thanked him. I was like, 'Thanks man! You did not have to say all that!' And he was very complimentary when I went up to him. He seems like a good guy. And not just because he complimented me!"[21]

Not unlike his mentor TobyMac's mix of hip-hop stylings and rock 'n' roll, Kearney's smooth rhythms and cool persona moved easily between rap and pop influences, but always with a sharp spiritual focus that consistently hinted at a deep belief in God and a traditionalist outlook on life. In one of his most interesting songs, "Girl America," Kearney effortlessly rapped and sang his way through a song that could be interpreted as chronicling either the life of a young girl or the downward trajectory of America (or both). Asked about his efforts to be accepted in the musical mainstream, Kearney was clear in his mission and purpose:

> I never made a record to be in the Christian market. So when I made my record it was to exist in all of the markets. . . . My faith is a part of who I am and the music I make. But it has to exist within the world that does not necessarily believe what I believe.[22]

At one time in America, the creation and maintenance of an industry devoted to making religious music and exclusively marketing it to fellow believers made sense, but in the world in which artists like Mat Kearney came of age, it no longer did, and he spoke for many when he seemed unable to explain the divide that had kept so many artists of faith out of mainstream popular culture:

> I don't know if I exactly know what Christian music is. . . . But I do not know if the notes and the chords—going from C to G to D—makes it Christian or not. . . . The record I made that works in the Christian market is the same record Columbia picked up and said they want to release.[23]

In part, the rationale had broken down because it represented a *break* with traditional Christian theology, which had always emphasized that all activities were to be done to the glory of God instead of being lumped into the categories of "sacred" and "secular." Despite the fact that modern evangelical Christians had constructed just such a framework with the creation of parallel religious-based institutions that mirrored their mainstream counterparts, artists like Kearney rejected the paradigm even as they professed devotion to God and to spreading the Christian message. In discussing artists who were Christians but didn't talk much about God from the stage, he said:

> I am not an evangelist. I am not a preacher. I am a musician. That is what I know how to do. I know how to write songs. I know how to write things that relate to my heart. I feel that I talk about God in every song, in everything I do—all of it!. . . . I totally feel that I am talking about God in everything I write about. Whether I am saying His name directly or whether I am talking about romantic love, it is all a part of the expression of faith that I have experienced and the grace that I have experienced. . . .
>
> God is in everything. He is in the mundane. Flannery O'Conner . . . said she looked for God in the mundane and . . . in the ordinary. . . . We are people that have to go to coffee shops. We have to live our lives. We have to be husbands and wives and students. We are all existing and God is in the middle of all of that for us. It is not just some bubble—only quoting scripture all day. So for me, I feel like I am talking about God all the time.[24]

One of the most consistent accusations that has been hurled at the genre of Christian rock through the years has been that it was derivative of the musical mainstream and that many CCM artists were merely pale pastel versions of their mainstream musical equivalents. It wasn't uncommon, for instance, for leaders at Christian record labels to describe their artists as being a "Christian version" of such and such artist. But to a new generation like Kearney, excelling artistically and being innovative was a priority, and it was clear from the way he approached his music that he was pushing the boundaries of genre with the way he wrote and recorded songs. A musician whose lyrics crossed over the borders that existed between the sacred and the secular, Kearney similarly crossed natural borders that separated musical genres. In many ways, artists like Kearney represented a passing of the torch from one generation of Christian-oriented artists to another. The first generation of Jesus rockers had retreated from the world and joined a corporate genre of Christian music. That, in turn, had given way to a new generation of artists, including Kearney, who were determined to sing for the entire world, and it would remain to be seen how successful and how difficult such a task would be. With his strong faith and a determination to sing in the mainstream music business, Mat Kearney would be an enigma to some and a hero to others. If he was out to convert souls to Jesus Christ, he set about to do it in a breezy manner that belied any such intensity, focusing instead on his desire to be real to his fans and tell them what was going on in his life and what motivated and inspired him. Asked what he hoped his audience would gain from listening to his music, he replied:

> Hopefully some of the life and the hope and the encouragement I have experienced in my life, in my own personal faith and personal day to day walk through life, has found its way into my music. Hopefully people can glean from that and can

receive some of that from listening to my music, no matter what walk of life they come from. That they will experience some of the grace or that they will be drawn closer to the grace that I have experienced in the middle of a harsh world, a world of pain that is struggling. That there is hope and there is redemption and there is grace available to people.[25]

THE BEDINGFIELDS

"She's a virgin!" blurted out an incredulous music executive at a meeting to discuss artists for a soundtrack for the film *Rocky Balboa* that I once attended, when I raised the name of pop singer Natasha Bedingfield as a possible collaborator. Although the soundtrack never did get produced, the outburst was another example of the culture clash that often ensued as Christians entered the mainstream and came face-to-face with entertainment executives who simply couldn't fathom them.

But in the case of Natasha Bedingfield, the entertainment culture would have not one but two such curiosities to deal with, since her brother Daniel was also an international pop star who had hit it big in the early 2000s with his hit songs "Gotta Get Thru This," and "If You're Not the One," both mainstays on American pop radio. But a cursory listen to his songs as background noise for shopping, waiting, or exercising would likely not have told the most interesting and surprising part of the story of Britain's newest pop phenom: Like his sister, he was a devout Christian, sometimes compared to a young Cliff Richard, who seemed unashamed of—and insistent upon—filling his songs of love with statements of devotion to God. Although Daniel broke into the pop music scene first, he was quickly followed by Natasha and her breakout single "Pocketful of Sunshine."

Christianity Today noted:

Turns out that [Daniel] Bedingfield's also an outspoken Christian. Depending which bio you read, his parents are either missionaries or social workers. He openly shares his faith in concerts and in some of his music. . . . The gentle acoustic "Honest Questions" . . . seems inspired by Psalm 63 and/or Isaiah 35. It's stunning to hear a song this faith-based on a mainstream release: "Oh look down and see the tears I've cried, the lives I've lived, the deaths I've died/You died them too, and all for me/You say, 'I will pour my water down upon a thirsty barren land/And streams will flow from the dust of your bruised and broken soul.'"[26]

While fans may have been enthralled with the singer, when it came to the sometimes hostile rock press, the arms were hardly outstretched. It wasn't entirely clear whether the harsh criticism Bedingfield sometimes encountered was because of his squeaky-clean Christian image or the fact that many critics simply looked down on his style of pop. Whatever the case, criticism was fast and furious in the music press. Critic Nicki Tranter noted:

Daniel Bedingfield's rise to the top of the charts, with esteemed publications like *Interview, Billboard* and *USA Today* singing his praises, is further proof that standards in the music industry have fallen. Everything on his album is so polished, so "electric," that even when it sounds good, it's impossible to distance yourself from how contrived the whole thing is. It's like the musical equivalent of Pamela Anderson: pretty but fake. It doesn't matter if Bedingfield can play an instrument, or even sing, because his computer is right beside him, ready to pick up any slack. . . .

Continuing the whole bizarre mess is how confident Bedingfield is when he sings such nonsense, as if he is so worldly wise and intelligent. "I could be James Dean / Of the music scene / I could be a big star / Like that man called Queen," he sings on his latest single "James Dean (I Wanna Know)," before going on to mention his "Brad Pitt smile" and Versace style. This ginormous ego is as perplexing as it is laughable, especially when he misuses words and phrases often in his songs, and has apparently never taken classes in basic grammar. Still, he somehow believes he's God's gift to music (which he threatens he's gonna make "till [his] brain is fried"). He even dedicates his album to "the creator, Yahweh" and "the four incredible girls that inspired my songs." Blah.[27]

Tranter seemed incensed not only by Bedingfield's expressions of faith, but also with his reliance on the computer for songwriting:

The 22-year-old Bedingfield has somehow found his way to the top of the charts in the US and the UK with his song *Gotta Get Thru This*, recorded in his bedroom on his PC. The song found its way onto a local pop record where it caught the attention of big time record producers. He was quickly signed to the Island label, wrote and performed the rest of his album in his underpants, and took his song to number one. The rest is music history.

This is all very nice for a boy from New Zealand raised in South London, but surely you would think with his obviously overwhelming ability to compose utter claptrap cleverly disguised as serious prophesizing, his lyrics might contain something a little more expressive than "If you're not the one / Why does my heart feel glad today / If you're not the one / Then why does my hand fit yours this way."[28]

In addition to his religion, his choice of a computer as a musical aid, and his brand of pop music, critics seemed to also resent what they perceived as his status as a sort of amateur philosopher. In the liner notes of his debut record, Bedingfield had noted:

> The blazing beauty of a tree, or the magnificent calm of the sky, our treasures are obscured and overshadowed, enveloped, swallowed by the meaningless dirge, the cry of oppression, the hopeless song of confused faces. . . . I often find myself swept downstream by the song's awful power humming along to its prevailing topline [*sic*]: Pain. But I also seek to express the whole journey. These brief moments of sight. These points of clarity, these expressions of hope, deliverance and the upward struggle of the searching soul. I point with my broken fingers toward the only safety I know—greater love hath no man than he.[29]

But Bedingfield's first two hits weren't exactly deep works of philosophy and, musically, were actually quite different from one another, leaving his music difficult to categorize. The calm and peaceful "If You're Not the One" was miles away from the frenetic "I Gotta Get Thru This," which seemed to be a perfect musical portrait of Bedingfield himself, a young man whose hyperactivity and dyslexia had required him to be medicated:

> I was a nightmare kid. . . . I couldn't behave, couldn't con-centrate unless I liked the subject. I couldn't remember the rules. I couldn't not be aggressive . . . bullying in a verbal

way. No, that's the wrong word, but you know when you just kind of get all your brothers and sisters to do what you want by going mad . . .

As a kid I'd say to an older woman, "Why do you have so much wrinkly fat on your legs?" I couldn't work out what was wrong with that. You know, I'd ask people about their wigs . . .

As a teenager I didn't like myself. I couldn't behave and I really wanted to. I did everything I could. Mum would say, "So what are the rules?" and I'd tell her, and five minutes later I'd have broken all of them. Then she would ask me afterwards what the rules were and I'd say I forgot.[30]

A diagnosis of hyperactivity resulted in a prescription for Ritalin, which Bedingfield credited with changing his life forever:

Three weeks later, I discovered I could think before I spoke; that there was a box to put the thoughts into, and then speak them. After a year I stopped taking it, and I could still use the box. I'm told that the most difficult time for anyone with hyperactivity is the transition from child to adult. And that's when they really recommend you taking it. At 18 I remember saying for the first time, "I like myself."[31]

As his career blossomed, the singer found himself in the enviable position of fielding offers from none other than Madonna, one of the world's biggest pop stars, who happened to have her own label, and whom Bedingfield eventually turned down in favor of Island/Def Jam: "I was very tempted, but Def Jam—which I think is a much better label—came and asked," he said of Madonna's efforts to sign him.[32]

Once upon a time, not too long ago, it had been exceedingly unfashionable to declare oneself a serious Christian in the music world. Artists such as Cliff Richard had been mocked mercilessly for holding to such ideals, but more recently it had become, if not fashionable, at least more common. From U2's Bono to Lenny Kravitz, professing Christians now populated rock.

Many churchgoing Christians simply tended to tune such folks out, focusing instead on the CCM market as the place where true believers gathered. But although inward faith could never be fully judged from the outside, there were tests that some Christians used to try to decipher whether or not artists were serious about their faith. One such test was an artist's attitudes about sexuality. On this front, both Bedingfields would likely pass any such test with flying colors. Not only did they have traditional views, but they also came off to observers as though they were products of a bygone era.

"He's so sweet, so innocent. I feel I'm back in the '50s with Richie Cunningham in *Happy Days*," observed one reporter of Daniel. "He's 23, but at times I could be talking to a 10-year-old with everything ahead, at others I could be with a nostalgic old man."[33]

And when it came to matters of sex, the hyperactive Christian articulated a most unusual (for the world of rock, anyway) worldview. When asked if he was a virgin, he declined to answer that question, but went on to define himself as a one-woman man: "Let's not even go there, man . . . that's not, that's not . . . that's completely too personal, but I'm definitely into shagging one person for life . . . Everything within me as a man wants to be committed. Everything."[34]

In such matters Bedingfield had as a role model his own

parents, married for twenty-five years. The singer describes them as "hippies who never needed drugs because they always had God," wrote the *Guardian*, and he appeared to deeply admire them.

"I've never seen my dad follow a woman with his eyes in my life. I'd love to be like that, wouldn't you?" he asked.[35]

But life as a freshly minted pop star would mean such things would have to wait, as Bedingfield described a lifestyle that did not put him into extensive contact with members of the opposite sex: "I have no interaction with the female of the species whatsoever at the moment. I'm too hard at work," he complained. "The only women I see are the ones who work for the record company. And fans at gigs—you get groupies trying it on, of course, but I don't like that. I love my fans, but no groupies, please."[36]

Bedingfield had a similarly conservative attitude toward drugs, which were once a mainstay of the mainstream music scene.

"Well, I once had a cigar," he admitted. "And Valium in the dentist's chair. That was wicked, man! I got such a buzz off Valium. . . . I reckon there are enough chemicals swimming around my brain already."[37]

Bedingfield's sister Natasha, who followed her brother's footsteps to fame and fortune in the mid-2000s, generally shared his conservative outlook on life. Although the two had performed as a trio on the Christian music circuit along with another sibling, both caught the ears of record executives, who quickly scooped them up and arranged for worldwide distribution of their records. Like her brother, Natasha spoke out forcefully on moral issues, recalling a time when she was asked to wear a skimpy outfit for a photo shoot:

When I first signed I was very clear that I wanted to be taken seriously, and they have gone along with it.

I like mystery, I don't like to reveal everything. I remember I turned up at a shoot once and they expected me to wear a bikini while lying on a glass table. I said, "I'm not doing that!"

As a woman in this business you have to stand up for yourself, to learn to say no, and people respect you for that.[38]

Like her brother's, Bedingfield's conservative outlook extended to alcohol:

It is hard, you have such a high while performing and then you get off stage and it all starts to crash. You feel so low, you criticize your performance, and that is why people take drugs or drink.

But I cope by having friends around me, we keep each other up. I like drinking but if I got drunk every night I wouldn't be able to catch a plane at 5am the next morning. Three glasses is my limit. I try to keep my life stable.[39]

Although Natasha didn't speak often in interviews about her faith other than to confirm that she was indeed a Christian, her music was doing plenty of talking, and critics were taking notice. Joanna Brokaw, a critic writing for Beliefnet.com, noted, "I saw her perform the song 'Pocket Full of Sunshine' on the Ellen DeGeneres show and thought to myself, 'Those lyrics could be slightly veiled religiously themed,' not even knowing about her Christian past.

"Watching the video for the song, I was struck by how benign it was—she's dressed modestly and yet very hip, no writing around on the ground, very sunny and positive."[40]

In many ways, "Pocket Full of Sunshine" was the perfect expression of the post-Christian music artist's sentiment, for the song was written from the perspective of someone with a secret world that those around her couldn't and wouldn't understand. While some fans thought the song to be about a drug trip, Bedingfield's Christian fans knew better, correctly understanding it as a nod to the faith that she held close to her in the middle of an industry that disagreed with everything she stood for. The song reached number five on the U.S. pop charts in 2008 and rocketed Natasha to new heights in the pop music pantheon.

The stories of unlikely pop stars like Daniel and Natasha Bedingfield were more evidence of a wave of young Christians who were inserting themselves into an industry that had been birthed in rebellion and reared among sex, drugs, and wild excess. For his part, Daniel saw role models in artists who themselves had navigated through the world of rock with a semblance of either strong religious devotion or spirituality:

"Bob Dylan, Sting and Bono," replied Bedingfield when asked to name some of his musical heroes. "They didn't try to be pop stars or turn themselves into icons. They're a celebration of being human."[41]

THE TRUE BELIEBER

"I'm a Christian, I believe in God, I believe that Jesus died on a cross for my sins. I believe that I have a relationship and I'm able to talk to him and really, he's the reason I'm here, so I definitely have to remember that. As soon as I start forgetting, I've got to click back and be like, you know, this is why I'm here."[42]

These words came not from the mouth of a television evangelist but from America's number one teen idol, Justin Bieber, who was yet another example of just how profoundly the exodus of people of faith out of the tidy genre of contemporary Christian music had affected American popular culture. The teen idol was the son of a devout Christian woman named Pattie Mallette, who, upon realizing her son's talent, was initially determined to steer him into the gospel music world.

For many people of faith, singer Sam Cooke's move from gospel to R & B and his subsequent murder by a woman who wasn't his wife had been a warning that those who left gospel music behind couldn't handle the temptations of the flesh that the popular music business offered. In the wake of difficulties for artists such as Cooke, Johnny Cash, Elvis, and others, many people of faith thought the way to avoid such downfalls was to operate within the relatively safe confines of gospel and Christian music. Bieber's mother, Pattie, was no exception and initially sought to direct her son's musical aspirations in that direction. Mallette attended the Jubilee Christian Fellowship in Stratford, Ontario, and sang in the church's "praise band." Cathleen Falsani, author of *Belieber! Fame, Faith, and the Heart of Justin Bieber*, noted:

> I would call it a charismatic or a Pentecostal church. The iteration of that looks a little different in Canada than it does [in the United States]. It looks like any number of our evangelical nondenominational churches, but with a lot more arms raised. Very, very prayerful. . . .
>
> Being young . . . [the praise band members] used to hang out, and [Mallette] would bring Justin. That's when they noticed this kid's got unbelievable rhythm. And he's 2.[43]

"She had not envisioned a future in mainstream pop music for him," observed the *New York Times* of Mallette. "'I said: "God, I gave him to you. You could send me a Christian man, a Christian label!"'"[44]

But God apparently had other plans for Mallette, a single mother raising her son Justin in their hometown of Stratford, in Ontario, Canada, when videos that her son posted at YouTube came to the attention of a young music promoter named Scooter Braun.

"The video was strictly intended for his grandmother to see in another province," she remembered.[45]

But when Braun first contacted Mallette, she was wary of what working with him might mean for her son's life. The *Jewish Journal* noted:

> But Braun won her over during a three hour conversation in which he described his values, his emphasis on family and stories about how Braun himself was raised. . . .
>
> Braun also had a question for Mallette: "I had seen a video of Justin singing some Christian songs and I found stuff online about how Christian Pattie was, so I said, "Look[,] I just want to bring up something right off the bat: I'm a Jew, does that make you uncomfortable?" It did not, and Braun went on to use the Internet in a unique marketing strategy that made Bieber, in a relatively short 18 months, the most popular teenager in the world.[46]

Similarly, the *New York Times* noted:

> Until recently, Justin was a regular boy who played hockey and soccer in Stratford, Ontario (population 30,000). He taught himself piano, guitar and trumpet, took drum lessons

and yowled pop tunes while he brushed his teeth. He lived in low-income housing with Ms. Mallette, who prayed that God would use her son as a modern Prophet Samuel, a voice to his generation.

A youth pastor, perhaps? Or even a singer on a Christian label, she thought?

So when an Atlanta-based hip-hop manager named Scooter Braun called nearly two years ago, Ms. Mallette was confused. "I prayed, 'God, you don't want this Jewish kid to be Justin's man, do you?'" she recalled.[47]

Mallette first recognized her son's talent when he was a toddler. "He would bang on things in time to music. He studied the drums for one year and then the trumpet when he was in school," she told *Catholic Online*.[48] In an interview with *Plugged In*, she said:

I could tell he had rhythm, so I always put instruments around him. He was also really coordinated when it came to sports, so I always wanted to get him involved in whatever he wanted to get involved in. I think it is really important to pay attention to what your kids are good at and what they enjoy doing because I think God gives us the desires of our heart and gives us our gifts and our talents.[49]

Braun won Mallette's permission to fly her son to Atlanta, where they recorded demos. Before long, after something of a bidding war that was said to have included offers from the likes of Justin Timberlake, Braun had quickly formed a production company with R & B star Usher, and the duo signed Bieber to Island Records, which released his first full album, *My World 2.0*.

Several cuts off of the record became smash hits and propelled Bieber to popularity both in the United States and around the world. Justin Bieber suddenly found himself in the middle of the kind of spectacular success that had tripped up devout performers before him, but his story was likely to have a different ending because of the constant presence of Mallette, who had definite ideas about her son's journey and destination:

"My prayer is for Justin to be protected against the temptations of this industry," Mallette said. "This is a dark industry. I'd like to think that Justin and his music is a light in the darkness."[50]

A central part of Mallette's regimen was keeping her son surrounded by a coterie of trusted advisers, something she believed would go a long way not only in keeping her son humble, but in keeping him out of trouble with the various sins of the flesh that often accompanied life in the pop star fast lane:

> I think the most important thing is to surround him with good people, people that are not necessarily yes men, but [people who] will help to create a sense of normalcy around him and be pouring into him what's right. I also just keep reminding him that he is here for a reason, that as much as it might look like it, it's not all about him, and that God has given him his gifts and talents for a reason, and to seek Him for what that is. Justin's manager is Jewish, and he comes from a great family background with a great moral base. Together we both felt it important to keep him surrounded with people that were first of all morally based and second of all faith based, if and when possible. Scooter knows how much my faith means to me. Justin's got a Christian tutor, he's got a travel pastor that comes with us now and again. So, yeah, we're always trying to keep him surrounded.[51]

For decades, rock 'n' roll had represented youth rebelling against the strictures of the adult establishment. Sex, it had seemed, was a central component of the rebellion, with youth predictably rebelling against the sexual morés of their parents' generation. But amazingly, with stars like Justin Bieber and others, that calculus was thrown on its head, for not only would Bieber take relatively conservative stands on such issues, but he would do so amid catcalls from American cultural figures old enough to be his grandparents. The controversy kicked into high gear when Bieber gave an interview to *Rolling Stone* in which he articulated a conservative stance on both abortion and sex before marriage.

"I don't think you should have sex with anyone unless you love them," he told the magazine, adding "I think you should just wait for the person you're . . . in love with."[52]

On abortion, Bieber was also clear in his thinking, declaring: "I really don't believe in abortion. It's like killing a baby."[53]

When the *Rolling Stone* reporter predictably leaned in with a question about whether he'd consider it in the case of rape, Bieber responded, "Well, I think that's really sad, but everything happens for a reason. I don't know how that would be a reason. I guess I haven't been in that position, so I wouldn't be able to judge that."[54]

Reaction from the "establishment" was swift and full of outrage and came first from the set of the hit TV talk show *The View*:

"He won't be in that position because he cannot give birth," said the show's guest cohost, KaDee Strickland. "He doesn't have a choice like that. He's a 16-year-old boy, as I understand it. That's a very hot-button thing to be talking about."[55]

Another panelist, Joy Behar, described Bieber's insinuation that a product of rape shouldn't be terminated as "really insulting to people who have been raped or victims of incest. There is no 'reason' for that."[56]

For her part, the show's creator, Barbara Walters, dismissed the comments by noting "You can look at it as something that's coming out of a young mind that is still growing."[57]

Bieber had a lone supporter in the form of the show's only non-liberal, Elisabeth Hasselback, who noted, "I don't think we can discount somebody's opinion because they happen to be 16. We have brilliant minds who are young [and] young minds who have created things that are now changing the world. To discount his opinion simply because he's 16, I think, is a disservice."[58]

Still others were horrified at the prospect of millions of young impressionable girls hearing such conservative sexual messages from the premier pop star of his generation. The *Yale Daily News*'s Kathryn Olivarus noted:

> Thanks, Biebs, for your stunning insight on something you obviously know nothing about and will never have to personally deal with for biological reasons.
>
> As Roe v. Wade is whittled down to a twig, even statements from a 16-year-old coming out with a 3-D movie called "Never Say Never," are not benign. Bieber, maybe unknowingly, is adding sound bytes to a scary political conversation that could affect women across the United States—the war on Planned Parenthood. . . .
>
> Justin Bieber is obviously no expert on reproductive rights. But statistics show that a large percentage of his tween-girl audience, screaming as he sings "Baby" at Madison

Square Garden, will need the services of Planned Parenthood at some point in their lives, even if they don't know it yet.[59]

In the 1950s, when Elvis was gyrating to the beat as girls swooned and adults gnashed their teeth over lost innocence, who could have possibly imagined that one day a young pop star would be articulating traditionalist moral ideas to the consternation of adults who had fought long and hard for sexual liberation and were not about to let a teenage pop star drag them back into a traditionalist culture they had walked away from? And yet, in the person of artists like Justin Bieber, that was exactly what was happening, and it was a direct result of the impact of mothers like Patti Mallette and churches like Jubilee Christian Fellowship, which were turning the page on a philosophy of escapism and engaging the mainstream world with artists of faith who were feeling increasingly emboldened to speak out about their beliefs.

But Bieber would not be without his vices. In 2014 the singer found himself accused of all manner of bad behavior, including visiting a brothel, urinating in a bucket in a restaurant, and being arrested for DUI. At a celebrity roast in March 2015, Bieber apologized for his behavior and vowed to turn over a new leaf.

However Bieber's story ultimately plays out, it is likely that he, though an adult, will continue to be guided by his mother:

> I think that we just stay focused on whose opinion matters. And God's opinion is the most important one. If Justin really feels like he is making God proud, then I think that is the most important thing. Other than that, I think you just need to do your best. You can't please everyone all the time, and so you

just need to feel good about yourself—for yourself and for God, for your family and the people closest to you. . . . In the biblical story of King Herod, he was elevated to such a place of honor in his culture that people were calling him god and praising him. He didn't say, "Yes, I am a god." He didn't encourage it, but just the fact that he didn't correct them and say "No, no, no, I am not God, there is only one God" led God to strike him dead. So I say," 'Justin, there is only one God, and you are not to be worshipped. You will be a role model, but you need to give credit where credit is due."[60]

SONS OF JONAS

"Well done the Jonas Brothers. Each wear a ring to say they are not going to have sex; I'd take them more seriously if they wore it around their genitals."[61]

So mocked Katy Perry's then fiancé, British comedian Russell Brand, during his hosting duties at the 2008 Video Music Awards. The target of his barbs was another in the flood of young pop artists who held traditional Christian views that would have been unthinkable in decades past and would challenge the very foundations of the pop and rock music cultures. People of faith had left the confines of the Christian subculture and descended upon the cultural mainstream in such large numbers that their effect was felt immediately, even in the reaction to Brand's comments: moments later, another artist, the devout Christian performer and *American Idol* contestant Jordin Sparks, leaped to the brothers' defense, declaring, "I just have one thing to say about promise rings. It's not bad to wear a promise ring, because not everybody—guy or girl—wants to be a slut."[62]

It was a stunning rejoinder that left Brand, the supposed star of the show, to sheepishly declare, "I've gotta say sorry because I said those things about promise rings; that was bad of me. I didn't mean to take it lightly. . . .

"I love Jonas Brothers," he added. "I think it's really good. I don't want to piss off teenage fans. . . . Promise rings, I'm well up for it, well done everyone."[63]

Apology delivered, Brand couldn't resist one last dig however: "It's just, a bit of sex occasionally, never hurt anybody."[64]

For their part, the brothers consisting of Nick, Kevin, and Joe, responded to the comments with characteristic aplomb: "For us, it's cool to see that he recognizes we are gentlemen," said Nick.[65]

Sparks's defense of the brothers was quickly echoed by other pop culture figures, including those not typically associated with religion and morality.

"I don't pick on them," said Paris Hilton. "That's something cool for a kid to keep, so don't pick on them for that."[66]

Even blogger Perez Hilton, known for his often-crass Internet commentary, chimed in: "I think those Jonas Brothers are good kids, and we shouldn't be making fun of them for promoting good values."[67]

The Jonas Brothers, homeschooled Christian kids from New Jersey, guided away from the Christian subculture and into the cultural mainstream by their minister father, were having a significant impact on the primary culture, causing it to debate casual sex, the relative merits of purity rings, and decisions to save sex for marriage. The Jonas Brothers' saga was different. Managed by their savvy father, who was said to be something of a musical prodigy himself, they would carefully navigate the difficult terrain where religion and the entertainment business met.

Kevin Sr. and Denise Miller met at a Christian training center in Texas, known as the Christ for the Nations Institute. Denise quickly fell in love with her bold and brash future husband.

"He talked like he was going to conquer the world," she recalled, though he had grown up poor, reared by a single mother. "He was talking about working at a summer camp with these young kids, and all his passion and heart for them. And I thought, 'He could be a wonderful father someday.'"[68]

They were soon married, and Kevin took a job with a New Jersey church that allowed him not only to hone his craft but also to learn the music business, both in nearby New York and Nashville.

"Kevin worked very diligently to learn the music industry from a songwriting perspective," Denise told *Good Housekeeping*. "He'd fly to Nashville—just walking the street, walking into different places."[69]

Being in New Jersey also put the rest of the family in close proximity to New York City, and the Jonas children quickly found work in the entertainment business. The entire family learned the importance of staying together and focused on the things that mattered. Kevin Jonas, Sr. recalled:

> I was pastoring a church when the boys were young and first started performing. Two of them were on Broadway and all three were doing commercials in NYC. Being a part of their lives was very important to us, so we spent our free time juggling being there. Maintaining involvement in our children's lives was impossible if we weren't around.[70]

For Kevin Jonas, staying involved in his sons' professional careers came with great personal sacrifice:

Certain shows would allow the parents to come in at the curtain call. Being a pastor, there was no way for me to afford a Broadway show every night, so I spent most of my time nearby—preparing sermons and doing meetings or phone calls while they were in their show. But, I would get back in time to see them bow on a Broadway stage.[71]

In the early years, attention was focused on the youngest Jonas brother, Nick, who found success on Broadway performing in plays such as *A Christmas Carol*, *Annie Get Your Gun*, and *Beauty and the Beast*. In 2002, a Christmas song he wrote and recorded came to the attention of INO Records, which released it to Christian radio, where it quickly became a hit. At the time, INO, a Christian-run record label led by a savvy music business veteran named Jeff Mosely, had an arrangement with Columbia Records, and Nick was soon signed to a solo record deal. When executives at Sony heard the rest of the brothers' work, they decided they would have a better chance at success as a threesome, After toying with the name Sons of Jonas, they finally settled on the Jonas Brothers, opening on the road for artists such as Kelly Clarkson, Backstreet Boys, and Jump5. Although the brothers' debut album, *It's about Time*, was released by Sony on a limited basis, it failed to catch fire. After moving to Disney-owned Hollywood Records in 2007, the brothers' next album was released later that year. Success quickly followed in both music and film as they went on to record a third record and starred in the movie *Camp Rock*. Through it all, their father was at their side, guiding their careers and making sure they impacted the world of pop music more than it affected them.

"We have done everything we can," he said, "including making some choices related to their team, choices that hopefully were wise in regards to spiritual support for their lives. We bring people out on the road to encourage the entire team. Some of those people I have known for a long time, and some are new friends. Some are well known, and some are not. They come to encourage these guys who aren't always around on a Sunday to attend church."[72]

Kevin Jonas Sr. once had musical ambitions of his own, and although he had been able to realize some of them over the years, he had never achieved the kind of success that his sons would. Although negative stereotypes of stage parents were legion, Jonas and his wife appeared to have their kids' best interests at heart and seemed to work together in a way that shielded their children from many of the excesses of the rock lifestyle. Jonas saw his own life as preparation for what his children were supposed to accomplish in the world. "I've spent much of my life in music, songwriting, and recording my own albums in the Christian world," said Jonas Sr. "I feel like my life created a platform that we could launch from."[73]

The Jonas Brothers were just one of dozens of bands and artists who found themselves in a brave new world of cultural engagement that few had ever contemplated when religion and rock first began their uneasy dance in the late 1960s. The answer in the early days of the so-called Jesus movement was to disengage from the culture and escape to the safe confines of the Christian music world, where temptations of the flesh still existed, but to a far lesser degree. With the collapse of the genre of "Christian music" came the need for a new model that would support artists of faith as they fanned out into the mainstream culture, and this included pastors who could travel with artists, ensuring they held to their beliefs and stayed on the straight and narrow even as they faced adoring fans and the pressures of life in the rock 'n' roll fast lane. For Kevin Jonas Sr., it was all a part of what he had set out to accomplish with his kids, and he considered it an integral part of his work with the band. "We believe in hospitality and in caring for people," he said. "We've made sure that the support team members are the best at what they do, and are people of character. . . . The band members are the boys' best friends in the entire world."[74]

From the Lohans to the Spearses, the parents of young pop culture icons hadn't always exhibited the best behavior, and many had detoured through divorce court on the way to their children's superstardom. The Jonas family, on the other hand, seemed to dodge many of the pitfalls that had ensnared others, and the family patriarch characteristically credited his wife with with the family's success: "I credit her with anything good that they have. She came from a wonderful family that taught her well. She has a strong faith, a discerning spirit, and the ability to speak truth in a way that is encouraging. I can't imagine doing this without her and our youngest son. She's a nurturer, a comforter, and a truth teller. She is the best living example I know of a faith-filled person."[75]

As the parents of singers such as Katy Perry could attest, whether the grand experiment of Christians in rock would succeed was an open question, and it would be up to artists like the Jonas Brothers to prove whether it was a good idea or not. Nick Jonas seemed to understand his mission and, in an early interview, laid out the band's focus: "We're going more mainstream with our music. We play mainstream music in the mainstream world. We have a light to shine in the dark world. We aren't saying we're perfect. We also don't want to shove anything down anyone's throat. We just want to be who we are so people can see there's something different."[76]

Kevin Jr. added:

That's our opportunity to witness. People are always saying, "Why don't you cuss? Why don't you smoke? What makes you different?" We ran into a girl today who saw us play at a Jesse McCartney concert. She said, "I just knew you were Christians!" We don't have to say anything. We love the quote, "Preach the Gospel, use words if necessary." To us, that's what we're really about. . . .

We surround ourselves with Christians, especially on our tour bus because that bus is our home. We walk into a building for a show and maybe 5 percent of the people there are Christians, so you want to have a core group of believers so you can go back to the bus and say, "Praise God!"[77]

THE HUNTER

A central premise of the Christian pop subculture—which had been argued for years by some devout Christians—was that non-Christians simply would not tolerate lyrics that explicitly talked about faith in God, or more specifically, faith in Jesus Christ, that most divisive of historical figures. But as more and more Christian artists flooded the mainstream music industry, that position became an increasingly difficult one to defend. When Kirk Franklin and his troupe God's Property rocked the charts with "Stomp," it became a favorite around the country despite its calls for a "Holy Ghost party." But when the duo

Mary Mary offered even more explicit praise and worship to God with their breakout song "Shackles," and that song became a major hit among clubgoers around the country, some Christians wondered about the appropriateness of a song that praised God being played at nightclubs on the nation's dance floors. The song was an unambiguously worshipful one that included lines such as "I just want to praise you . . . I once was lost, but now I'm found, I've got my feet on solid ground, thank you, Lord."[78] As Christians continued their march into the center of pop culture, they were showing up in some very unexpected places indeed.

A British DJ named Andy Hunter took the phenomenon of Christian-themed club music to the next level, however, when his music became a favorite on dance floors around the country, and he too would face the difficult question of how far believers should go in mixing the sacred with the profane. While Franklin and Mary Mary's music clearly referenced their faith, Hunter's music was of the subgenre known as "worship music," that is, music that was relatively free of earthly concerns and focused almost exclusively on the vertical relationship between man and God, none of which kept him or his songs from climbing the mainstream charts. One track, "Amazing," was on the American dance charts, and his music was prominently featured in the television show *Alias* and in a number of feature films. Tribalmixes.com noted:

> Combining a passion for God with a strong creative vision, UK bands like Delirious sparked the modern worship movement in the mid 1990's. At roughly the same time, decks and dance music were being merged on both sides of the Atlantic

by DJ artists like Moby and Fat Boy. At some point along the way, the two movements became a little jumbled in the backwaters of Bristol, England, and "Trance and Electronica" dj, worship leader, Andy Hunter, found his calling. This might bear a little explaining.[79]

Hunter had come to faith a few years earlier. And he said he has attended church his whole life but didn't become a Christian until he was fourteen.

"A lot of those kids were into the DJ and dance music scene," Hunter recalled, "so I bought some turntables and some vinyl, and really started to get into it as a means of building relationships."[80]

Those experiences showed Hunter and his associates the importance of creating relevant music for a new generation that was not always interested in hymns:

> We began to ask ourselves "How do we teach these kids about worship?" . . . They had never set foot in a church before. The old hymns, as rich as they are, were too great a leap culturally. To sing those would have been like asking them to speak another language. But most of them were solidly into dance music so we decided to start experimenting and trying to lead worship with the turntables. Because I was already a DJ, I landed in that role as worship leader.[81]

Hunter got his vinyl start in 1997 when, along with partner Martin King, he released an album, *Cultural Shift*, and continued to add new musical elements to his repertoire. M-Audio noted: "To focus on solo projects, Hunter moved to Swansea in South Wales in 1999. Starting up a drum n bass night called

Absolute Drum n Bass (from 1999–2000), Hunter expanded his sonic palette to include progressive house, techno and trance."[82]

Exodus was Hunter's major-league debut, an album that would bring his music to hundreds of thousands of fans around the world and serve to further shake up the philosophical foundations of the very notion of the separation of music and faith. Hunter wrote the album over the course of a year and a half and before long had assembled enough material for his record, which had been inspired by the Old Testament:

> The theme of Exodus started when I was spending time in God's Word, reading through the book of Exodus . . . As a response to what I was reading, I just felt moved to go to the turntables and begin to worship God. I started spinning tracks and the idea came of using the themes of Exodus and coming up with a full set like a DJ in a club would use. Only this would be for the church, and it would be a whole worship journey.[83]

One of Hunter's songs, "Amazing," was inspired by a vision he had received from God:

> It was basically God holding out his hand and saying, "Andy, will you come and fly with me? Will you take me by my hand, and will you fly with me in the heavens and soar above the clouds and let me whisper things to you, let me show you things that must take place in the nations?" and things like that, and that sense of intimacy. So that whole track was birthed out of something that God was speaking to me about. And again, you know it's amazing what happened with that track. Within the mainstream club world, it was released as

a promo, and on the U.K. club charts, it got to number four, and now in Holland it's number five.[84]

One reviewer noted:

With titles like "Go," "Amazing," "Show," "Strange Dream," "Intercessional," and "Translucent," Andy Hunter's *Exodus* grew into a pulsing, driving set that mirrored the themes of the book of Exodus. The structure effectively leads concert-goers down a path that begins with a call to worship, moves through a time of praise, and then focuses on God's call and the direction of one's life and dreams in relation to it. The Exodus project closes with a prayer of intercession and resolve to pursue God and His plans.[85]

Though surprised on one level that music so vertically inclined could strike a chord with those who did not share its basic message, Hunter also admitted that he had hoped and believed by faith that his music would be widely accepted:

For me, it's amazing, you know I have to kind of pinch myself, but on the other hand, you know God's a faithful God, and it's not surprising in that sense, if you see what I mean. So I've got this sort of dual personality approach where I had faith for it to happen, so it's not a surprise, but then the human side of me is totally blown away and like, "Wow, I can't believe it's happening!" So it is amazing, just the goals that we set for it in terms of breaking down barriers—even within the Christian industry, that it would cross over and maybe make people think about what worship actually is—is it really about the genre? . . .

Part of me is quite surprised [at the success of *Exodus*], but part of me isn't, I mean, because God had been speaking to me a few years ago about the whole project and theme of Exodus. I guess I've always had a confidence in God and faith; you know, it's almost like God saying, "Just hold on Andy; wait until we see what happens," and the things we've been praying for, obviously, God's answering those prayers . . . the licensing thing on the album with it coming out on the final *Matrix* trailer and things like that.[86]

The movement of Christians into mainstream music was often populated by those believers who were wary of being perceived as being on a mission to spread their faith. Some were intent on emphasizing that their music was merely a form of self-expression, not intended for any utilitarian purposes or to be used in any way for evangelization. Andy Hunter, however, had no such inhibitions and managed to strike a balance between the two polarized camps: those who saw their music as strictly a method of proselytizing and those who just wanted to create art. Hunter carefully and methodically balanced the two.

"I think if we can bring that message of worship through our music, that's great," he said. "I don't want to champion the cause of dance music and see it really successful. I mean, I love dance music, but more importantly, it's the mission that God's given to me to challenge lifestyles and worship and say hey, it's not about music, it's about lifestyles."[87]

In the meantime, Hunter's music continued to break new ground in film, television, and in commercials, and he seemed particularly excited about an opportunity to have his music used by Microsoft:

I was in Australia at the time in January doing some festivals, and I got an email from Microsoft for a program called Insider Live (TechTV) about featuring the new Windows Media Player 9. They just wanted to talk to me as an artist about that project and how important high-end quality is, once you've finished and produced your music, and how it sounds once you've downloaded it and are listening to it through Media Player. So that was a great opportunity.[88]

In some ways, Hunter appeared to have dual careers running simultaneously. On the one hand his music was finding a path to the musical mainstream through various platforms and on the other, he was continuing to expand his presence in the UK's burgeoning church culture. As time went on, however, it appeared as if his two worlds were merging, and Hunter found himself bringing unsuspecting listeners to a heavenly place:

> Every time I do a show I want to take people into God's presence. I want them to worship, to experience God intimately, and to leave re-centreed and refocused on God's plan and priorities for their life. The fact that there are very few lyrics in my music makes it conducive to this sort of thing. You're not bound by a particular theme or lyric so there's room to think and ponder about what God might be showing you. Before I play an instrumental track, I'll use the microphone like a worship leader to read scripture and give some pointers, but once the music starts I step back and leave room for God to speak to their hearts.[89]

To critics in the Christian community who questioned the mixing of dance culture and worship music, Hunter had clearly and powerfully demonstrated that his music was able to reach across religious and denominational lines; however, he also hoped that it might also be able to cross generational lines and relished telling a story of an older woman he had encountered at one of his shows:

> I had a fifty-five year old woman come up to me after a show recently . . . who was completely unfamiliar with Trance music. But she told me that she had just had the best worship experience of her life. She felt like she had really experienced God's presence. For her, it was the most freeing and powerful time of worship she'd ever had. That means a lot to me because it confirms the fact that it's not about the genre. It's about worshipping God and focusing on God and finding new ways of doing that. God is a creative God, and the church is a creative body where there's room for a lot of expression.[90]

Andy Hunter had scaled walls that had, for years, kept religion out of dance music and God off the dance floor. Traditionalist voices would continue to voice skepticism about whether revelers were paying any attention to the lyrics of DJ Andy Hunter, or even remotely understanding his musical purpose, but Hunter would keep on, bringing God's story to a new generation in the music of their times at places they might have least expected to hear it:

> I was really excited about that plan . . . because I wanted to see how people respond in that setting to a song that's all about soaring to an intimate place with God. My goal is just to take Jesus to the furthest reaches of youth culture. That's

why I do club shows in the first place. I want to bring Jesus to people whether they're Christians or not. I know it seems an unlikely method, but God is using these turntables to turn hearts to himself.[91]

THIS YEAR'S "MODEL"

Hailing from the tiny town of Rocky Mount, North Carolina, Dana Glover was yet another example of a new generation of artists who, despite their Christian convictions, nonetheless forged paths into the mainstream music scene.

When the CCM world first developed in the early 1970s, it had, over time, produced a subculture that was largely walled off from the primary one. Thus, for a typical American who lived and breathed in the greater pop culture, the year 1981 meant listening to the music of artists such as Billy Joel, Hall & Oates, or Kool & the Gang. But for young Christian kids growing up in the Christian subculture, it meant listening to the Imperials, Sweet Comfort Band, Amy Grant, and David Meece.

Leading the pack were the Imperials, who had first gotten their start backing up Elvis and over the years had several incarnations as various members came and went. By the time young Dana Glover discovered them, they had made the jump from country to pop/rock after hooking up with producer Michael Omartian, who had worked the boards for artists such as Christopher Cross, Rod Stewart, and Donna Summer. Omartian and his wife, Stormie, became the Imperials' unofficial fifth and sixth members, producing and cowriting many of the songs beginning with the 1979 album *One More Song for You*, and on to *Priority*, *Let the Wind Blow*, and one of the group's final and finest efforts, *This Year's Model*. Although unknown to most artists today, the Imperials were a major inspiration to Glover. "To me, gospel music was the cool stuff," she revealed. "Though not well known in the mainstream, their songs spoke to me."[92]

But there were other gospel influences too. "I was always especially drawn to the people who sounded like they were singing from the heart," she said. "I'd listen to the Winans a lot, and that just pushed me; that sound moved me. I'd also hear the black choir from the neighboring church, and they would sing and just kill it, just kill it. I'd think, "That is the real deal.""[93]

Although many Christian kids were forbidden to listen to "secular" music, Glover also had her share of those influences as well, like George Michael and Whitney Houston.

"My world was small," she said. "I wasn't shut off—we had a TV—but there was a lot I didn't get. . . . I would look for that kind of music on the radio. That sound would grab me immediately. I remember when I first heard Mariah Carey. Her voice definitely affected me, partly because she also drew from the same influences and styles.[94]

Glover started playing the piano when she was just five. "I think I could have been much better if I'd studied," she admitted, "but playing by ear was much more fun."

"My mom was the biggest influence of all," she said. "She grew up playing the piano, so there was what I guess you could call 'ear' in our family. And we learned to harmonize from a really young age."[95]

In the eighth grade, the Glover family moved from Rocky Mount to Asheville, where her musical evolution continued.

"Asheville was a big, positive change for me because I got to become something different," she remembered. "That's when I began to form my own musical identity. Even though I was barely a teenager, I was sure music was my true love. I had a solo at a talent show and I played 'St. Elmo's Fire' on the sax. I knew I was connecting with the crowd, and that moment defined me."[96]

Before long, the family moved again and her parents divorced, making Asheville a memory, but looking back on that difficult period in her life, Glover found purpose in what otherwise seemed mere happenstance.

"It's almost like it served its purpose for me, just enough to mold me a little bit outside of where I'd grown up," she said. "And then as quickly as we got there, we left. . . . Life was not always easy. My mom is an amazing person and she has always taken on quite a bit. She was the rock for our family."[97]

Glover had begun to consider a career in modeling and, at sixteen, signed with the Ford modeling agency and made her way to New York.

"I'd started thinking about it because I'm tall," she explained. "It did become a priority for a while once I started doing it, but I still knew music was my road, even if I didn't know how I was going to get there. No matter what else I've done, I've always felt I was a musician first."[98]

Working in the big city as a model provided Glover with an opportunity to grow as a person, but if life in New York and Milan were causing Glover to rethink the Christian values she was brought up around, she also found other places and communities that served to reinforce them.

"I'd frequently take the train to hear the Brooklyn Tabernacle Choir and was always inspired. It was a constant reinforcement of my passion," she remembered.[99]

Early work as a fashion model soon gave way to singing

backup, and at eighteen Glover moved to Nashville. But for a singer with mainstream pop aspirations, Music City was not the place to go, and she quickly realized the town was not where she belonged:

"I didn't know if California was the place for me to pursue music, but I knew Nashville wasn't," she said. "I'd already known North Carolina wasn't, and I'd ruled out New York, so that really only left California. I didn't know how I was going to create my life there, but I was somehow certain it was the right place for me."[100]

Although she was intent on making a career for herself in the music world, Glover also had a "plan B" in mind, making sure that she kept the modeling option open in case things didn't work out as planned, but before long, Glover made a solid connection with attorney Alan Mintz, who arranged for several showcases for Dreamworks executives Jared Levine and Robbie Robertson:

> He really connected to my music. Alan felt something in it that spoke to the music he'd grown up on. . . . I played to just Jared and Alan and two other people in the room, and it was torture—I was so nervous. . . . I wasn't fully aware of who Robbie was. I knew his songs from The Band but didn't put it all together. It helped that I didn't realize it because I got to know him on my own without being intimidated. And because he's an artist himself, he knew how important it was for me to find my own voice.[101]

Robertson likely understood the perils of signing an artist who had gotten her start as a model—the chances of her developing a fan base among guys who merely liked the way she looked and falling flat with women who resented her genetics were high—but he saw in Glover the potential of transcending that dynamic. Dreamworks soon signed her to a recording contract. That in turn led to her ballad "It Is You I Have Loved All Along" being used in the end credits of the hit film *Shrek* and with Dreamworks' support, Glover hooked up with Matthew Wilder, the singer of the '80s hit "Break My Stride," who had morphed from one-hit-wonder recording artist to a top producer for artists such as No Doubt, Christina Aguilera, and others.

"The process with Matthew [of recording her debut album] and [the sound engineer]. . . was so special because they really embraced my style and became like family," she said.

"The first time I heard the Train song 'Drops of Jupiter' on the radio," she explained further, "I called Jared [her A&R man at Dreamworks]. I got his voicemail, so I put the phone to the radio, going, 'this is the sound—this is it: I want this kind of string sound.' And we got the same amazing guy, Paul Buckmaster, for my record!"[102]

Glover knew exactly what she wanted to title her album.

"I had a dream that *Testimony* was the name of the album," she remembered. "It was very vivid and very specific and when I woke up I thought, 'I don't really know what the finished product is going to sound like, but that's the title.'"[103]

One lesson numerous Christians who operated in the mainstream culture had learned was that it was best to be subtle, especially in the early going, about their beliefs in order to survive and make it past the gatekeepers and tastemakers. None, perhaps, had perfected this art as had Bono of U2, who teased reporters with feints and dodges, carefully hiding his rather orthodox Christian beliefs behind irony and self-deprecating humor. If that was the formula, then Glover had apparently not heard of it, for calling her debut album *Testimony*, a word most commonly associated with Christianity and the church, would do anything but camouflage her faith or her beliefs and Glover set about writing songs for her debut. As is often the case, a song birthed in turmoil, "Thinking Over," would quickly become one of her signature songs. Remembering the time she wrote the song as "the scariest time in my life," Glover observed:

> It was scary because it was so intense I didn't know if I was going to be doing the right thing so I didn't have peace of mind about either outcome and that scared me to death . . . I thought I'm just going to be unhappy the rest of my life, even though I knew that wasn't true. About the only outlet I had was to write out my fear. I don't know if people take it as fearful when they hear it, but when I wrote it, I was really fearful. . . .
>
> You can interpret the song a lot of different ways, but when it comes to the bridge, it pretty much spills it all. So it's in there, if people are listening.[104]

The first thing publicists look for in marketing their artists is a "hook," or something unique in their story that set them apart from the rest of the pack. In the case of Glover, in addition to her good looks, her story as a model who left behind her career to sing proved irresistible to her handlers. The other angle used to sell her to the music-buying public was her background in the church. Pitching her as a Southern belle who was raised singing in the church may have been just another "hook" for her publicists, but it was one that Glover seemed happy to embrace, in spite of the dangers that it could lead to her being stereotyped.

Hoping to put to rest certain stereotypes that music journalists tended to have about Southern Christianity, Glover insisted that her experiences in the church had been deep and rich. The old adage that you could take the girl out of the South but not the South out of the girl could just as easily have applied to Dana Glover's faith as well as her geography. In an industry in which believers were often racked with insecurity and self-doubt, Glover seemed remarkably content with who she was and what she believed, in terms of both her music and her faith.

LECRAE'S REACH

In September 2014 a hip-hop artist named Lecrae shocked the music industry by selling eighty-eight thousand copies of his album *Anomaly* in its first week of release, making it the number one record in the country. Although a new name to many in the mainstream music business, Lecrae had been making a name for himself in Christian circles as a devout Christian who not only released records on his own label, Reach Records, but marched to his own drumbeat in other ways. Like many other artists of his generation, Lecrae wasn't interested in promoting "Christian music" or in his case "Christian rap" but rather sought to integrate himself and his music into the mainstream. Yet unlike others who, it was argued by some, had sold their souls to get there, Lecrae's spiritual fervor had followed him all the way to the top of the charts. He said:

> My music is not Christian—Lecrae is, and you hear evidence of my faith in my music[105]. . . . My whole ambition was to create good music and I think a lot of people have this presupposition that when a Christian is creating art that

he's instantly trying to give answers, and so they already assume what's going to happen when they get it. But, I'm interested in telling great stories. I'm interested in asking great questions and not always trying to shove an answer down everyone's throat.[106]

For those who followed the evolution of Christian thought on the subject of faith and the arts, such comments from Lecrae would hark back to a number of Christian thinkers of whom he had clearly imbibed deeply. One of those influences was the philosopher Nancy Pearcey, a disciple of the late philosopher Francis Schaeffer, who had himself deeply influenced a previous generation of Christians in the arts. Pearcey's book *Total Truth* had been cited by numerous political leaders on the Right, and she also counted Lecrae among her admirers.

"Lecrae recommended that the team read Pearcey's book *Total Truth* to get a better understanding of what it means to bring a Christian worldview into all of life, including pop culture," noted Houston Baptist University in a Facebook post about the influence of one of its star professors.

"When my husband Rick and I met Lecrae, he related that when he first became a Christian, he thought he could write only about spiritual subjects," said Pearcey. "But when he learned about Christianity as a worldview, partly from reading my book *Total Truth*, he was 'liberated' to realize he could write about *any* subject from a Christian perspective."[107]

Responding to a Twitter follower who had written: "I read all the Nancy Pearcey books you recommend plus some Keller stuff and Steve Turner so it is pretty clear what you mean to me!" the artist responded: "Right on bro! Those books are the biz!"[108]

The reference to Steve Turner involved a book by a British biographer of the Beatles, Johnny Cash, U2, and others who had also written one of the most important books in the area of faith and popular culture, entitled *Imagine: A Vision for Christians in the Arts.*

The contents of *Imagine* had originally been developed as a speech given to the Renaissance Group, a group of artists who met regularly in Corona Del Mar, California, and occasionally in Nashville to wrestle with issues related to being men and women of faith in the arts in a mainstream context. The group regularly heard from artists and thinkers such as Charlton Heston, Os Guinness, Chuck Colson, and others and when Turner gave his talk, he so impressed the audience that one in attendance, recording artist Steve Taylor, took it upon himself to publish it as a booklet entitled *Being There: A Vision for Christians in the Arts.* The booklet was later expanded and published by Intervarsity Press as *Imagine.*

Although Lecrae was a part of the mass exodus of young Christians out of the ghetto of the Christian subculture and into the mainstream of American life, a cursory review of his lyrics and his public statements made it clear that there was a philosophical and religious underpinning to his life and work that set him apart from many of the others who had followed an otherwise similar path. And unlike some of those whose faith seemed to fade as their fame increased, Lecrae seemed to double down in his desire to spread his faith through his music:

"I believe that success is accomplishing what God created you to accomplish," he stated. "And hopefully I would have left not just inspiring people, but creating people who would carry the same mission with the same type of passion and integrity."[109]

In *Total Truth* Pearcey had made the case for seeing Christianity as more than just a religious obligation to be fulfilled on Sunday mornings or in Bible studies, but rather, a worldview that was to be implemented in every area of a believer's life. The formulation was based on the idea that while many Americans claimed a Christian faith, a much smaller subset actually had a "worldview" that could be called Christian. For instance while public opinion polls regularly identified that upwards of 84 percent of Americans believed in God, surveys by the Barna Group, a polling firm specializing in analyzing religious trends, sometimes pegged the number of Americans who had a "Biblical worldview" at 4 percent. In *Total Truth* Pearcey had carried on the work of her mentors Schaeffer and Chuck Colson in pushing the notion of the importance of that "worldview," and in Lecrae she seemed to have found a disciple of her own.

"We've limited Christianity to salvation and sanctification," he said. "Christianity is the truth about everything. If you say you have a Christian worldview, that means you see the world through that lens—not just how people get saved and what to stay away from."[110]

While plenty of rock artists and rappers had been known to spout God-talk—Kanye West's "Jesus Walks," for example—few imbibed deeply of the kind of philosophy that Pearcey and others were known for and likely wouldn't even have been familiar with the term itself.

Author David Noebel, who had written several books on the subject, explained: "A worldview is the framework from which we view reality and make sense of life and the world. It's any ideology, philosophy, theology, movement or religion that provides an overarching approach to understanding God, the world and man's relations to God and the world."[111]

Author Del Tackett, a writer affiliated with Focus on the Family, added:

> Someone with a biblical worldview believes his primary reason for existence is to love and serve God. Whether conscious or subconscious, every person has some type of worldview. A personal worldview is a combination of all you believe to be true, and what you believe becomes the driving force behind every emotion, decision and action. Therefore, it affects your response to every area of life: from philosophy to science, theology and anthropology to economics, law, politics, art and social order—everything. For example, let's suppose you have bought the idea that beauty is in the eye of the beholder (secular relative truth) as opposed to beauty as defined by God's purity and creativity (absolute truth). Then any art piece, no matter how vulgar or abstract, would be considered "art," a creation of beauty.[112]

Worldview in tow, Lecrae was increasing in prominence in the culture, and his fame was providing him a large pulpit from which to expound his views. Yet, the artist who had become one of the Christian faith's most prominent warriors himself came from a less-than-religious background.

Born and raised in Houston, the future hip-hop star was shuttled between Dallas, Houston, and San Diego. After a rough childhood, under the influence of his devout Christian grandmother, he began attending church. Lecrae later remembered:

> I think it was just accumulation. I think for me it was seeing like, "OK, I keep running into this dead end." Just having a

grandmother who was rooted in the church it was like, "OK, maybe this is the direction I need to turn." I really didn't have a faith or know what that looked like and didn't explore it.

A girl invited me to come out to a Bible study and I said, "Why not? I don't have anything to lose." I went and, to my surprise, I saw people that loved God, but they were not square or rigid. They were just people like me. They read the same books and listened to the same music. Their character was just different. They were loving and that's really what drew me in. After that, it was just hearing them talk about their faith, hearing them talk about Jesus specifically. That was it for me. . . .

[It was] right after high school. Not even a year after high school. So I was 19 and I had done everything from 16 to 19. I had done more than the average adult. And even after me saying, "Ok God I really want to live for you," it wasn't overnight. It was a process. And so I spent a lot of time making bad decisions.[113]

Before long he found himself a part of the Christian-influenced hip-hop group known as the Cross Movement, a media/ministry conglomerate that became the breeding ground for young Christian rappers and hip-hop artists. Lecrae noticed a difference in the members of the group, noting that he saw "guys who had been shot from being in gangs, girls who were extremely promiscuous in the past, I see rappers, dancers and singers; I see people who came from the same background I came from, and they still embodied who they were culturally, but they were all in love with Jesus and I had never seen that before."[114]

His affiliation with the Cross Movement led to the release

of his first record, but not to signing with any major labels most of whom had been notoriously clumsy in helping to cultivate hip-hop artists who were Christians and who were mostly left to fend for themselves without the support of Christian labels. That would leave Lecrae on his own in terms of marketing and distributing his music, a fact that would make his eventual success even more noteworthy.

Though the largely white-dominated Christian music establishment may have been unable to get its arms around hip-hop, failing to nurture, sign, and market large numbers of artists as their mainstream counterparts had, it was a group of high-profile white Christian ministers who came alongside Lecrae and other hip-hop artists who were Christians, and among these was theologian, author, and pastor John Piper.

In an online article in which he cited a dozen or so examples of such artist/pastor interaction, blogger Tim Challies noted:

> I have come across an interesting and unexpected influence on these artists: none other than John Piper. Sometimes he is the one who has inspired the song and, even more often, he actually appears within the song. . . .
>
> Let's get started with what is probably the most notable and most popular of these Piper references. "Don't Waste Your Life" by Lecrae may not actually feature Piper's voice, but it is named after one of his most popular books.[115]

Pop stars and their preachers were nothing new in American popular culture, of course, for long before Lecrae and John Piper, Elvis had had Rex Humbard, Johnny Cash had Billy Graham, and shockingly, John Lennon had corresponded with Oral Roberts about the nature of salvation and even called in for prayer on Pat

Robertson's ministry hotline. But the duo of an African-American rapper and a straight-laced white minister from Minnesota was the unlikeliest of all such pairings. In a most unusual video posted at YouTube, the minister updated his audience on a lunch he had just shared with Lecrae before urging the artist to discuss his hopes for what he wanted to accomplish with his music. Lecrae replied without missing a beat:

> First and foremost I see myself as an indigenous minister in an urban culture. And my music, my artistry, is really generating a platform for me to be able to articulate the revealed will of God and His manifold wisdom in that He desires to accomplish his work in and through the church, and so one of my strong burdens and passions is to see churches planted and created specifically in the urban context and urban environments that articulate solid biblical truths and are Christ-centered and God-centered. And so for me, I carry a unique burden with using my music, which, for the urban context is many times a philosophical voice. It allows me to be a thought leader in the urban context. And so if I want to maximize what I'm doing, it's going to be encouraging churches to be established; it's going to be encouraging biblical communities where people can grow and be discipled and be raised up to accomplish the work of the Lord. And so that's really where my passion lies; that's really why I do what I do; that's why I take the engagements, to be able [to] garner a platform to have influence to influence people to not only plant these churches but become part of these churches.[116]

People of faith were now firmly in the middle of American pop culture. The once-mighty Christian music industry had now been reduced to a ghost of what it once was and consisted primarily of worship music and a thriving DVD movie distribution business. Dozens, perhaps hundreds of Christian-oriented artists were now working in the mainstream music business, yet not a few had lost their way spiritually, critics would argue. Rumors of sexual escapades followed Justin Bieber on his tours around the world, while Miley Cyrus grinded her way across concert stages and Katy Perry delivered a Grammy performance that caused E! News to tweet: "Um, did we just witness actual witchcraft during Katy Perry's #Grammys performance?"[117]

But Lecrae was a different kind of artist, one who seemed intent on keeping his wits about him and faithfully delivering the spiritual message that he felt he had been entrusted with. Although drawing inspiration from a number of Christian philosophers and preachers, he was clearly his own man and was perhaps the best example of what many of his forefathers had dreamed was possible, that a generation would emerge who were strong enough to be in the world and not be unduly influenced in negative ways by it. And he was clearly in it for the long haul, hoping to influence the next generation as well, to be, in biblical parlance, fully in the world, but not of it.

"When I'm dead and gone I would hope that other people would come and say, I'm just carrying on the mantle that was set in place by someone like Lecrae."[118]

TAKING THE HILL

When thousands of mourners gathered to honor the life of Michael Jackson, it was a young woman named Judith Hill who stole the show with a soulful rendition of the recently deceased artist's song "Heal the World." It was a bittersweet moment for

Jackson's fans, and for Hill herself, for the then twenty-five-year-old singer had been practicing long hours preparing for what was to have been Jackson's return to the concert stage. The tour never happened when the fifty-year-old pop star passed away and instead, Hill's budding collaboration with Jackson was relegated to scenes from their rehearsals featured in the full-length documentary *Michael Jackson's This Is It*. It would not be the *last* of Hill's high-profile appearances at a pop star's funeral, however. Several years later, when Prince passed away, it was once again Hill who would appear among the mourners, this time for another musical genius who had also taken her under his wing, in this case, producing her debut album.

But long before her collaborations with Prince and Jackson, Hill got her start as a child prodigy listening to her parents perform. Her father, known professionally as Pee Wee Hill, and her mother, Michiko, met while playing in the Chester Thompson Band in the 1970s and collaborated with artists such as Rufus and Sly Stone. The two gave Hill a musical foundation and a love for music at an early age.

"She dictated to me what chords to play on the piano, she hummed it," recalled her mother of Hill's first recording at age four.[119]

Growing up in the Los Angeles area, Hill proceeded to Biola University, which had also given birth to the band Cold War Kids. She graduated in 2005 with a degree in music composition and soon found her place in the music world when she toured Europe with a French singer named Michel Polnareff. In 2013 Hill made waves on the popular TV show *The Voice* when she advanced to the top eight before being eliminated. But it was her collaboration with Jackson that was her biggest career break. Jackson had invited Hill to be one of his singers on the "This Is

It" tour, and the two had rehearsed together extensively. When Jackson suddenly and unexpectedly died from an overdose of a drug he was using for sleep disorders, Hill's life suddenly became very public after both her performance at his funeral and the subsequent release of the rehearsal footage as a film became a national sensation.

"That was a very tragic and crazy time," she recalled. "We were thrown into the limelight in a weird way. All of a sudden, there was a film that came out about us rehearsing. I look back at that chapter and it's so bittersweet. Because it's like, man, Michael Jackson, the King of Pop, the beautiful last few hours that we spent with him and what he shared with us. It was a circus after he died, it really was. We were caught in the whirlwind. I was really young and green at the time, and it was kind of scary."[120]

In 2015 Hill began her collaboration with Prince on her debut album, *Back in Time*. Hill had casually mentioned Prince as a dream collaborator in an interview, and when the pop icon heard about it, he contacted her.

"I got a personal call from him, which was crazy! That was the beginning of the adventure," Hill remembered.[121]

"I've been a big fan of his since I was really young," she added. "My dad was the first to introduce me to Prince's music. In our household, we celebrate all funksters. But, Prince is special because of his unique sound and fresh take on funk music."[122]

Hill was quickly invited to visit him at Paisley Park, the singer's recording complex and home in Minnesota, and before long the two were collaborating on what would become Hill's record.

"The first time I went over there, there was no agenda or talk of a record; just jamming on stuff," Hill recalled. "A Thursday in, he asked me to play some of my songs and he would come up with these cool arrangements for these songs I had already written."[123]

In another recollection about that meeting, she added, "Both of us were so excited about how great the arrangements sounded! So we decided to record it. It took about three weeks to actually complete all the work. It was a very quick and fun process."[124]

Acknowledged widely as a musical genius, Prince didn't disappoint in his interactions with Hill and emphasized to his new protégé the importance of creativity in the songwriting and production process.

"One of the biggest things I was impressed by was his imagination," she said. "He has such amazing ideas and made them come to life on stage and musically . . . It really did inspire me."[125]

Hill was particularly astonished by the legendary pop singer's work ethic and his instinctive musical abilities:

"I'm surprised and impressed by how prolific he is," she told me. "He can write lyrics in five minutes. Ideas just flow out of him constantly. Songs are written every day and records are being made all the time. He's a hit factory.[126]

In a story from *Billboard*, Hill said of Prince, "He challenges me to be my best. I like that challenge, because with him, it's do-or-die on that stage. I think that I've really been challenged to step it up, and I'm happy for that extra push."

Hill was that most unusual musician who had been afforded the gift of working closely and intimately with two of the greatest pop performers of the twentieth century. Few had had such opportunities, and Hill compared the experiences of working with the two: "There's a lot of great similarities in terms of their epicness and how they approach things," she said of Prince and Jackson. "The attention to detail, being very specific about everything they want. They see the big picture and they're very involved. I just learned as an artist that it's so important to be hands-on."[127]

Sandwiched between the funerals of Prince and Michael Jackson was another funeral at which Hill also sang. Although not as well-known as the two pop legends, gospel singer Andraé Crouch had also deeply influenced Hill, and the singer recalled Crouch fondly: "Andrae Crouch was someone I always admired and would see from time to time as my parents worked with him," she recalled. "He was one of the best songwriters of our time. His music is so simple yet cutting to the heart. I was deeply moved to see all my friends and legendary gospel singers celebrate his legacy at the service. It's amazing to hear all the songs we know and realize, 'Andrae wrote that too!'"[128]

In October 2015 her collaboration with Prince, *Back in Time*, was released to critical acclaim, and Hill was eager to describe the songs that populated the album.

"With songs like 'Cry, Cry, Cry,' 'Angel in the Dark,' and 'Beautiful Life,' there is a reoccurring theme about persevering through hard times," she said. "I also celebrate my family and community with 'My People' 'Turn Up' and 'Jammin' in the Basement.' Lastly, I speak heavily about the race issues and police brutality we have been facing in America recently. 'As Trains Go By' is a powerful statement about such things."[129]

For Hill, the product of two talented musicians who had been playing music all her life, her debut album came at a momentous time in her life.

"This has just been a long time coming. This is a day I've dreamed for since I was 10 years old, so it's really an exciting time," she said.[130]

Hill was a unique fusion of several cultural influences,

including her African-American and Japanese heritage, her parents' musical talents, and a rigorous Christian education. All of these inspirations had together formed a most interesting artist.

"I love listening to traditional Japanese music and instruments," she revealed. "I've always been fascinated and deeply connected to ancient and exotic musical traditions. Every time I go to Japan, I find a deep sense of serenity and comfort as if it is a distant homeland I've always known. And, of course, I grew up around gospel and soul music. I would say I identify with my African American side a little stronger since I was born in America and have always seen my dad's family a little more."[131]

While some artists shied away from public pronouncements of their faith for fear of being labeled and marginalized, Hill was straightforward in interviews about her beliefs.

"Being a Christian should influence every aspect of our lives," she said. "We take our faith wherever we go, whether we are working at a store or driving. For me, music is probably the main thing I do in life and my faith in Christ always comes up in lyrics and my overall worldview.

"When I write messages of hope, love, relationships, struggles, pain, there is an underlining message of hope in Christ and I think that is what drives the hope in my life and I take that wherever I go."[132]

Hill was equally candid about how her own struggles informed both her music and her faith.

"I've always been sort of a melancholy person, battled with different depressions and things but I always found restraint in looking up to God and knowing He will get me through," she said. "I want my music to inspire people and get them through those difficult times.'

As Judith Hill continued to spread her wings and bring her music and her faith to the world, those closest to her, her parents, who had guided her in both her musical and faith journeys, were proud of the path she had gone down.

"Outside the stage, she might be a little shy, quiet and sometimes nervous," her mother once admitted. "But when she gets on stage," her father chimed in, "she's at home. She's in her element. That's the gift that comes from the Lord."[133]

UNBREAKABLE

"Buy good music," wrote rapper LeCrae on an Instagram posting, "Stirs the mind body and soul. Plus they are stand up people."[134]

The hip-hop star whose album had recently landed atop the charts was talking about a fellow artist and devout Christian named Tori Kelly, whose album "Unbreakable Smile" had, like LeCrae's, reached the top of the charts. Although she had unsuccessfully auditioned for *American Idol* in her teens, Kelly had signed with Justin Bieber's manager, Scooter Braun. Over time she had developed a soulful sound and vocal style that was inspired by Crystal Lewis, who had debuted in Christian music circles in the 1980s but had rarely been heard outside of that world.

Christian music may have been sequestered in its own universe for most of the '70s, '80s, and '90s, but that didn't mean it wasn't influencing the next generation of artists and Kelly was among these. Taking to Twitter, Kelly had once written of her favorite CCM artists of another era: "Stacie Orrico, Crystal Lewis, Rachael Lampa, Out of Eden . . . they all inspired me at such a young age! Their music makes me reminisce."[135]

In a brave new social media universe in which even the most

mundane of conversations now took place in public, Lewis responded to Kelly on her own social media account: "And now you inspired me."

When the two later met up at a concert, Kelly once again took to Instagram: "Crystal Lewis came to see me at MSG. Dead. I love you so much!!!"

Later, speaking to a music reporter who had likely never heard of Lewis, Kelly tried to explain: "There's one singer, Crystal Lewis, who on a technical level, her voice is just so spot on. When I was three years old I was trying to mimic her."[136]

"Laura Kelly (Tori's Mom) and I actually met as children, believe it or not," recalled her muse, Lewis. "My father was a Nazarene pastor and her family attended our church for a time. Over the course of the last three or four years, as we've reconnected, it's been fun to realize that we actually knew each other way back when. Tori and I became friends through social media as well as through mutual friends. It's been such a beautiful honor to have her acknowledge me as an influence vocally. She's incredibly talented and it means the world to me that she includes me as someone she's learned and gleaned from."[137]

Kelly got her start in 2004 when she won the America's Most Talented competition, and although her nascent career stalled when she was eliminated early in the process in season nine, much as Justin Bieber had done, she built a strong following online.

"Kelly wisely turned to YouTube as a way of reaching the masses and quickly created a community of online fans," noted Yahoo! News. "When her cover of Frank Ocean's 'Thinkin Bout You' went viral in 2012, (it has over 23 million views), she was back on the music industry's radar. 'I really credit everything to the fans because they're the ones who discovered me on YouTube and pushed everything out there,' says the artist. . . .

"'I never had a plan B, even in kindergarten when they would ask what you want to be when you grow up — everyone would giggle but I would always say singer,' she says. 'It felt like it was just in my veins. I had to do it.'" [138]

"I was signed when I was 12 years old, which is where a lot of these lyrics come from, because I learned a lot," she told another interviewer. "As a kid, I didn't know it would be so political. It was such a blessing in disguise that nothing happened then because I got to really grow up." [139]

Though Kelly had signed to the mainstream powerhouse Interscope, what was to be the prepubescent singer's debut album never materialized and she was released from her recording contract. The singer hinted at the reasons behind the parting:

> The things they were expecting me to do and wear and stuff like that—that's where I pulled inspiration from for *Unbreakable Smile*. That's when I took the independent route. I'm thankful that happened because now I can look at the industry without bitterness, but say: "this is how we can work together . . . I'm not going to let you guys walk all over me but at the same time, I'm not going to be stubborn and think that I know everything either." [140]

"I went to the [label] office and there were music videos playing with female singers wearing hardly any clothes and, as a 13-year-old, I was confused because it didn't feel right. I want to send a message to people that they don't have to do that," Kelly asserted. [141]

Although Kelly rarely got into details of what exactly had been asked of her that made her uncomfortable, she had hinted strongly at the issues when she noted in one of her songs, "Maybe I can sell out shows without taking off my clothes."[142]

"I would like to be somebody young people, young girls, can look up to," she once said. "I just want to give them a new way of looking at things because I remember how young I was when I would watch these shows. I would be so sad if a six-year-old was watching TV and was like 'Oh, I must have to be like that to be successful.' And that's what these kids are thinking. We're the ones, whether we admit it or not, that have a really big impact on these kids. Not that I've ever necessarily aimed for that, but I guess recently I feel more of a responsibility."

"I'm not going to speak badly on anyone else," she said, when questioned about her contemporaries' example, "but I'm just going off what other people are saying that they've seen. I'm really just being myself. I'm not trying to do it as a gimmick or anything like that, I just want people to know you're allowed to be modest and it will work."[143]

A few years later, Kelly got another major break when she appeared on *American Idol* before Simon Cowell and three other judges. While the other three reacted positively to Kelly, Simon was unimpressed, labeling her "almost annoying."[144] While many an artist might have been severely discouraged by such an encounter with a heavyweight of the music business, Kelly remained upbeat.

"Some people think it was my only setback, but no," she recalled. "I was only sixteen, so I think for me, I was more just curious how I would do on the show because I had been a fan. That was the first time I'd really been in front of cameras. And it was a lot of cameras—they want to catch any moment they can. Looking back on that, it's the same thing as before: it's good that I didn't make it because right after that, I started posting YouTube videos. I was just over it and thought 'I'm going to do this myself.'"[145]

Newly emboldened by the positive reaction she received from the other judges, Kelly continued to chart an independent course, utilizing social media to build a strong fan base on YouTube and beyond. She also had a canny strategy in mind to maximize her online persona, one that involved posting covers of well-known pop songs followed by her originals:

> I remember consciously thinking, "Okay, I'm gonna post this cover right now, and then immediately after, I'm gonna give people this original that I just wrote." I always wanted to keep that balance just to make sure that people knew that I was a songwriter too. Even if the songs that I wrote weren't getting as popular, I always wanted to put that out there, just for even my own sake. But it was cool to see that at first, the covers were really big, and then to see people latch onto my originals. Eventually, those became even bigger [than] the covers sometimes. For me, that was the most fulfilling thing.[146]

That hard work paid off when Kelly came to the attention of manager Scooter Braun, who had guided a similarly Internet-based career of one Justin Bieber to superstardom. Significantly, Braun, unlike some music executives of the past, didn't try to squelch either Kelly or Bieber's spirituality, freely allowing their Christian sentiments to permeate their music. In Kelly's case, both faith and her attitude toward the music industry and her critics permeated her music as she prepared songs for her debut record.

"'Unbreakable Smile' was based off one of the songs I wrote for the album—it was actually the first song I wrote for the album, without realizing it yet," she remembered of a song that could easily be interpreted as a salvo at Cowell and other detractors. "I think I wanted to name the album that, because it seemed like that was just the theme of that chapter in my life, and just the theme of all the songs put together. When I was writing that song in particular, I was just holding in so many feelings for a while; I wasn't saying them. I think when I finally did write that song, it just unlocked a whole other layer of me as an artist, and me as a songwriter. I just felt so much more confident about my music. So I just wanted that to be the overall message: that I don't have a breakable smile. And I wanted people to be able to take away something from that."[147]

Christians like Kelly who were in the mainstream often released songs filled with double entendres that could be interpreted as being about either God or a significant other. One of Kelly's signature songs, "Hollow," may have sounded like one of those to some of her fans, but Kelly was clear in the song's deeper meaning:

> "Hollow" . . . came to me in a crazy way because I was just right in the thick of . . . promoting the album and we wanted to put out another single and I heard the song. It wasn't fully finished—I went to the studio the night that I heard it and finished the song. And I find out later that my friend had actually written it and I had no idea that I'm the one singing his song that he's been like trying to get out there. I think just the message behind it was for both of us really was it's directly connected to our faith and just how a lot of times we feel

really hollow inside and every time I try to fill that space with something, it's like Jesus for me is just the only thing that has ever filled that. So it's been really cool just to hear the feedback that the song is getting and I'm happy people like it.[148]

Of course, Tori Kelly wasn't the first artist to attempt to inject her faith into her music, nor would she be the last, but as the pop star continued to gain traction, the music press began to take notice of her faith, and increasingly, profiles of the singer focused on that aspect of her music.

"The message is very much rooted in her faith," noted the *Guardian*'s Caroline Sullivan in a profile piece on the singer. "Kelly refuses to call herself religious, terming it 'a relationship with God.' Her Twitter biography refers to Psalm 91:4, which she quotes to me, looking it up on her phone to check the wording: 'He will cover you with his feathers and under his wings you will find refuge.'"[149]

Refuting suggestions that she would seek to impose that faith on her fans, Kelly bristled at the insinuation but made it clear that she wouldn't back down from letting her faith continue to inform her music. "It's something I wouldn't want to force onto people but I'm also not going to hide it or be ashamed of it or anything like that," she said. "I'm kind of just, you know, living life and that's a part of my life so it naturally kind of bleeds into my music."[150]

A generation ago, other artists who also refused to keep their faith from "bleeding" into their music were effectively kept out of the musical mainstream by various forces both within and without their communities. Kelly's mentor, Crystal Lewis, a powerful vocalist and performer who reached the heights of the Christian music industry, was one of these who looked on with pride at what the next generation of artists of faith had accomplished.

"I'm thrilled that Tori was so ahead of the curve and was able to pretty much bypass the CCM market completely," she said. "It can be a narrow and limited space to be confined to. There is a place, dare I say *need,* in the mainstream market for more artists that are authentic *and* extraordinarily talented *and* positive. Tori ticks all those boxes. It's often difficult for artists to change lanes and cross over the lines of various genres, yet she seems to be navigating her way around those obstacles with ease. And it makes me immensely proud and happy!"[151]

Tori Kelly was part of a new generation of artists who were not content with staying in the world of religious rock yet not comfortable with being in the mainstream music business if she wouldn't be allowed to sing about her faith in God. For naysayers who used artists such as Katy Perry to say that it was impossible for an artist with Christian convictions to stand strong for them in the pop music world, Kelly was one example that it was indeed possible. As her star power increased in the pop music scene, Kelly looked back over her already long career and saw the guiding hand of Providence.

"It feels like everything is playing out the way it was always supposed to," she said. "Ten years or more sounds like a really long time but being in it, it feels like I literally had to be knocked down a couple of times to become the artist that I am right now."[152]

STRESSED OUT

Once upon a time, young Christians with musical talent were ushered into the offices of Christian music labels like Word, Sparrow, and Benson and later, to hipper ones, like Frontline.

There, with few exceptions, their music would be targeted, laser-like, at fellow Christians, and awareness of said artists by those who didn't shop at Christian retail, listen to Christian radio, or follow the Christian touring circuit would be negligible.

If they'd been born a decade or two earlier, Twenty One Pilots, an Ohio-based band consisting of two friends, Tyler Joseph and Josh Dun would likely have ended up on one of those labels and never come to the attention of mainstream music fans. Signed to the mainstream indie label Fueled by Ramen, the two childhood friends took a completely different path and with their breakout hit, "Stressed Out," were on their way to major-league success and many observers were taking note.

"Twenty One Pilots are one of the hardest-to-categorize hit acts in years, mixing angsty lyrics, Macklemore-style rhymes, Ben Folds–like piano pop, 311-ish reggae beats, hard-rock energy and the occasional ukulele ballad," observed *Rolling Stone* in a profile on the band. "Onstage, Joseph plays bass, piano and uke when he's not stalking around in smeared makeup and a bondage mask. Dun, a chilled-out former skater with an easy grin and gauges in his ears, helps them sound like a band, triggering prerecorded backing tracks as he plays. It's a seemingly odd combination that makes total sense to their teen fan base."[153]

The venerable bible of the rock and pop music industry also noted that Twenty One Pilots was composed of two suburban Christian kids whose angst about life didn't extend to matters of faith, for in that area at least, they seemed relatively at peace with the notion that they would be in a mainstream music world that was often at odds with their beliefs. The band's unusual name didn't have any religious meaning behind it, but instead is a reference to the Authur Miller play *All My Sons*.

It's about a guy who's creating and developing parts for airplanes in war time, when it comes to his attention that some of these parts were faulty. He was faced with a decision: Do I send the parts out and risk people getting hurt and potentially dying, or do I recall the parts and most likely hang my name and probably end this business? That was a huge decision, and ultimately he decides to send the parts out, and as a result 21 pilots die. There ends up being no correlation between the deaths and the parts, but one of the pilots killed happens to be one of his sons, and his daughter blames him for his death the rest of the play. At the end, he kills himself.

The way we apply that to our band is that all of us are constantly faced with decisions. It could be a moral decision or just a small decision, like, should we watch the opener play? Maybe a bigger decision like, should we sign this publishing deal? Or which label should we sign with? It's been surprising how many times we've used that reference throughout the last couple years to help us base our decisions that we've made.[154]

Both Joseph and Dun were reared in conservative Christian households, and Joseph's father was a principal at a Christian school. Part of that upbringing meant that media was heavily scrutinized and often consisted of Christian alternatives to what their secular friends were listening to and watching:

"I'd hide albums like Green Day's *Dookie* under my bed," remembered Dun. "Sometimes [my parents would] find them and get real mad. They'd find a Christian alternative, like Relient K, and make me listen to that."[155]

Dun rebelled against the strict upbringing and remembered

that it almost got him kicked out of the house.

"I just had this aggression. They almost sent me to a military school," he recalled. "They didn't know what to do with me, and I was always in detention. I never got into drugs or alcohol, but I would yell at my parents and just treat them terribly. Everything was an argument. Looking back, they were trying their best."[156]

While declarations of faith by bands like Cold War Kids had seemed to stall their careers, for Twenty One Pilots, whose members never seemed to hide their faith or act like it was anything odd, critics seemed to yawn at their frequent mentions of and allusions to their faith in God. Although the duo didn't go out of their way to talk religion, they were always ready with an answer when asked about it by members of the music press.

"It's never been Josh & I's goal to stand up on a stage with a microphone and tell people what to believe," said Joseph. "That being said, what I do believe is very important to me, and absolutely is going to always be present whenever I create something, whenever I'm working through something. I think what someone believes can define them, even if it's that they don't believe anything, and for me and my faith, it will always be a big part of my music, whether it's directly or indirectly."[157]

"We're always questioning things," Dun told another interviewer, "but I guess it's safe to say that we're both Christians."[158]

And fans, especially Christian ones, were noticing the many declarations of faith contained in the Pilots' music. "Twenty One Pilots confounds secular critics, shows Gen-Y & Z a way to faith," blared one headline in an online publication. Writers Michael Ashcraft and Mark Ellis reported that the band had "declared its musical manifesto" as far back as 2013 in the song "Car Radio": "I will try with every rhyme to come across like I am dying to let you know you need to try to think."[159]

"Even though they are open about their faith, the band continues to sneak like a hacker through the world's default gospel-rejection mechanism," the writers continued. "While the dialectic voice confuses secular reporters, the message of salvation carries through to their listeners."[160]

It was a sign of the times, perhaps, that in a nation where 80 percent of its citizens considered themselves to be Christians, some critics felt the band had to sneak around in plain sight when it came to its members' faith, but they really weren't doing that much sneaking at all, with lyrics that were rather up front in presenting their struggles in light of that faith.

"While 'Stressed Out' is an innocuous ditty about young adults yearning for the carefree days of childhood, other songs on their two albums—*Vessel* and *Blurryface*—pack plenty of gospel punch," noted Ashcraft and Ellis, adding:

> In the "Holding on to You" video, Tyler escapes the clutches of zombies. "I'm taking over my body, back into control. It seems a lot like flesh is all I got. Not any more, flesh out the door. I must've forgot, you can't trust me . . . You should take my life. You should take my soul."
>
> Sinners who consider suicide when lonely at night are encouraged to "fight it. Take the pain, ignite it. Tie a noose around your mind loose enough to breathe fine. Tie it to a tree, and tell it, 'You belong to me. This noose is just a leash. You must obey me.'"
>
> The language is just the type of poetry this generation relates to, but it's also unadulterated Bible message. The song hails from Jer. 17:9: "The heart is deceitful about all things and desperately wicked. Who can understand it?"

Tyler is giving a modern voice to Pauline doctrine. The song echoes the Roman longing for freedom from fleshly desires, and Tyler breathes new life into Paul's paradox that death to sin is life in Christ and freedom from sin is obedience to Christ.

In "Heavydirtysoul," Tyler says, "Death inspires me like a dog inspires a rabbit. Can you save my heavy dirty soul?"

And in "Car Radio," the singer exposes how sinners deaden internal pain with meaningless lyrics put to a catchy tune.

"There are things we can do, but from the things that work there are only two. And from the two that we choose to do, peace will win and fear will lose," Tyler sings. "There's faith and there's sleep. We need to pick one please because faith is to be awake, and to be awake is for us to think, and for us to think is to be alive. And I will try with every rhyme to come across like I am dying to let you know you need to try to think."[161]

It wasn't just critics who were taking note of the duo's inspiring lyrics. So were fans.

"Josh and Tyler's music has really had a positive influence on the way I view myself and my depression," wrote a fan named Carlynn. "I've never heard songs about mental illness before that are obviously trying to make a change in the listener's life, and listening to their songs make me feel empowered, not more sad. Their music also made me realize I'm not alone."[162]

"When I first listened to their music I was like, 'I'm not alone,'" noted another fan, named Mattie. "I thought I was the only one. Twenty One Pilots really did save my life in more ways than one."[163]

Unlike some pop culture figures who disavowed any notion

that they should be role models to their fans, artists such as Tori Kelly and Twenty One Pilots had a sense that with fame came a responsibility to their fans:

"There are artists that I am fans of that have helped me through a lot," noted Joseph. "And because I know what that feels like, to be on the receiving end of something that someone created, I understand the weight and the importance and the honor in someone saying that our music has helped them in that same way. There's nothing more important in our career than hearing that."[164]

"I feel a heavy responsibility to continue not only creating or playing music, but also working on my own life, and trying to be a person that's worthy of somebody looking up to, I guess," added Dun.[165]

Unafraid to address issues teens faced, the duo was willing to go where even parents many feared to tread: suicide.

"It's a real thing that's pretty common, especially with teens," noted Dun. "A lot of times, parents will avoid talking about it, or they'll say, 'Let's not think about that.' But why not grant people the permission to think about it and redirect those feelings and thoughts to something different and creative? That's kind of the mindset behind a lot of the content and lyrics on *Vessel*."[166]

That formula was obviously effective, as 2016 turned out to be a pivotal year for the band as the duo's track "Stressed Out," dominated multiple formats, reaching the number one position on the pop chart, the adult pop chart, the alternative songs chart, and the rock chart, an unprecedented hat trick that propelled the band to national recognition.

"From the minute the album came out, 'Stressed Out' was raising its hand as a hit record," noted Mike Easterlin, president of the band's label, Fueled by Ramen. "It was streaming and selling strongly, even as [lead *Blurryface* single] 'Tear in My Heart' was doing well. I could have never imagined that ['Stressed'] would stay at the top of the Alternative Songs chart for so long or cross to pop so fast, but I think we all felt like we had a hit song."[167]

For decades, young Christians like Joseph and Dun had tried, often in vain, to make sure their music would be heard outside of the Christian community and a Christian music industry that sprang up around them often made it even more difficult to reach beyond its boundaries. Part of that could be attributed to Christian label A&R directors who often encouraged these artists to write one-dimensional songs that were exclusively about their faith. There were notable exceptions, of course, with powerful songs like "She's Gone," by Bloodgood, which addressed suicide; "Kiss Me Like a Woman" by Charlie Peacock and "Endless Flight" by Richie Furay, both unabashed love songs; and "No Such Thing as Divorce" by Bob Bennett, a folky reminder to his children that their parents' marital status wouldn't affect them. But while Twenty One Pilots were never shy about weaving their faith into their lyrics, they had become skilled at writing and performing "normal" songs that non-Christian fans could relate to. The band's smash hit "Stressed" was a prime example of this.

"Their current hit, the rap-rock throwback 'Stressed Out,' is about the harsh end of adolescence ('Used to dream of outer space, but now they're laughing at our face/Saying, "Wake up, you need to make money"')," noted *Rolling Stone.*[168]

The song was also in many ways a lyrical counterpunch to the very organizing principles of rock, the notion that kids and their parents had almost nothing in common, that they wouldn't be understood by their forbears, and that they could defy parental expectations of their children developing independent and responsible lives. For Twenty One Pilots however, rebellion was not the dominant theme of its members' music. Raised in relatively healthy families with respect for God and family, the duo went so far as to include their family members in the video for the song, featuring siblings and parents yelling at them in their beds "Wake up! You have to make money!"[169] It wasn't just a throwaway line, however, as Joseph remembered a time when his father had taught him an important lesson that later came out in his music.

"I said to my dad, 'Are you disappointed that I'm working a minimum-wage job and I didn't go to college?'" he remembered. "I'll never forget his response. He said, 'It's not about how much money you make or what your job is, but it's more about your character. For that, I'm proud of you.' It gave me motivation."[170]

Tyler Joseph and Josh Dun seemed galaxies away from their forbears who started rock and roll. With egos that appeared to be firmly in check, and deeply connected to God and family, they were charting a course in rock that had little to do with hedonism and excess, and more to do with enjoying the creative process and using their art to give back to those they loved.

"Growing up, money is important," Joseph said. "And now I have a career where I'm making enough money to live. But I really want to give it to my parents, my family, charities and people around me."[171]

7

INTO THE GREAT WIDE-OPEN

As more and more young and outspoken Christians left the world of contemporary Christian music for the uncharted waters of the musical mainstream, others stayed behind to fill the gaps left behind by the exiting artists. Among the artists who remained in the CCM industry, a subcategory known as "worship music" continued to grow, while still other pop/rock Christian artists felt market pressures to take a break from their "Christian records" and record even more lyrically obvious "worship records." Artists who followed this track, such as Michael W. Smith and Third Day, were often rewarded handsomely with increased sales for their subsequent albums.

Others, including Jars of Clay, which tried to avoid what had by then come to be seen as a bandwagon, saw their sales taper off and the group eventually disbanded. But a backlash was clearly brewing against the increasing commercialization of "worship." Christa Farris, then an editor at *CCM* magazine, once observed, "It's gotten to the point where if one more worship CD comes across my desk I'm going to scream. . . . Artists are responding to what consumers seem to want . . . It seems like a good thing because we're giving worship to the Creator, but the Psalms talk about singing a new song unto the Lord. I think we're all waiting for these new songs to emerge. . . . How many more times can you hear 'I Could Sing of Your Love Forever?'"[1]

For those artists who remained in the CCM industry, it seemed to become increasingly popular to abandon rock band status and claim that they were "worship bands," with the unspoken implication that such artists were more committed to serving God than were those artists who had crossed over into the musical mainstream. Perhaps the most interesting example of this phenomenon was the "worship band" Rock 'n' Roll Worship Circus, whose members made it clear that they were not there to merely "entertain" but to lead Christians in worshipping their God. But the members of Rock 'n' Roll Worship Circus had a problem: they didn't look like a "worship band" and constantly dealt with critics who said they were more goth than worship. It was just another development in the sometimes-confusing world left in the wake of so many young Christians trying to make sense of things in a post-Christian music culture, one that had been constructed on questionable logic and theology. But a musician who was actually an integral part of that Jesus movement, John Fischer believed strongly that the Jesus music movement was birthed not by artists who were trying to worship God among fellow Christians, but rather by those who sought to take their music and message to the masses, only to find those efforts thwarted by those whose focus was to do business and market their music to fellow believers:

> I would say that we lost the mission some time ago. When I think of Christian Music, I go back to the beginnings that I'm familiar with, which would be "Jesus Music." That was very much a "reach the world" agenda. And we did, we had the world's ear then, but it was nothing to do with "Christian Music." Then as we got more sophisticated, we went through a period where the mission changed and turned inward. It turned into—in its best sense—teaching and encouraging Christians, and in its worst sense, just entertaining Christians. But I think as of late, I am encouraged that there at least are channels for Christian artists to move out into the world. So I would say, yeah we lost it, but I think we're getting it back, at least in some form.[2]

Others also remained troubled by the unspoken implication that seemed to linger in the air, that only the truly committed musicians made worship music while those lesser in the faith took the music out of the church. Dan Haseltine of Jars of Clay observed:

> The radio and record companies have placed their stamp of approval on the worship movement and by the choices they have made, have contributed to the idea that this is the only legitimate musical form for Christian Music. Unfortunately,

artists who believe that art finds its greatest voice in the pro-
phetic form will take a huge risk by following their calling. It
is important for Christians to describe the world as they see
it, through the eyes of faith. Testimony is one of the most
important and vital forms of faith building.[3]

Haseltine might also have been speaking of artists like Kevin
Max, the onetime member of the supergroup dc Talk. The band
had made a name for itself first in the CCM world and then
later via Virgin Records in the mainstream, but had stopped
its group activity as its members embarked on solo careers.
Michael Tait and TobyMac had put out their records to wide
applause in the CCM community, but the group's third singer,
Max, had made a left-of-center record that sought a broader
audience. While TobyMac and Tait's records sold respectably,
Max's *Stereotype Be* fell flat and he was eventually released from
his contract with his CCM label, but not before being told by
its president, "You're a Francis Schaeffer artist in a Billy Graham
world." What the president of Forefront likely had in mind was
Max's high-concept album that may have gone right over the
heads of dc Talk fans. Max recalled:

> It was meant as a concept for me to show how the excesses
> of rock & roll and fashion can leave you lonely. I wanted
> to throw that into the imaging, that it's not all about what
> you look like, it's not how we appear. That's the idea behind
> *Stereotype Be*, that you can't stereotype somebody from an
> appearance. But none of them really got that. They just
> thought, "Oh, that's just Kevin Max trying to push the
> envelope." What people don't realize about me, is that I
> really think things out before I do them. It's not just me on a

whim doing whatever. Sometimes I do that, but a lot of times when it comes to a concept, I've really thought about this, I've really tried to come up with some kind of philosophy behind what I'm doing.[4]

Max and his two partners in dc Talk had collectively made their label millions of dollars over the span of a nearly fifteen-year career. But when it came to catching their longtime artist's vision, helping him solidify his core fan base, and finding new fans in the mainstream market, Forefront seemed disinterested. Max said:

It's a mystery. I want to say that I think the timing wasn't right, for me as a person, maybe. And that's a God thing. But I feel like, when it comes to the business end, I don't think that Forefront had a clue on how to market the project. I don't think they even tried to market it. I think they just put it out there expecting the dc Talk crowd to buy it, regardless of anything besides the fact that I'm one-third of dc Talk. They didn't put a lot of prep work into it. I remember, all of the ideas that went into it were coming from me. Nobody ever challenged me on anything. It was just like, "Okay, this is what you're doing, okay these are the photos you want to take . . ." Nobody ever said, "You know, I think the feather boa might be too much for the Christian audience."[5]

Max's experience was in stark contrast to the two records that Virgin had successfully marketed to the mainstream for his band:

Before *Stereotype Be*, I was on Virgin Records, with Supernatural and Jesus Freak, and I remember sitting around a round table with the whole staff of Virgin, getting behind the project, from the venue to the marketing of the project, to the manufacturing of the project, to radio, to whatever. They talked about this stuff. With *Stereotype Be* and Forefront, none of these things were ever talked about. It was just kind of like, "Okay, we'll throw it out there." . . . I'm not trying to slam Forefront, I'm saying it hoping to encourage them to learn from the mistake.[6]

Soon after the *Stereotype Be* fiasco, Forefront was able to take one of its artists, Stacie Orrico, into the mainstream by deftly partnering with another label in the EMI family, Virgin Records, and developing her jointly and successfully marketing her to the mainstream music world. But the label's inability to do the same for one of the market's most talented but under-rated artists, Max's fellow dc Talk member TobyMac, meant the label still had a long way to go. At least one executive who ran a traditional Christian music label understood Max's dilemma and was working hard to solve the problems that plagued the CCM industry. Barry Landis, at that time with Word Records, one of the oldest and most respected CCM labels, had worked to break down the walls that kept his artists out of mainstream circulation. Landis was a disciple of the late Bob Briner, the author of the book *Roaring Lambs*, in which Briner had argued for an exodus of Christian artists into the mainstream music industry. Landis had been introduced to Briner's book by a friend in the early '90s and found it to be a life-changing read:

I was struggling with whether I should remain in the Christian music industry or whether I should try to segue into the mainstream music world, which had a significant presence in Nashville. My opinion of the Christian music industry was that it was far more interested in selling records to Christians than it was in venturing into new opportunities out in the world to tell the good news. I rushed out to buy *Roaring Lambs* the very day I heard about it. I thought it might hold some answers for me, and I was not disappointed. It was a book that made so much sense that I couldn't believe someone was just getting around to saying these things in print. It was a quick read, but the effect it had on my life will be eternal. As I read the pages, I was reminded of the calling on my life as a youngster and that God was continuing to work in me.[7]

Landis quickly reached out to Briner for advice and was not disappointed:

I wrote to Bob immediately. I'm just the kind of person who likes to fax authors I enjoy reading. I really was amazed to have a response from Bob within the same day. That completely boggled my mind because at the time, the method of operating in the Christian music business was anything but thoughtful and professional. Calls and faxes went unanswered for many days (if they're answered at all) because, in my opinion, most of the men and women who run the affairs of Christian music hadn't learned the rudiments of proper business techniques. . . . That started a very fast friendship, one that was built on mutual respect of and help for each other, although he helped me a great deal more than I ever helped him. I was at a crossroads in my career, thinking that I needed to escape the mindset of the Christian music industry in order to "roar." Bob helped me see I should use the equity built up over nearly twenty years in the music field and pray that God would show me a path to leverage my strengths and reach out to new avenues of marketing Christian music for the kingdom's sake.[8]

To critics who charged that mainstream success for his artists was impossible to accomplish from within the CCM industry, Landis countered:

> It is hard, but not impossible. When you think about it, the only way to change the world is from within. You have to be filled up with the Holy Spirit before you can go out into the world to be His witness. I think it's about calculating strategic influence. Far too many times, Christians think they have to shout Jesus' name if they have the opportunity. I think we have failed many times with that strategy. We need to think and pray long and hard about the opportunities God gives us and we need to strategically consider what He wants us to do. Very few people examine their lives in terms of a long life span and what can be done over that period of time. The more we think about that, I think the more we will have effective, long-lasting impact on the culture.[9]

Another label head, Brandon Ebel, had smartly walked the line between the two worlds and maintained that his goal was to make his music available to all people regardless of their religious affiliation and had done just that with his label Tooth & Nail Records. Still, critics such as John Fischer bemoaned the continued focus on selling records to fellow believers. "I think what happened is that we became too big and powerful," he said. "There's a big Christian industry machine now. And it's making too much money. And the world is even in on it now, making their money off of it. So yeah, there's too much invested."[10]

Dan Haseltine had seen success in both the mainstream and CCM markets with his band Jars of Clay, and though he supported those artists with a different calling, he saw his as being a part of the mainstream:

> We have to be able to write in a language that is decipherable to the watching world. I feel like it is simply the church language we use that can make a song irrelevant to a non-church person. But to write a song about personal life from the perspective of another Christian gives the church a chance to be discipled. It gives the body of Christ a chance to see their world from another faith angle. Like putting three people in a room and asking them to describe the painting in front of them. They will all give different descriptions based on their point of focus. And yet they will all still be describing the same painting. This is the beauty of a Gospel and a God that is more than one-dimensional. We all benefit from different faith perspectives. Even if they are diabolically different than our own. . . . it forces us to think and to be challenged.[11]

Offering advice to a young artist who sought to incorporate his faith into his music, Haseltine suggested:

> I would encourage budding musicians to make the best art they can. Be the best poet they can be, be the best songwriter, communicator they can be. Do not cheapen the value of the Gospel by encasing it in a mediocre melody or a boring musical idea, do not devalue truth by laying it in a bed of poor musicianship. God deserves our best. No matter where it gets played or what kind of platform a person is given.[12]

John Fischer had been around since the very beginnings of "Christian rock" in the late 1960s. With a style of music often compared to James Taylor, the traveling troubadour had logged thousands of miles singing around the country before becoming a prolific author who wrote and thought deeply about such issues. Looking to the future with confidence, Fischer saw no letup in the onslaught of devout Christians invading mainstream rock:

> It must be God's timing for it to be happening now, because these attempts to break down the walls around Christian Music have been going on since pretty much its beginning. And somewhere along the way we got comfortable in preaching to ourselves. Regarding why, I can think of two reasons. One: the music has gotten better. . . . The second reason is that the world has recognized that Christians, or at least the more conservative listener, is a big market out there. So they're not as hesitant as they used to be about going there. Because there is a market for it.[13]

From his perch as keen observer of the Christian music movement, Fischer drew lessons to be learned by future generations of artists who wanted to impact the larger world. The origins of the problem were a faulty worldview, Fischer noted, and could only be corrected by acquiring a correct one:

> Christians don't know, generally, how to think about the world. What they tend to do is think about it in a sort of sacred/secular realm, as if the world is divided up into these two camps. And worldviews are almost impossible to change—they take a long time. Because a worldview is

something that you aren't even aware of. It's a way you think that you grew up with, and everybody around you thinks the same way. That's why these things are so hard to talk about, because you can't change them. When you've got two people talking, they're both coming from two different worldviews and two different realities. So even the words they're saying don't necessarily mean the same thing. To get somebody from a real conservative worldview—you know, "Christians against the world"—to see the value of a Christian being in the world as an artist, period—that's a real stretch. That's like assigning yourself over to the enemy.[14]

Rock and religion, unlikely bedfellows, were now clearly intertwined. If the results were watered-down songs where God was always referred to as "You" but were otherwise indistinguishable from typical love songs, it's likely that devout Christians of the future would rue the day when they went along with the experiment. Likewise, the rock world might regret the day it allowed religion into its tent if the result was music that was unable to be related to by the common man, Christian or not. And for people of faith who had a long history of not being able to keep the faith amid the crushing demands of fame and the prospect of unlimited financial success, it would most clearly be judged a failure if their favorite artists were to choose mammon over God:

"If anyone can handle fame, it should be Christians," noted John Fischer. "Because Christians have been first humbled to even know Christ, to even know God, we become broken and humbled and we see our sins. So if there's any hope of anybody who can handle it correctly, it's with Christians."[15]

From the Chance the Rapper to the Cold War Kids, from Mumford & Sons and Justin Bieber to Twenty One Pilots and Megadeth, the religious had clearly invaded rock, and rock was grudgingly ceding ground that had once been the near-exclusive domain of hedonism. Yet, in biblical terms, rock seemed full of two types of Christians—those who modeled themselves after the biblical character Daniel, unaffected by his surroundings and fervently focused on serving God, and those described in a prophecy by the apostle Paul, who wrote that in the end times would come those "having a form of religion, but turning their backs on the power of it."

Long hailed as "the Devil's music," rock 'n' roll had now gotten religion, understanding the power of spiritual transformation and harnessing that power, and popular culture would never be the same.

NOTES

CHAPTER ONE: ROCK GETS RELIGION

1. Lauren Johnston, "Old Time Rock & Roll." CBS News, August 15, 2004, http://www.cbsnews.com/news/old-time-rock-roll/.
2. Steve Jelbert, "Praise Be: God and Top of the Pops," *Belfast Telegraph*, June 17, 2003, http://www.belfasttelegraph.co.uk/imported/praise-be-god-and-top-of-the-pops-28153406.html.
3. Ibid.
4. Anthony DeBarros, "Music in a New Light," *USA Today*, October 5, 2002.
5. Kim Campbell, "Bible Belters Change Their Tune," *Christian Science Monitor*, February 6, 2004, http://www.csmonitor.com/2004/0206/p16s02-almp.html.
6. Lou Carlozo, "The Faith Factor," *Chicago Tribune*, September 1, 2002.
7. Ibid.
8. Ibid.
9. Ibid.

10. Mark Joseph, "Why Should the Church Have All the Good Music?" *Today's Christian Music*, June 16, 2005, http://www.todayschristianmusic.com/artists/various/features/why-should-the-church-have-all-the-good-music/.

11. Ibid.

12. Ibid.

13. Switchfoot, "Meant to Live," in *The Beautiful Letdown*, Columbia/Sony BMG, 2003; lyrics available at http://www.metrolyrics.com/meant-to-live-lyrics-switchfoot.html.

14. "Rockers Depart from 'Christian Music' Label," Entertainment, *Christian Today*, August 15, 2006, http://www.christiantoday.com/article/rockers.depart.from.christian.music.label/7277.html.

15. "Songs & Beliefs," Todays Christian Music, accessed March 22, 2017, http://www.todayschristianmusic.com/artists/various/features/songs-beliefs/.

16. Charlie Peacock, *At the Crossroads: An Insider's Look at the Past, Present, and Future of Contemporary Christian Music* (Nashville: Broadman & Holman, 1999).

17. Joseph, "Why Should the Church Have All the Good Music?"

18. Jason Byassee, "Eschatological Innovation," *Faith & Leadership*, August 3, 2009.

19. Sonny Sandoval, in an interview on the *Howard Stern Radio Show*, March 18, 2000.

20. Bart Millard, interviewed at CMCentral.com.

21. Ibid.

22. Jars of Clay, "Revolution," by Stephen Daniel Mason et al., in *The Eleventh Hour*, Essential, 2002.

23. Joseph, "Why Should the Church Have All the Good Music?"

24. John Fischer, interview with the author, 2006.

25. Tommy Coomes, in interview with author, 2006.

CHAPTER TWO: GOD'S IDOLS

1. Melody Green and David Hazard, *No Compromise: The Life Story of Keith Green*, upd. exp. ed. (Nashville: Thomas Nelson, 2008), 208.

2. Josh Tyrangiel, "Building a Better Pop Star," *Time*, October 5, 2003, http://content.time.com/time/magazine/article/0,9171,493242,00.html.

3. Ibid.

4. CNN, "Taking the 'Measure' of Clay Aiken," October 15, 2003, http://www.cnn.com/2003/SHOWBIZ/Music/10/15/sprj.caf03.clay.aiken/.

5. Associated Press, "Christian Version of 'American Idol' to Debut," *Today*, June 21, 2004, http://www.today.com/id/526167e8/ns/today-today_entertainment/t/christian-version-american-idol-debut/.

6. Ramin Setoodeh, "Religion and 'Idol': Could Adam Lambert Be Heading Home?," *Newsweek*, May 12, 2009, http://www.newsweek.com/religion-and-idol-could-adam-lambert-be-heading-home-220788/.

7. Devlin Donaldson, "Billy Ray Hearn," *CCM Magazine*, June 1998, 46.

CHAPTER THREE: RELATIONSHIP STATUS: IT'S COMPLICATED

1. Caroline Graham, "'Shameful and Disgusting': The No1 Song Which Has Sparked Outrage—from the Singer's Own Parents," *Daily Mail*, updated August 16, 2008, http://www.dailymail.co.uk/tvshowbiz/article-1046018/Shameful-disgusting-The-No1-song-sparked-outrage--singers-parents.html.

2. Ibid.

3. Ibid.

4. Jocelyn Vena, "Katy Perry Poses in Lingerie, Talks Religion in *Rolling Stone*," MTV News, August 3, 2010, http://www.mtv.com/news/1644948/katy-perry-poses-in-lingerie-talks-religion-in-rolling-stone/.

5. Vanessa Grigoriadis, "Sex, God & Katy Perry," *Rolling Stone*, August 19, 2010, http://www.rollingstone.com/music/news/sex-god-katy-perry-rolling-stones-2010-cover-story-20110607.

6. Ibid.

7. James Dinh, "Katy Perry Says Mixing Sex and Religion Makes 'Bad Things Happen,'" MTV News, August 5, 2010, http://www.mtv.com/news/1645124/katy-perry-says-mixing-sex-and-religion-makes-bad-things-happen/.

8. Grigoriadis, "Sex, God & Katy Perry."

9. Ibid.

10. PageSix.com Staff, "Katy's Boobs Traumatize Mom," *Page Six*, March 28, 2011, http://pagesix.com/2011/03/28/katys-boobs-traumatize-mom/.

11. Ibid.

12. Richard Price, "Katy Perry's Parents Condemn Her Lifestyle While Cashing In on Her Eternal Damnation," *New York Post*, June 12, 2011, http://nypost.com/2011/06/12/katy-perrys-parents-condemn-her-lifestyle-while-cashing-in-on-her-eternal-damnation/.

13. Benge Nsenduluka, "Katy Perry's Pastor Mother: 'God' Will Use Divorce to Boost Church," *Christian Post*, January 6, 2012, http://www.christianpost.com/news/katy-perrys-pastor-mother-god-used-divorce-to-boost-church-66576/.

14. "Katy Perry's Preacher Dad: 'My Daughter Is a Devil Child,'" news.com.au, May 2, 2013, http://www.news.com.au/entertainment/celebrity-life/katy-perrys-preacher-dad-my-daughter-is-a-devil-child/news-story/d44df8076d6342ab2123f8c79486605f.

15. Price, "Katy Perry's Parents Condemn Her Lifestyle."

16. Nsenduluka, "Katy Perry's Pastor Mother."

17. Gordon Smart, "Katy Perry: My Music Is about to Get F****** Dark," *Sun* (UK), April 7, 2012, http://www.thesun.co.uk/sol/homepage/showbiz/bizarre/4244886/Katy-Perry-news-Singer-says-she-wants-to-sing-miserable-songs-folloowing-her-marriage-breakdown-to-Russell-Brand.html.

18. "Camille Paglia: Miley, Go Back to School," *Time*, August 17, 2013, http://ideas.time.com/2013/08/27/pops-drop-from-madonna-to-miley/.

19. Ibid.

20. Chris Heath, "Mr. Hannah Montana's Achy Broken Heart," *GQ,* March 1, 2011, http://www.gq.com/entertainment/celebrities/201103/billy-ray-cyrus-mr-hannah-montana-miley?currentPage=5;.70.

21. Ibid.

22. Audrey Hingley, "Hosanna, Montana!" Christianity.com, accessed March 22, 2017, http://www.christianity.com/11622758/.

23. Ibid.

24. Ibid.

25. Ann Oldenburg, "Miley Cyrus Fulfills Her Destiny," *USA Today,* January 14, 2007.

26. Kimberly Dillon Summers, *Miley Cyrus: A Biography* (Santa Barbara: Greenwood, 2009), 2.

27. Heath, "Mr. Hannah Montana's Achy Broken Heart."

28. Mark Joseph, "Rock and Religion: A Potent Mix," Crosswalk.com, January 13, 2004, http://www.crosswalk.com/culture/books/rock-and-religion-a-potent-mix-1240747.html.

29. David Hooper, "Ashlee Simpson Revisited." Music Marketing [Dot] Com, November 7, 2004, http://www.musicmarketing.com/2004/11/ashlee_simpson_.html.

30. Ibid.

31. Ibid.

32. Ibid.

33. Ibid.

34. Ibid.

35. Ibid.

36. Ibid.

37. Ibid.

38. "Ashlee Simpson, Autobiography, Album Review, Plugged In," *Plugged In,* http://www.pluggedin.com/music/albums/2004/ashleesimpson-autobiography.aspx.

39. Jenny Eliscu, "Avril Lavigne: Little Miss Can't Be Wrong," *Rolling Stone,* March 20, 2003, http://www.rollingstone.com/music/news/little-miss-cant-be-wrong-20030320.

40. Ibid.

41. NBC News, "All about Avril Lavigne," NBCNews.com, December 9, 2003, http://www.nbcnews.com/id/3080073/ns/dateline_nbc-newsmakers/t/all-about-avril-lavigne/#.WNLd7_nyuUk.

42. Ibid.

43. Eliscu, "Avril Lavigne."

44. McQueen, "Avril's Wild Ride to Stardom."

45. Lorraine Ali, "Anarchy on MTV? Tough Gals, Rejoice." *Newsweek,* December 29, 2002, http://www.newsweek.com/anarchy-mtv-tough-gals-rejoice-141321.

46. Ibid.

47. NBC News, "All about Avril Lavigne."

48. Mike Ross, "Avril's Living a Dream," Canoe.com, April 21, 2003, http://jam.canoe.ca/Music/Artists/L/Lavigne_Avril/2003/04/21/pf-746830.html.

49. NBC News, "All about Avril Lavigne."

50. Ibid.

51. Ibid.

52. Ibid.

53. Ibid.

54. Ibid.

55. McQueen, "Avril's Wild Ride to Stardom."

56. Ibid.

57. Ibid.

58. NBC News, "All about Avril Lavigne."

59. Jane Stevenson, "'Whatever,'" CANOE JAM!, May 28, 2004, http://jam.canoe.ca/Music/Artists/L/Lavigne_Avril/2004/05/28/pf-746820.html.

60. Eliscu, "Avril Lavigne."

61. Ibid.

62. "Avril Lavigne: Let Go: Album Review," *Plugged In*, accessed March 23, 2017, http://www.pluggedin.com/music/albums/2002/avrillavigne-letgo.aspx.

63. Stevenson, "Whatever."

64. Ibid.

65. Ali, "Anarchy on MTV?" *Newsweek*, December 29, 2002, http://www.newsweek.com/anarchy-mtv-tough-gals-rejoice-141321;.

66. Ann McQueen, "Avril Lavigne Likes Saying the 'F' Word," *tg media* (blog), September 22, 2004, http://tg-media.blogspot.com/2004/09/avril-lavigne-likes-saying-f-word.html.

67. Ibid.

68. Eliscu, "Little Miss Can't Be Wrong."

69. McQueen, "Avril's Wild Ride to Stardom."

70. Eryn Sun, "Kings of Leon Tap into Their Pentecostal Roots in New Documentary 'Talihina Sky,'" *Christian Post*, April 7, 2011, http://www.christianpost.com/news/kings-of-leon-tap-into-their-pentecostal-roots-in-new-documentary-talihina-sky-49739/.

71. Matt Conner, "Kings of Leon's Faith Journey," *Relevant* magazine, October 19, 2010, http://www.relevantmagazine.com/culture/music/features/23184-kings-of-leons-faith-journey.

72. Neil McCormick, "Kings of Leon: With God on Our Side," *Telegraph*, September 17, 2008, http://www.telegraph.co.uk/culture/music/3560771/Kings-of-Leon-with-God-on-our-side.html?mobile=basic.

73. Jordan Levin, "Meet the New Kings of Rock 'n' Roll," *PopMatters*, May 1, 2009, http://www.popmatters.com/article/73891-meet-the-new-kings-of-rock-n-roll/.

74. Sun, "Kings of Leon Tap into Their Pentecostal Roots."

75. Ibid.

76. Levin, "Meet the New Kings of Rock 'n' Roll."

77. Ibid.

78. "Kings of Leon," *Pollstar*, September 29, 2003, http://www.pollstar.com/hotstar_article. aspx?ID=41523.

79. McCormick, "Kings of Leon."

80. Chris Scharen, "Kings of Leon—Running Away from God (Sort Of)," *Broken Hallelujahs* (blog), October 3, 2007, https://scharen.wordpress.com/2007/10/03/kings-of-leon-running-away-from-god-sort-of/.

81. Ibid.

82. Sun, "Kings of Leon Tap into Their Pentecostal Roots."

83. Ibid.

84. Adam R. Holz, "Kings of Leon, Come around Sundown, Album Review," *Plugged In*, accessed March 23, 2017, http://www.pluggedin.com/music/albums/2010/kingsofleon-comearoundsundown.aspx.

85. Barry Divola, "Bear Witness to Kings of Leon's Caleb Followill," *Entertainment Weekly*, April 12, 2007, http://www.ew.com/ew/article/0,,20034325,00.html.

86. Steve Beard, "Elvis Presley's Spiritual Journey," the website of Russ Kelly, http://www.tithing-russkelly.com/elvis/id15.html.

87. McCormick, "Kings of Leon."

88. Scharen, "Kings of Leon—Running Away from God."

89. Sun, "Kings of Leon Tap into Their Pentecostal Roots."

90. Scharen "Kings of Leon--Running Away from God."

91. "The Nod Squad," *Chicago Tribune*, September 15, 2004, http://articles.chicagotribune.com/2004-09-15/news/0409160419_1_stellar-awards-american-music-awards-gospel.

92. Andree Farias, "The College Dropout," January 1, 2004, http://www.crosswalk.com/11617281/.

93. Ibid.

94. Dan Aquilante, "Kanye Dig It—West on Janet: 'Sweet' and Lil Kim 'Raunchy,'" *New York Post*, August 15, 2004, http://nypost.com/2004/08/15/kanye-dig-it-west-on-janet-sweet-and-lil-kim-raunchy/;.

95. Ibid.

96. "Think Kanye smokes?" discussion on IGN, comment posted by "JTeel54," on February 8, 2008, http://www.ign.com/boards/threads/think-kanye-smokes.159779239/, citing an interview on GotVape.com (no longer accessible).

97. Loren Eaton Bob Smithouser, "Kanye West: The College Dropout: Album Review," *Plugged In*, accessed March 23, 2017, http://www.pluggedin.com/music/albums/2004/kanyewest-thecollegedropout.aspx.

98. Ibid.

99. Kim Jones, "Gospel Artist Micah Stampley's Thoughts on Kanye West," http://christianmusic.about.com/od/editorial1/f/What-Does-Micah-Stampley-Think-About-The-Kanye-West-Controversy.htm. Article no longer available.

100. "Stranger Things interview with Ben Moody (September 2000)," originally posted at http://www.evboard.com/495355-post16.html (no longer accessible); cached on *EvThreads* (posted by "Ring," July 1, 2013), http://evthreads.proboards.com/thread/1466/stranger-interview-moody-september-2000.

101. Gabe Wilson, "Enclave Interview 1998," notachristianband.com, accessed March 23, 2017, http://www.notachristianband.com/enclave.shtml.

102. Ibid.

103. Ibid.

104. Ibid.

105. Enrique Lopetegui, "Evanescence Comes Back Strong While Keeping Jesus (Mostly) out of It," *San Antonio Current*, October 11, 2011, http://www.sacurrent.com/sanantonio/evanescence-comes-back-strong-while-keeping-jesus-mostly-out-of-it/Content?oid=2242627.

106. Joe Dangelo, "Evanescence's Label Tells Christian Outlets to Yank Fallen," MTV News, April 16, 2003, http://www.mtv.com/news/1471313/evanescences-label-tells-christian-outlets-to-yank-fallen/.

107. Zach Baron, "How Chance the Rapper's Life Became Perfect." *GQ*, August 24, 2016, http://www.gq.com/story/how-chance-the-rappers-life-became-perfect.

108. Tomi Obaro, "Why Chance the Rapper's Black Christian Joy Matters," Buzzfeed News, May 19, 2016, https://www.buzzfeed.com/tomiobaro/why-chance-the-rappers-christian-joy-matters?utm_term=.ad2JGyvGL#.mgDom3kmw.

109. Justin Sarachik, "Chance the Rapper Losing God Helped Him Create Music as 'Christian Man,'" *Rapzilla*, May 26, 2016, http://www.rapzilla.com/rz/features/13483-chance-the-rapper-losing-god-helped-him-create-music-as-christian-man.

110. Ibid.

111. Watson Jones III, "This Year's Summer Jam Is All about the Love of God," *Christianity Today*, June 9, 2016, http://www.christianitytoday.com/ct/2016/june-web-only/chance-rapper-coloring-book.html.

112. Ibid.

113. Ibid.

114. Phil Mushnick, "Challenge to White Sox, ESPN hosts: Recite Chance the Rapper Lyrics," *New York Post*, April 11, 2016, http://nypost.com/2016/04/11/challenge-to-white-sox-espn-hosts-recite-chance-the-rapper-lyrics/.

115. Ibid.

116. Twitter.com/chancetherapper; no longer visible.

117. Lil Chano from 79th@chancetherapper, "I'm leaving cigarettes in January," Twitter, January 1, 2016, https://twitter.com/chancetherapper/status/683003026446114816?lang=en.

118. "King's X—Over My Head (Video)," YouTube video, 4:57, by Atlantic Records, October 26, 2009, https://www.youtube.com/watch?v=J2SYPzKzD94.

119. Joe Coscarelli, "Kendrick Lamar on His New Album and the Weight of Clarity," *New York Times*, March 16, 2015, https://www.nytimes.com/2015/03/22/arts/music/kendrick-lamar-on-his-new-album-and-the-weight-of-clarity.html?smid=nytimesarts&_r=1.

120. Ibid.

121. Kendrick Lamar, "Sherane a.k.a Master Splinter's Daughter," Genius, accessed March 30, 2017, https://genius.com/Kendrick-lamar-sherane-aka-master-splinters-daughter-lyrics.

122. Gavin Edwards, "Billboard Cover: Kendrick Lamar on Ferguson, Leaving Iggy Azalea Alone and Why 'We're in the Last Days,'" *Billboard*, January 9, 2015, http://www.billboard.com/articles/news/6436268/kendrick-lamar-billboard-cover-story-on-new-album-iggy-azalea-police-violence-the-rapture.

123. Reggie Ugwu, "The Radical Christianity of Kendrick Lamar," BuzzFeed Music, February 3, 2015, https://www.buzzfeed.com/reggieugwu/the-radical-christianity-of-kendrick-lamar?utm_term=.wnjXEagE8#.nebXJ8aJD.

124. Ibid.

125. Ibid.

126. Yoh. "Get God on the Phone: How Kendrick Lamar Quietly Became Music's Biggest Christian Rapper," DJBooth, March 18, 2016, http://djbooth.net/news/entry/2016-03-18-kendrick-lamar-religion-hip-hop-christianity.

127. Ugwu, "The Radical Christianity of Kendrick Lamar."

128. Ibid.

129. Ibid.

130. Yoh, "Get God on the Phone."

131. Ibid.

132. Ugwu, "The Radical Christianity of Kendrick Lamar."

133. Insanul Ahmed, "Turn the Page." *Complex*, August 2014, http://www.complex.com/covers/kendrick-lamar-interview-turn-the-page-2014-cover-story/.

134. Ugwu, "The Radical Christianity of Kendrick Lamar."

CHAPTER FOUR: A CROSS AND A SONG WHERE I DON'T BELONG

1. Mark Joseph, "Why Should the Church Have All the Good Music?" Crosswalk.com, May 11, 2005, http://www.crosswalk.com/culture/music/why-should-the-church-have-all-the-good-music-1329733.html.

2. Steve Carney, "Band's Faith Pays off," *Los Angeles Times*, June 27, 2003, http://articles.latimes.com/2003/jun/27/entertainment/et-carney27>.

3. Bart Millard quoted in CMCentral.com.

4. Ibid.

5. Crystal Caviness, "Christian Music Hits Mainstream Radio," UPI, July 8, 2003, http://www.upi.com/Odd_News/2003/07/08/Christian-music-hits-mainstream-radio/91311057689448/.

6. Ibid.

7. Ibid.

8. Ibid.

9. Bart Millard quoted in CMCentral.com.

10. Ibid.

11. Ibid.

12. Corrie Moss, "Stacie Orrico Won't Be 'Stuck' with Christian Tag," MTV News, April 23, 2003, http://www.mtv.com/news/1471487/stacie-orrico-wont-be-stuck-with-christian-tag/.

13. "Open-Ended Interview with Stacie Orrico," JesusfreakHideout.com, June 1, 2003, http://www.jesusfreakhideout.com/interviews/StacieOrrico.asp.

14. Moss, "Stacie Orrico Won't Be 'Stuck' with Christian Tag."

15. "Open-Ended Interview with Stacie Orrico."

16. Ibid.

17. Ibid.

18. Parrish, "Interview 2."

19. Nathan Spicer, "The Civil Wars: *Barton Hollow*," *Paste* magazine, January 31, 2011, https://www.pastemagazine.com/articles/2011/01/the-civil-wars-barton-hollow.html.

20. James C. McKinley Jr., "Their Year of Living Almost Famously," *New York Times*, October 25, 2011, http://www.nytimes.com/2011/10/26/arts/music/talking-to-joy-williams-and-john-paul-white-of-the-civil-wars.html.

21. Simmy Richman, "How We Met: Joy Williams & John Paul White," *Independent*, March 18, 2012, http://www.independent.co.uk/news/people/profiles/how-we-met-joy-williams--john-paul-white-7574200.html.

22. Ibid.

23. Goforth, "Finding Her Own Voice."

24. Ibid.

25. Ibid.

26. Gilligan, "The Musical Marriage of the Civil Wars."

27. Ernie Thomas, "Chevelle Online, Articles," Chevelle Online, November 1, 1999, http://chevelleonline.net/main/content/media/Print-Articles/rev_midbeat_nov99.htm. No longer accessible.

28. Ibid.

29. Joe Dangelo, "Chevelle Rev High With New Single, Tour," MTV, January 30, 2003, http://www.mtv.com/news/1459767/chevelle-rev-high-with-new-single-tour/.

30. Ibid.

31. "Chevelle Bucks 'New Metal' on Epic Debut," *Billboard*, November 4, 2002, http://www.billboard.com/articles/news/73584/chevelle-bucks-new-metal-on-epic-debut.

32. Andree Farias, "Chevelle This Type of Thinking (Could Do Us In) (Epic)," *Christianity Today*, January 1, 2004, http://www.christianitytoday.com/ct/2004/januaryweb-only/thistypeofthinking.html. Archived at https://web.archive.org/web/20071218201636/http://www.christianitytoday.com/music/glimpses/2004/thistypeofthinking.html.

33. Chuck Boring, "ChevelleOnline, Interviews," Chevelle Online, December 12, 2002, http://chevelleonline.net/main/content/media/Print-Interviews/chevelle_ei_dec1202.htm. No longer accessible.

34. Farias, "This Type of Thinking (Could Do Us In)."

35. Ibid.

36. Catherine Lee, interviewer, "Video Vision: Exclusive Interview," Video Vision, March 4, 2000, http://videovision.org/interview-chevelle.html.

37. Switchfoot, "Meant to Live" by Jon Foreman and Tim Foreman, in *The Beautiful Letdown*, Columbia/Sony BMG, 2003, compact disc.

38. Chris Owen, "Switchfoot Interview," Learning2Breathe.com, accessed March 24, 2017, http://www.learning2breathe.com/lifeandloveandwhy/interview.html.

39. Ibid.

40. Ibid.

41. Andy Argyrakis, "Switchfoot Focuses on Life's Beauty over Letdowns," Crosswalk.com, January 1, 2003, http://www.crosswalk.com/11617767/.

42. "Benson," *Thinking New Thoughts* (blog), January 30, 2003 , http://blog.besologic.com/2003/01/, citing "Q&A with Jon Foreman," *Relevant* magazine, link no longer accessible.

43. "Benson," *Thinking New Thoughts.*

44. Frank Schaeffer, *Bad News for Modern Man: An Agenda for Christian Activism* (Wheaton, Ill.: Crossway Books, 1984).

45. Argyrakis, "Switchfoot Focuses on Life's Beauty over Letdowns."

46. Switchfoot, "This Is Your Life" by Jon Foreman, in *The Beautiful Letdown.*

47. Switchfoot, "On Fire" by Jon Foreman and Daniel Victor, in *The Beautiful Letdown.*

48. "Benson," *Thinking New Thoughts,* January 18, 2003, http://blog.besologic.com/2003/01/cause-youre-on-fire-when-hes-near-you.html?m=1.

49. Ibid.

50. Owen, "Switchfoot Interview."

51. Kim Flanders, "Purple Door Festival 02," cMusicWeb, September 1, 2002, http://www.cmusicweb.com/features/purpledoor02/switchfoot.shtml.

52. Mark 4:9, paraphrased.

53. Argyrakis, "Switchfoot Focuses on Life's Beauty over Letdowns."

54. Ibid.

55. Switchfoot, "The Beautiful Letdown" in *The Beautiful Letdown.*

CHAPTER FIVE: ROCK IN A HARD PLACE

1. AskMen Editors, "Interview: Dave Mustaine News," AskMen, accessed March 24, 2017, http://www.askmen.com/celebs/interview_100/149_dave_mustaine_interview.html.

2. Jeff Kerby, "Reviews: Megadeth *The System Has Failed*," KNAC.com, September 14, 2004, http://www.knac.com/article.asp?ArticleID=3241.

3. Ibid.

4. Mark Moring, "The Confessions of Scott Stapp," *Christianity Today*, September 18, 2012, http://www.christianitytoday.com/ct/2012/october/confessions-of-scott-stapp.html.

5. Mark Moring, "Stapp: I Am a Christian," *Christianity Today*, August 9, 2004, http://www.christianitytoday.com/ct/2004/augustweb-only/scottstapp-0804.html.

6. Tim Adams, "With Arms Wide Open," Todays Christian Music, November 29, 2009.

7. Mark Moring, "I Am a Christian," crosswalk.com, August 9, 2004, http://www.crosswalk.com/11617886/.

8. Adams, "With Arms Wide Open."

9. Moring, "Stapp: I Am a Christian," Crosswalk.com.

10. Ibid.

11. Scott Stapp, Interview with author, 2003.

12. Moring, "Stapp: I Am a Christian," Crosswalk.com.

13. Lynn Vincent, "Scott Stapp's New Creed," *World*, September 25, 2004, http://www.worldmag.com/2004/09/scott_stapp_s_new_creed/page2. No longer accessible.

14. Ibid.

15. Moring, "Stapp: I Am a Christian," Crosswalk.com.

16. Adams, "With Arms Wide Open."

17. Moring, "Stapp: I Am a Christian," Crosswalk.com.

18. Ibid.

19. Vincent, "Scott Stapp's New Creed."

20. Moring, "Stapp: I Am a Christian," Crosswalk.com.

21. Stephen, "Scott Stapp," *Faithmaps Blog*, November 21, 2004, http://faithmaps.blogspot.com/2004_11_01_archive.html, citing *World* magazine.

22. Moring, "Stapp: I Am a Christian," Crosswalk.com.

23. Adams, "With Arms Wide Open."

24. Ibid.

25. Ibid.

26. Moring, "Stapp: I Am a Christian," Crosswalk.com.

27. Adams, "With Arms Wide Open."

28. Ibid.

29. Vincent, "Scott Stapp's New Creed."

30. David (reviewer), "Cold War Kids—Robbers & Cowards," Silent Uproar, October 9, 2006, http://silentuproar.com/reviews/1563/cold-war-kids/robbers-cowards/.

31. Ibid.

32. Jim Macnie, contrib., "U2 Bio," *Rolling Stone*, 2001, http://www.rollingstone.com/music/artists/u2/biography.

33. David, "Cold War Kids."

34. Seth Combs, "Down with the Jesus Freaks!" *San Diego CityBeat*, January 17, 2007, http://sdcitybeat.com/news-and-opinion/jesus-freaks/.

35. Ibid.

36. Ibid.

37. Ibid.

38. Combs, "Down with the Jesus Freaks!"

39. Andrew McCoy, "Artist to Watch: Cold War Kids," *Sacred Heart*, October 10, 2008, http://www.sacredheartspectrum.com/news/view.php/663165/Artist-to-watch-Cold-War-Kids, citing *Rolling Stone* (p. 122). No longer accessible.

40. C. S. Lewis, 9 August 1939, in *The Collected Letters of C. S. Lewis*, Slp ed. (Harper San Francisco, 2005).

41. Christian Scharen, "A Deliberately Spiritual Thing," *Cresset*, January 1, 2014, http://thecresset.org/2011/Michaelmas/Scharen_M11.html.

42. Austin Scaggs, "Marcus Mumford on Backing Dylan, Naked Songwriting and Why Arcade Fire Rule His World," *Rolling Stone*, March 4, 2011, http://www.rollingstone.com/music/news/marcus-mumford-on-backing-dylan-naked-songwriting-and-why-arcade-fire-rule-his-world-20110304.

43. Scharen, "A Deliberately Spiritual Thing."

44. Laura Barton, "The Almighty Power of Mumford & Sons." *Guardian*, February 11, 2011, http://www.theguardian.com/music/2010/feb/11/mumford-sons-sigh-more.

45. Ibid.

46. Ibid.

47. Andrea Swensson, "Interview: Mumford & Sons' Marshall Winston Chats Backstage," *City Pages*, May 26, 2010, http://www.citypages.com/music/interview-mumford-and-sons-marshall-winston-chats-backstage-6632913.

48. Dustin Christensen, "Christianity Needs a Better Story," *Relevant* magazine, June 16, 2011, http://www.relevantmagazine.com/god/deeper-walk/features/25927-christianity-needs-a-better-story.

49. Ben Schumer, "Mumford & Sons *Sigh No More*," *Pop Matters*, February 17, 2010, http://www.popmatters.com/review/120255-mumford-sons-sigh-no-more/.

50. Nick Tosches, "Over the Influence Mylon," Rolling Stone, February 15, 1973, 58.

51. Mikael Wood, "Switchfoot, 'Oh! Gravity' (Columbia)," *Spin*, January 5, 2007, http://www.spin.com/reviews/switchfoot-oh-gravity-columbia/.

52. "Larry Norman, Why Should the Devil Have All the Good Music Lyrics," Lyrics Mania, accessed March 27, 2017, http://www.lyricsmania.com/why_should_the_devil_have_all_the_good_music_lyrics_larry_norman.html.

53. Schumer, "Mumford & Sons."

54. Rachel Dovey, "Mumford & Sons: Sigh No More," *Paste* magazine, March 30, 2010, http://www.pastemagazine.com/articles/2010/03/mumford-sons-sigh-no-more.html.

55. Scharen, "A Deliberately Spiritual Thing."

56. Leah Greenblatt, "Mumford & Sons: An EW Q&A with Frontman Marcus Mumford," *Entertainment Weekly*, October 1, 2010, http://www.ew.com/article/2010/10/01/mumford-sons-marcus-interview.

57. Adam Holz, "Mumford & Sons Sigh No More: Album Review," *Plugged In*, February 16, 2010, http://www.pluggedin.com/music/albums/2011/mumfordandsons-sighnomore.aspx.

58. Ibid.

59. Jonathan Bautts, "Matt Thiessen and Matt Hoopes of Relient K," chorusfm, 2013, https://chorus.fm/interviews/matt-thiessen-and-matt-hoopes-of-relient-k/.

60. Ibid.

61. Ibid.

62. Jackie A. Chapman, "Under the Radar?" Crosswalk.com, February 19, 2007, http://www.crosswalk.com/11618114/.

63. Ibid.

64. Ibid.

65. Steve Taylor, "Meltdown (at Madame Tussaud's)," in *Meltdown*, Sparrow, 1984.

66. Krishana Kraft, "Mood Rings, Chap Stick and Pink Tuxedos," *Brio* magazine, June 1, 2005, http://www.tradema-rk.net/press/interviews/brio-magazine-mood-rings-chap-stick-and-pink-tuxedos/.

67. Steve Knight, "Story Behind the Song: Relient K's Matt Thiessen Talks About 'My Girlfriend,'" Todays Christian Music, http://www.todayschristianmusic.com/artists/relient-k/features/story-behind-the-song-relient-k-s-matt-thiessen-talks-about-my-girlfriend/.

68. Ibid.

69. Ibid.

70. Kraft, "Mood Rings, Chap Stick and Pink Tuxedos."

71. Stan Friedman, "Into the Fray," Crosswalk.com, July 17, 2006, http://www.crosswalk.com/11618063/.

72. Jeremy Hunt, "Interview: The Fray," *Relevant* magazine, September 1, 2006, http://www.relevantmagazine.com/culture/music/features/3404-interview-the-fray.

73. Friedman, "Into the Fray."

74. Hunt, "Interview."

75. Friedman, "Into the Fray."

76. ChristianMusic.com, "The Fray Bio," *Christian Music*, accessed March 29, 2017, http://www.christianmusic.com/fray/fray.htm.

77. Friedman, "Into the Fray."

78. David Sessions, "The Fray," Patrol magazine, February 4, 2009, archived on Douban.com, at https://www.douban.com/note/27227406/.

79. Jon Dolan, "The Fray: Scars & Stories," *Rolling Stone*, February 7, 2012, http://www.rollingstone.com/music/albumreviews/scars-stories-20120207.

80. Friedman, "Into the Fray."

81. Ibid.

82. OneRepublic, Twitter, 7:45 a.m., August 30, 2011, https://twitter.com/OneRepublic/status/108550893779161088.

83. Ibid., 7:50 a.m., https://twitter.com/OneRepublic/status/108552182462300160.

84. Joey Guerra, "Keep an Eye on One Republic," *Houston Chronicle*, January 17, 2008, http://www.chron.com/entertainment/music/article/Keep-an-eye-on-OneRepublic-1754864.php.

85. *Flint Journal* staff, "OneRepublic Unleashes New Sound on Latest Album," Michigan Live, October 28, 2009, http://www.mlive.com/entertainment/flint/index.ssf/2009/10/onerepublic_unleashes_new_soun.html.

86. Joey Guerra, "Keep an eye on One Republic," *Houston Chronicle*, January 17, 2008, http://www.chron.com/entertainment/music/article/Keep-an-eye-on-OneRepublic-1754864.php.

87. Guerra, "Keep an Eye on One Republic."

88. Guerra, "Keep an Eye on One Republic."

89. Dave Swanson, "49 Years Ago: John Lennon's 'Beatles More Popular Than Jesus' Story is Published," Ultimate Classic Rock, March 4, 2015, http://ultimateclassicrock.com/john-lennon-beatles-more-popular-than-jesus/.

90. "Misery Business", AZ Lyrics, http://www.azlyrics.com/lyrics/paramore/miserybusiness.html

91. paramoreband (signed by Hayley), "redemption. it's a long story," *Live Journal*, June 27, 2007, http://paramoremusic.livejournal.com/1305652.html.

92. Ibid.

93. Trish Bendix, "An Interview with Tourmates Tegan Quin and Hayley Williams of Paramore," After Ellen, September 7, 2010, http://www.afterellen.com/more/78940-an-interview-with-tourmates-tegan-quin-and-hayley-williams-of-paramore.

94. Tony (Pascarella?, "Interviews: Q & A with Paramore," ParamoreFans.com, http://paramorefans.com/paramore/interviews/tonyp.php.

95. Ibid.

96. Josh Farro, "Josh and Zac's Exit Statement," *Blogspot*, December 21, 2010, http://joshnfarro.blogspot.com/2010_12_01_archive.html, blog removed; reposted in "Josh Farro 'finally tells the truth' about Paramore," Alternative Press, December 22, 2010, http://www.altpress.com/news/entry/josh_and_zac_farro_finally_tell_the_truth_about_paramore/.

97. Ian Youngs, "Talking Shop: Paramore," BBC News, February 6, 2008, http://news.bbc.co.uk/2/hi/entertainment/7226757.stm.

98. John Sellers, "15 Questions for Paramore's Hayley Williams," *Spin*, October 6, 2009, http://www.spin.com/2009/10/15-questions-paramores-hayley-williams/.

99. Joey Guerra, "Paramore's Path Mixes Members' Fame, Faith," *Houston Chronicle*, May 29, 2009, http://www.chron.com/entertainment/music/article/Paramore-s-path-mixes-members-fame-faith-1744427.php.

100. Shelby, response to Alex, "Did Paramore break up?" Yahoo! Answers, 2011; accessed March 29, 2017, https://answers.yahoo.com/question/index?qid=20101219115611AAR6gX0; borrowed from Paramore.net.

101. Josh Farro, in Danielle Bacher, "[Updated with Statement from the Farros] Paramore's Josh and Zac Farro Leave the Band," *OC Weekly*, December 22, 2010, http://www.ocweekly.com/music/updated-with-statement-from-the-farros-paramores-josh-and-zac-farro-leave-the-band-6569583.

102. Leah Greenblatt, "Paramore Responds to Departing Band Member's Exit Statement: 'Yeah, it hurts'," *Entertainment*, January 4, 2011, http://ew.com/article/2011/01/04/paramore-responds-hayley-williams-josh-farro/.

103. Jeff Schwachter, "Full Interview with Flyleaf's Lacey Mosley," *Atlantic City Weekly*, May 19, 2010, http://www.atlanticcityweekly.com/arts_and_entertainment/features/full-interview-with-flyleaf-s-lacey-mosley/article_8bdca4be-edc2-5820-a024-afa972e97f87.html.

104. Ibid.

105. Ibid.

106. Ibid.

107. Ibid.

108. Ibid.

109. Greg Maki, "Flyleaf Singer Making the Most of Her Opportunity," *Star*, December 18 2009, http://www.stardem.com/community/article_95aa28af-3542-5230-aea9-e92f8cba3cb3.html.

110. Angel, "Flyleaf Cries Out "Memento Mori," NewRelease Today, November 23, 2009, http://www.newreleasetuesday.com/article.php?article_id=292.

111. Ibid.

112. Bob Paulson, "A Conversation with Flyleaf's Lacey Mosley," Billy Graham Evangelistic Association, June 30, 2009, http://billygraham.org/decision-magazine/july-august-2009/a-conversation-with-flyleafs-lacey-mosley/.

113. Angel, "Flyleaf Cries Out "Memento Mori."

CHAPTER SIX: HIDING IN PLAIN SIGHT

1. Amy Larocca, "The Real Miley Cyrus," *Harper's Bazaar*, January 6, 2010, http://www.harpersbazaar.com/celebrity/latest/news/a462/miley-cyrus-cover-interview-0210/.

2. *60 Minutes*, "Taylor Swift Sees Fame as a Responsibility," CBS News, November 16, 2011, http://www.cbsnews.com/news/taylor-swift-sees-fame-as-a-responsibility/.

3. *60 Minutes*, "Taylor Swift: A Young Singer''s Meteoric Rise," CBS News, May 19, 2013, http://www.cbsnews.com/news/taylor-swift-a-young-singers-meteoric-rise-19-05-2013/.

4. Vanessa Grigoriadis, "The Very Pink, Very Perfect Life of Taylor Swift," *Rolling Stone*, March 5, 2009, http://www.rollingstone.com/music/news/the-very-pink-very-perfect-life-of-taylor-swift-20090305.

5. Richard Rys, "Exit Interview: Taylor Swift," *Philadelphia* magazine, October 21, 2008, http://www.phillymag.com/articles/exit-interview-taylor-swift/.

6. Ibid.

7. Ibid.

8. Nisha Diu, "Taylor Swift Interview: 'I Won't Do Sexy Shoots'," *Telegraph*, April 3, 2011, http://www.telegraph.co.uk/culture/music/8421110/Taylor-Swift-interview-I-wont-do-sexy-shoots.html.

9. Eunice Oh, "Taylor Swift Says She Is Not Pregnant," *People*, November 6, 2008, http://www.people.com/people/article/0,,20238686,00.html.

10. Rys, "Exit Interview."

11. Dan Macsai, "Taylor Swift on Going Pop, Ignoring the Gossip and the Best (Worst) Nickname She's Ever Had," *Time*, October 19, 2012, http://entertainment.time.com/2012/10/19/taylor-swift-on-going-pop-ignoring-the-gossip-and-the-best-worst-nickname-shes-ever-had/#ixzz29lV0bNx5.

12. Taylor Swift: "@CivilWars Show. Belcourt Theatre. Caitlin and I bought t-shirts cause we're superfanssss. they RULE Live!" Twitter, February 2, 2011, https://twitter.com/taylorswift13/status/33005091195723776.

13. *60 Minutes*, "Taylor Swift Sees Fame as a Responsibility."

14. MTV News Staff, "Mase on His Faith, Retirement: 'The Realest Thing You've Ever Seen,'" MTV, April 26, 1999, http://www.mtv.com/news/1431886/mase-on-his-faith-retirement-the-realest-thing-youve-ever-seen/.

15. "Mase: Rap and Gospel Don't Mix," MTV, May 24, 1999, http://www.mtv.com/news/1431885/mase-rap-and-gospel-dont-mix/.

16. Andree Farias, "Welcome Back," *Christianity Today*, January 1, 2004, http://www.christianitytoday.com/ct/2004/januaryweb-only/welcomeback.html.

17. Jase Luttrell, "Mat Kearney: *Nothing Left to Lose: A brainwavez.org Music Review*," Brainwavez.org, December 1, 2006, http://www.brainwavez.org/music/reviews/2006/20061201001-01.html.

18. Kim Flanders, "Mat Kearney," cMusicWeb.com, July 2005, http://www.cmusicweb.com/modernrock/matkearney/interview.shtml.

19. Ibid.

20. Ibid.

21. Ibid.

22. Ibid.

23. Ibid.

24. Ibid.

25. Ibid.

26. Russ Breimeier, "Gotta Get Thru This," *Christianity Today*, January 1, 2003, http://www.christianitytoday.com/ct/2003/januaryweb-only/gottagetthruthis.html.

27. Nikki Tranter, "Daniel Bedingfield: Gotta Get Thru This: Ego-a-go-go," *PopMatters*, October 31, 2002, http://www.popmatters.com/review/bedingfielddaniel-gotta/.

28. Ibid.

29. Ibid.

30. Simon Hattenstone, "I'm Absolutely Nuts," *Guardian*, July 28, 2003, http://www.theguardian.com/music/2003/jul/28/artsfeatures.popandrock.

31. Ibid.

32. James Ellis, "Daniel Bedingfield," *Metro News*, October 27, 2009, http://metro.co.uk/2009/10/27/daniel-bedingfield-636626/.

33. Hattenstone, "I'm Absolutely Nuts."

34. Ibid.

35. Ibid.

36. Ellis, "Daniel Bedingfield."

37. Hattenstone, "I'm Absolutely Nuts."

38. Liz Jones, "Is Natasha Bedingfield God's Gift to Pop Music?" *Daily Mail Online*, May 12, 2007, http://www.dailymail.co.uk/home/you/article-451155/Is-Natasha-Bedingfield-Gods-gift-pop-music.html.

39. Ibid.

40. Joanne Brokaw, "Natasha Bedingfield's Christian Music Past," *Gospel Soundcheck* (blog), http://www.beliefnet.com/columnists/gospelsoundcheck/2008/07/natasha-bedingfield-christian.html.

41. Ellis, "Daniel Bedingfield."

42. Elizabeth Snead, "Justin Bieber Gets Jesus Christ Tattooed on His Leg," *Hollywood Reporter*, January 5, 2012, http://www.hollywoodreporter.com/fash-track/justin-bieber-jesus-tattoo-278814.

43. Christine Thomasos, "Justin Bieber Story: The Origin of His Faith," *Christian Post*, September 26, 2011, http://m.christianpost.com/news/justin-bieber-story-the-origin-of-his-faith-56555/.

44. Jan Hoffman, "Justin Bieber Is Living the Dream," *New York Times*, January 2, 2010, http://www.nytimes.com/2010/01/03/fashion/03bieber.html?_r=0.

45. Greg Goodsell, "Exclusive Interview: Mom of Pop Sensation Justin Bieber Asks for Your Prayers," *Catholic Online*, February 14, 2011, http://www.catholic.org/news/ae/music/story.php?id=40340.

46. Naomi Pfefferman, "Justin Bieber's Jewish Father Figure, Scooter Braun," *Jewish Journal*, February 8, 2011, http://www.jewishjournal.com/the_ticket/item/my_interview_with_scooter_braun_justin_biebers_jewish_father_figure_2011020.

47. Hoffman, "Justin Bieber Is Living the Dream."

48. Goodsell, "Mom of Pop Sensation Justin Bieber Asks for Your Prayers."

49. Adam Holz, "Pattie Mallette's Mission as a Mom," *Plugged In*, February 14, 2011, http://www.pluggedin.com/upfront/2011/pattiemallettesmissionasamom.aspx, no longer accessible.

50. Goodsell, "Mom of Pop Sensation Justin Bieber Asks for Your Prayers."

51. Holz, "Pattie Mallette's Mission as a Mom."

52. Vanessa Grigoriadis, "Justin Bieber Talks Sex, Politics, Music and Puberty in New 'Rolling Stone' Cover Story," *Rolling Stone*, February 16, 2011, http://www.rollingstone.com/music/news/justin-bieber-talks-sex-politics-music-and-puberty-in-new-rolling-stone-cover-story-20110216.

53. Ibid.

54. Ibid.

55. Shari Weiss, "Justin Bieber's Abortion Comments Slammed by 'The View'," *NY Daily News*, February 18, 2011, http://www.nydailynews.com/entertainment/gossip/justin-bieber-abortion-comments-rolling-stone-slammed-view-article-1.135801.

56. Ibid.

57. Ibid.

58. Ibid.

59. Kathryn Olivarius, "Opinion, Olivarius: Bieber's Abortion Comments Are Not Benign," *Yale Daily News*, February 17, 2011, http://yaledailynews.com/crosscampus/2011/02/17/opinion-olivarius-biebers-abortion-comments-are-not-benign/.

60. Holz, "Pattie Mallette's Mission as a Mom."

61. *Now Magazine*, "Russell Brand Apologises for Jonas Brothers Gag," *Celebs Now*, September 9, 2008, http://www.nowmagazine.co.uk/celebrity-news/273091/russell-brand-apologises-for-jonas-brothers-gag.

62. Jocelyn Vena, "Jordin Sparks: 'I Don't Regret' Promise-Ring Outburst at VMAS," MTV News, September 10, 2008, http://www.mtv.com/news/1594549/jordin-sparks-i-dont-regret-promise-ring-outburst-at-vmas/.

63. Hollie McKay, "Jordin Sparks Fires Back at MTV Video Music Awards Host over Purity Rings," Fox News, September 8, 2008, http://www.foxnews.com/story/2008/09/08/jordin-sparks-fires-back-at-mtv-video-music-wards-host-over-purity-rings/.

64. Ibid.

65. Jocelyn Vena, "Jonas Brothers Respond to Russell Brand's VMA Comments," MTV News, September 9, 2008, http://www.mtv.com/news/1594439/jonas-brothers-respond-to-russell-brands-vma-comments/.

66. Ibid.

67. Ibid.

68. Amanda Robb, "Meet Denise Jonas," *Good Housekeeping*, June 2, 2009, http://www.goodhousekeeping.com/life/inspirational-stories/interviews/a16687/jonas-brothers-mom-denise-jonas/.

69. Ibid.

70. Allen Weed, "Papa Jonas Interview," *Anything Diz*, July 17, 2010, http://anythingdiz.livejournal.com/3126812.html.

71. Ibid.

72. Ibid.

73. Ibid.

74. Ibid.

75. Ibid.

76. *Christianity Today*, "Before They Were Stars," *Ignite Your Faith*, January 1, 2008, http://www.christianitytoday.com/iyf/2008/fall/37.37.html.

77. Ibid.

78. MaryMary, "Shackles," by Erica Atkins, Tina Atkins, and Warryn Campbell, in *Thankful*, Columbia, 1999, compact disc.

79. Slash, "Andy Hunter," Tribalmixes.com, accessed March 28, 2017, http://www.tribalmixes.com/djlist2.php?id=866.

80. Slash, "Andy Hunter."

81. Ibid.

82. M-Audio, "Andy Hunter," M-Audio.com, accessed March 28, 2017, http://www.m-audio.com/artists/profile/andy-hunter.

83. Slash, "Andy Hunter."

84. *Relevant*, "Andy Hunter: Breaking Down Barriers," *Relevant Magazine*, May 13, 2003, http://www.relevantmagazine.com/culture/music/features/2833-andy-hunter-breaking-down-barriers.

85. Slash, "Andy Hunter."

86. *Relevant*, "Andy Hunter."

87. Ibid.

88. Ibid.

89. Slash, "Andy Hunter."

90. Slash, "Andy Hunter."

91. Ibid.

92. AT40, "Artists: Dana Glover," American Top 40 with Ryan Seacrest, accessed March 28, 2017, http://www.at40.com/artist/dana-glover/2007.

93. Ibid.

94. Ibid.

95. Ibid.

96. Ibid.

97. Ibid.

98. Ibid.

99. AT40, "Artists: Dana Glover."

100. Ibid.

101. AT40, "Artists: Dana Glover."

102. AT40, "Artists: Dana Glover."

103. Ibid.

104. Kristi Singer (*Star News* correspondent), "Dana Glover Remembers Wilmington." Kristi Singer website, February 7, 2003, http://kristi_singer.tripod.com/id177.htm.

105. Emma Green, "America's New Hip-Hop King Lecrae Claims: My Music Is Not Christian, But I Am," *Huffington Post*, October 8, 2014, http://www.huffingtonpost.com/2014/10/08/lecrae-christian-rapper_n_5946496.html.

106. Denver 7, "One-on-One with Lecrae, First Christian Rapper to Top Billboard 200," ABC 7 Denver, October 13, 2014, http://www.thedenverchannel.com/thenow/one-on-one-with-lecrae-first-christian-rapper-to-top-billboard-20010132014.

107. Author interview, May 2017.

108. Lecrae, on Twitter, April 16, 2012, https://twitter.com/lecrae/status/191965551428501506.

109. Denver 7, "One-on-One with Lecrae."

110. Emma Green, "Lecrae: 'Christians Have Prostituted Art to Give Answers,'" *Atlantic*, October 6, 2014, http://www.theatlantic.com/entertainment/archive/2014/10/lecrae-christians-have-prostituted-art-to-give-answers/381103/.

111. David Noebel, "Worldview," Richmond Center for Christian Study, accessed March 29, 2017, http://www.richmondstudycenter.org/worldview.

112. Del Tackett, "What's a Christian Worldview?" Focus on the Family, accessed March 29, 2017, http://www.focusonthefamily.com/faith/christian-worldview/whats-a-christian-worldview/whats-a-worldview-anyway.

113. *Complex*, "Interview: Lecrae Talks about Going from 'Crazy Crae' to Christian Rapper," *Complex* magazine, June 8, 2012, http://www.complex.com/music/2012/06/interview-lecrae.

114. Eryn Sun, "Christian Hip-Hop Artist Lecrae on Troubled Past," *Christian Post*, September 18, 2011, http://m.christianpost.com/news/christian-hip-hop-artist-lecrae-on-troubled-past-source-of-significance-56671/.

115. Tim Challies, "John Piper's Unexpected Career in Hip-Hop," *Challies* (blog), February 10, 2012, http://www.challies.com/a-la-carte/john-pipers-unexpected-career-in-hip-hop.

116. "John Piper Interviews Lecrae," YouTube video, 6:10, Lecrae explains "what he and his friends at Reach Records want to see God do through their music," posted by Desiring God, January 5, 2011, https://www.youtube.com/watch?t=91&v=Mu0OFi5pScE.

117. E! News on Twitter, January 26, 2012, https://twitter.com/eonline/status/427616198465835008.

118. Denver 7, "One-on-One with Lecrae."

119. The Los Angeles News Group, "'The Voice' Contestant Judith Hill Is No Stranger to the Spotlight," *Denver Post*, April 11, 2013, http://www.denverpost.com/2013/04/11/the-voice-contestant-judith-hill-is-no-stranger-to-the-spotlight/.

120. Lyndsey Parker, "Judith Hill on Jamming with Prince, Remembering Michael Jackson, and What 'The Voice' Taught Her about America," Tumblr, accessed March 30, 2017, http://lyndsey-parker.tumblr.com/post/131653597883/judith-hill-on-jamming-with-prince-remembering.

121. Mark Joseph, "Judith Hill Goes Back in Time," *Huffington Post*, November 29, 2015, http://www.huffingtonpost.com/mark-joseph/judith-hill-blends-east-w_b_8597546.html.

122. Ibid.

123. Malorie McCall, "Judith Hill 'Happy for That Extra Push' from Prince to Step Up First Album 'Back in Time,'" *Billboard*, October 23, 2015, http://www.billboard.com/articles/columns/the-juice/6738244/judith-hill-prince-new-album-back-time.

124. Joseph, "Judith Hill Goes Back in Time."

125. The Los Angeles News Group, "'The Voice' Contestant Judith Hill Is No Stranger to the Spotlight."

126. Joseph, Mark. "Judith Hill Goes Back in Time." *The Huffington Post*, November 29, 2015, http://www.huffingtonpost.com/mark-joseph/judith-hill-blends-east-w_b_8597546.html.

127. Parker, "Judith Hill on Jamming with Prince."

128. Joseph, "Judith Hill Goes Back in Time."

129. Ibid.

130. McCall, "Judith Hill 'Happy for That Extra Push' from Prince to Step Up First Album 'Back in Time'.".

131. Joseph, "Judith Hill Goes Back in Time."

132. Josephine Vivaldo, "Michael Jackson's Back-Up Singer, Biola University Team Up for Japan," *Christian Post*, March 23, 2011, http://www.christianpost.com/news/michael-jacksons-back-up-singer-biola-university-team-up-for-japan-49539/#YbHIZCls2qF4RZKK.99.

133. The Los Angeles News Group, "'The Voice' Contestant Judith Hill Is No Stranger to the Spotlight."

134. Jeannie Law, "Pop Sensation Tori Kelly Shares Heart of Worship During Concerts; Hillsong United, Lecrae & More Show Support," Breathecast, June 29, 2015, http://www.breathecast.com/articles/pop-sensation-tori-kelly-shares-heart-of-worship-during-concerts-hillsong-united-lecrae-more-show-support-video-29206/.

135. Tori Kelly, https://twitter.com/torikelly.

136. Alexandra Perron, "Tori Kelly on Her Rise to Fame and the Importance of Following Your Passion." Yahoo! News, October 13, 2015, https://www.yahoo.com/news/tori-kelly-tk-114107067.html.

137. Author interview, April, 2017.

138. Perron, "Tori Kelly on Her Rise to Fame and the Importance of Following Your Passion."

139. David Ellis, "Tori Kelly, Interview: 'I Just Want People to Know You're Allowed to Be Modest and It Will Work,'" *Evening Standard*, October 16, 2015, http://www.standard.co.uk/goingout/music/tori-kelly-interview-i-just-want-people-to-know-you-re-allowed-to-be-modest-and-it-will-work-a3092531.html.

140. Ibid.

141. Caroline Sullivan, "Tori Kelly: 'Believe in Yourself and Don't Be Bullied,'" *Guardian*, October 8, 2015, https://www.theguardian.com/music/2015/oct/08/tori-kelly-vma-justin-bieber-carly-rae-jepsen.

142. Tori Kelly, "Unbreakable Smile," in *Unbreakable Smile*, Capitol Records and Schoolboy Records, 2015, compact disc.

143. Ellis, "Tori Kelly, Interview."

144. Sullivan, "Tori Kelly."

145. Ellis, "Tori Kelly, Interview."

146. Iyana Robertson, "Who's That Girl: Allow Tori Kelly to Introduce You to Her 'Unbreakable Smile,'" *Vibe*, June 29, 2015, http://www.vibe.com/2015/06/tori-kelly-unbreakable-smile-interview/.

147. Ibid.

148. Marc Inocencio, "Tori Kelly," *On Air with Ryan Seacrest* (video), October 29, 2015, http://onairwithryan.iheart.com/onair/ryan-seacrest-52241/tori-kelly-explains-vulnerable-message-behind-14079035/.

149. Sullivan, "Tori Kelly."

150. "Tori Kelly Talks Faith, Music, and Performing Alongside Some BIG Names (Like Britney)." *The Bert Show,* http://thebertshow.com/tori-kelly-talks-faith-music-and-performing-alongside-some-big-names-like-britney/.

151. Crystal Lewis, interview with author, March 2017.

152. Ellis, "Tori Kelly, Interview."

153. Andy Greene, "Twenty One Pilots: Inside the Biggest New Band of the Past Year," *Rolling Stone,* January 14, 2016, http://www.rollingstone.com/music/features/twenty-one-pilots-inside-the-biggest-new-band-of-the-past-year-20160114.

154. Valerie Reich, "Ohio's Twenty One Pilots Graduate from Hometown Heroes to the Major Leagues (Q&A)." *Hollywood Reporter,* August 7, 2013, http://www.hollywoodreporter.com/earshot/ohios-twenty-one-pilots-graduate-597242.

155. Greene, "Twenty One Pilots."

156. Ibid.

157. Matt Crane, "15 things We Learned about Twenty One Pilots Today," Alternative Press, April 24, 2015, http://www.altpress.com/features/entry/15_things_we_learned_about_twenty_one_pilots_today.

158. Greene, "Twenty One Pilots."

159. Michael Ashcraft and Mark Ellis, "Christian Band Twenty One Pilots Confounds Secular Critics, Shows Gen-Y & Z a Way to Faith," *God Reports* (blog), April 1, 2016, http://blogs.christianpost.com/god-reports/christian-band-twenty-one-pilots-confounds-secular-critics-shows-gen-y-z-a-way-to-faith-27476/.

160. Ibid.

161. Ibid.

162. Ibid.

163. Ibid.

164. Crane, "15 Things We Learned about Twenty One Pilots Today."

165. Ibid.

166. Reich, "Ohio's Twenty One Pilots Graduate from Hometown Heroes to the Major Leagues (Q&A)."

167. Gary Trust, "Twenty One Pilots 'Mean So Many Things to So Many People,' Says Fueled by Ramen Exec (Exclusive Q&A)," *Billboard,* January 7, 2016, http://www.billboard.com/articles/columns/chart-beat/6835380/twenty-one-pilots-mike-easterlin-interview.

168. Greene, "Twenty One Pilots."

169. "twenty one pilots: Stressed Out [OFFICIAL VIDEO]." YouTube, 3:45, from the album *Blurryface*, posted by Fueled by Ramen, April 27, 2016, https://www.youtube.com/watch?v=pXRviuL6vMY.

170. Greene, "Twenty One Pilots."

171. Ibid.

CHAPTER SEVEN: INTO THE GREAT WIDE-OPEN

1. The *Washington Times*, "Christian Quandary," *Washington Times*, August 13, 2003, http://www.washingtontimes.com/news/2003/aug/13/20030813-093528-9573r/?page=all.

2. John Fischer, Interview with author, 2006.

3. Dan Haseltine, quoted in Robin Parrish, "The New Roaring Lambs Movement," 2003.

4. "What Corrupt Christian Music Says," Defending_Artists: The TRUTH About Christian Music . . . Kevin Max, http://darthhobbit.tripod.com/defendingartists/id6.html.

5. Robin Parrish, "The New Roaring Lambs Movement: Kevin Max," Kevin Max on Tripod, February 19, 2003, http://kfker.tripod.com/cmcentral.htm. The feather boa mentioned in this quote was, Max said, "meant as a concept for me to show how the excesses of rock & roll and fashion can leave you lonely." Ibid.

6. Ibid.

7. Barry Landis, interview with author, April 2017.

8. Ibid.

9. Ibid.

10. Dan Haseltine, interview with the author, March 2017.

11. Ibid.

12. Dan Haseltine, interview with the author, 3/17.

13. John Fischer, interview with the author, 2006.

14. John Fischer, interview with the author, 2006.

15. Ibid.

INDEX

A

ABC News, 48–49, 147
Absolute Punk (now chorusfm), 171
Adams, Yolanda, 10
Adams, Tim, 153
Adele, 186
Aguilera, Christina, 48, 58, 108, 250
Aiken, Clay, 26, 27, 28–29, 31
Allen, Kris, 26, 31–32
A&M, 110
American Idol, 3, 26–32, 34, 232, 266, 269
Americans with a "Biblical worldview," percent of, 255
Arcade Fire, 167
Ardent Records, 16, 100
Art of Anarchy, 157
Ashcraft, Michael, 276–78
Atlantic Records, 3, 11, 13, 192
Aveiro, Matt, 160

B

Backstreet Boys, 235
Bailey, Philip, 85
Bakker, Jim, 70
Band, the, 167

Baptist Standard, 7
Barna Group, 255
Barton, Laura, 164
Bautts, Jonathan, 171
Beach Boys, 196
Beatles, 170, 189, 196, 254
Becker, Greg, 118
Bedingfield, Daniel, 25, 216–22, 223, 224
Bedingfield, Molly and John, 222
Bedingfield, Natasha, 216, 221, 222–24
Behar, Joy, 230
Beliefnet.com, 223
Bennett, Bob, 280
Bennett, Chancelor. *See* Chance the Rapper
Bennett, Ken, 83
Benson (music label), 273
Bernall, Cassie, 196
Berry, Chuck, 170
Berlin, Rick, 153–54
Beyoncé, 186
Bhaattacharya, Sameer, 199
biblical worldview, 255, 256. *See also* Christian worldview
Bieber, Justin, 224–25, 226–32, 260, 266, 267, 270, 293
Big Gay Steven, 19, 20, 101, 107

Billboard charts, 5, 7
Biola University, 158–60, 261
Blanton, Mike, 99
Blender, 21
Bloodgood, 280
Bono, 71, 75, 189, 221, 224, 250–51
Brand, Russell, 35–36, 40, 232–33
Brann, Matt, 63
Braun, Scooter, 226, 227, 266, 270
Briner, Bob (author, *Roaring Lambs*), 287, 288–89
Brokaw, Joanna, 223
Brown, James, 42
Buckmaster, Paul, 250
Butler, Chad, 14–15, 24, 129
Butler, Chuck, 14, 24
Buzzfeed, 83–84, 92, 94

C

Calvary Chapel, 12, 13, 17, 18
Campbell, Kim, 5–6
Capitol Records, 100, 172
Carey, Mariah, 38, 194, 247
Carlisle, Bob, 2, 16
Carney, Steve, 101
Carter, Jimmy, 8
Cash, Johnny, 84, 85, 160, 225, 254, 258
Catania, Bob, 102–4
Catholic Online, 227
Caviezel, Jim, 75
CBA (Christian Booksellers Association), 10, 11
CBS News, 5, 203
CCM (or, contemporary Christian music), 2–3, 6, 10–15, 17, 18, 22, 23, 25, 27, 64, 66, 77, 79, 100, 107–12, 117–19, 121–23, 129, 130, 143, 186, 199, 215, 221, 225, 246, 266, 273, 282, 283, 285, 287, 289, 290
CCM (magazine), 24, 283

Chagall Guevara, 122
Challies, Tim, 258
Chance the Rapper, 82–89, 90
Chapman, Gary, 98
Chapman, Steven Curtis, 23, 92, 178
Chester Thompson Band, 261
Chevelle, 3, 122–28, 134
Chicago Tribune, 6–7, 20
Chorusfm, 171
Christian Booksellers Association. *See* CBA
Christianity Today, 72, 86, 87, 126–27, 143, 144–45, 152, 175, 217
Christian Music Trade Association (CMTA), 10–12
Christian Science Monitor, 5–6
Christian SoundScan, 11
Christian worldview, 112, 123, 125, 253. *See also* biblical worldview
Civil Wars, 116–18, 121, 208
Clapton, Eric, 22
Clark, Jason, 192–93
Clarkson, Kelly, 188, 235
CMTA (Christian Music Trade Association), 10–12
Cobain, Kurt, 200
Cold War Kids, 157–60, 162, 167, 261, 276, 293
Colson, Chuck, 254, 255
Columbia Records, 3, 13, 15, 131, 133, 185, 187, 213, 235
Coniff, Tamara, 50
contemporary Christian music, 2, 6, 9, 107, 117, 199, 225, 282. *See* CCM
Cooke, Sam, 85, 225
Coomes, Tommy, 13, 23, 24–25
Coomes, Tyler and Eric, 25
Cowell, Simon, 30, 269, 271
Creed, 15, 144, 145, 146, 148–53, 157
Cross, Christopher, 246
Cross Movement, 257
Crouch, Andraé, 22, 264

Crouch, Matt, 30
Cua, Rick, 143
Culpepper, James, 199
Curb, Mike, 102
Curb Records, 102–3
Cyrus, Billy Ray, 42–47
Cyrus, Cody (son of Billy Ray), 42
Cyrus, Miley, 41–43, 45–47, 203, 260
Cyrus, Ron (grandfather of Miley), 42
Cyrus, Tish, 42, 43

D

Dash, 173
Daughtry, Chris, 26, 32
Davis, Clive, 27–28, 29, 32, 62
Davis, Jeremy, 192, 195
dc Talk, 172, 178, 192, 193, 212, 285–87
Dead Kennedys, 176
Def Jam (label), 220
DeGarmo, Diana, 26, 27
DeGarmo, Eddie, 27
DeGarmo & Key, 16
Delirious, 239
Destiny's Child, 109
Disney, 41, 45, 46, 235
DJBooth (website), 95–96
Doc (TV series), 44
Donnie Trumpet and the Social Experiment, 86
Dorsey, Thomas A., 84
Dove awards, 99, 117
Downtown Records, 157, 160
Dr. Dre, 97
Dreamworks, 11, 249, 250
Dun, Josh, 274, 275–76, 278, 279, 280, 281
Dwane, Ted, 165
Dylan, Bob, 18, 163, 175, 224

E

Earth, Wind & Fire, 85
Easterlin, Mike, 279–80
Ebel, Brandon, 289
Ebony magazine, 94
Ellis, Mark, 276–78
Emanuel, Rahm, 83, 88, 89
EMI, 11, 108, 287
Eminem, 91, 102, 128
Enclave (music site), 78
E! News, 260
English, Joe, 143
Entertainment Weekly, 20, 68, 76
Epic, 3, 123, 182
Evanescence, 3, 15, 76–82, 122, 124, 127
EW.com, 195

F

Faith, Paloma, 165
Faith, God & Rock 'n' Roll (Joseph), 1, 3
Falsani, Cathleen (*Belieber! Fame, Faith, and the Heart of Justin Bieber*), 225
Falwell, Jerry, 8
Fantasia, 26
Farris, Christa, 283
Farro, Josh, 192–94, 195
Farro, Zac, 192, 193, 194, 195
Fat Boy, 240
Filkins, Zach, 185
Fischer, John, 24, 283–84, 289, 291–92
Flyleaf, 3, 196–97, 199–202
Focus on the Family, 60, 68, 256
Followill, Betty Ann, 64, 65
Followill, Caleb, 64–65, 67, 68–71
Followill, Ivan Leon, 64, 54, 70
Followill, Jared, 65
Followill, Matthew, 65
Followill, Nathan, 64–70
Forefront (CCM label), 108, 110, 285, 286, 287

Foreman, Jon, 129–30, 131–36, 137–38, 167, 173

Foreman, Tim, 14, 15, 128–29

Franklin, Kirk, 23, 71, 83, 85, 89, 92, 238, 239

Fray, the, 177–85

Frontline (music label), 273

Fueled by Ramen (indie label), 192, 274, 280

Furay, Richie, 280

G

Gatlin, Wendy, 104

Geffen, David, 32

Geffen Records, 20

Gibson, Mel, 143, 144, 146, 147, 150, 155

Gifted (TV show), 30

Gill, Vince, 98–99

Glover, Dana, 246, 247–52

God's Property, 238

Goff, Philip, 8

Good Housekeeping, 234

gospel music, origin of, 84

Gospel Music Association, 11, 23

Gotee (label), 172

GQ magazine, 43

Graham, Billy, 53, 258, 285

Grant, Amy, 2, 23, 98–99, 111, 112, 129, 192, 246

Green, Al, 85, 210–11

Green, Keith, 27–28

Green, Steve, 23

Green Day's *Dookie*, 275

Griffith, Andy, 10

Guardian, 164–65, 222, 272

Guinness, Os, 254

Gunn, Jadda, 71

H

Hall & Oates, 246

Ham, Greg, 110

Hamill, James, 69

Hamilton, Anthony, 25

Hannah Montana (TV show), 43, 44–45, 46

Harris, Louis, 8

Hartmann, Jared, 199

Haseltine, Dan, 22, 284–85, 290

Hasselback, Elisabeth, 230

Hawkins, Edwin, 2

Heard, Mark, 13

Hearn, Billy Ray, 28, 32

Heath, Chris, 43–44

Helton, RJ, 26

Herrera, Mike, 173

Heston, Charlton, 254

Hetfield, James, 140

Hill, Faith, 57

Hill, Judith, 260–66

Hill, Lauryn, 143, 161

Hill, Michiko, 261, 266

Hill, Pee Wee, 261, 262, 266

Hilton, Paris, 233

Hilton, Perez, 233

hippies, 17, 101, 222

Hollywood Records, 235

Hoopes, Matt, 171–72

Hoppus, Mark, 144

Horton, Chad, 95

Houston, Whitney, 27, 247

Houston Baptist University, 253

Houston Chronicle, 193–94

Howard Stern Radio Show, 19

Hudson, Keith, 39–40

Hudson, Mary, 33–35, 38–40

Huff, Dann, 23

Humbard, Rex, 258

Hunger Games, 208

Hunter, Andy, 239, 240–46

I

Imagine: A Vision for Christians in the Arts (Turner), 254

Imperials, 246–47
Independent (UK), 4
INO Records, 102, 104, 235
Insane Clown Posse, 128
Interscope (label), 268
Interview, 217
Island/Def Jam, 220
Island Records, 227

J

Jackson, Janet, 20, 29
Jackson, Jesse, 89
Jackson, Mahalia, 84
Jackson, Michael, 38, 260–62, 263, 264
Jagger, Mick, 42
Jars of Clay, 2, 15, 19, 22, 23, 192, 283, 284, 290
Jay Z, 97
Jeopardy (game show), 9–10
Jesus movement, 12, 236, 284
Jesus music, 2, 12–14, 16, 24, 25, 129, 284
Jewish Journal, 226
Joel, Billy, 27, 246
Johnson, Robert, 189
Jonas, Denise Miller, 233, 234, 236, 237
Jonas, Joe, 207
Jonas, Kevin, Jr., 233, 238
Jonas, Kevin, Sr., 233, 234–36, 237
Jonas, Nick, 233, 235, 237–38
Jonas Brothers, 187, 207, 232, 233, 235–37
Jones, Watson, III, 87
Joplin, Janis, 27
Joseph, Tyler, 274, 275, 276, 278, 279, 280, 281
Jubilee Christian Fellowship (Stratford, ON), 225, 231
Jump5, 235

K

Kadish, Kevin, 110

Kasha, Al, 18
Kearney, Mat, 211–16
Kelly, Laura (mother of Tori), 267
Kelly, R. (Robert Sylvester Kelly), 7–8
Kelly, Tori, 266–73, 279
Ken, Thomas, 167
Key, Dana, 16, 22, 100
Kierkegaard, Søren, 161
King, Joe, 178
King, Martin, 240
Kings of Leon, 64–70
King's X, 15, 90, 128
KNAC.com, 142–43
Kool & the Gang, 246
Kravitz, Lenny, 221

L

Lachey, Nick, 50–51
Lady Gaga, 35, 36–37, 206
Lamar, Kendrick, 90–97
Lambert, Adam, 31–32
Lampa, Rachael, 266
Landis, Barry, 287–89
Late Great Planet Earth, The (Lindsay), 181
Lavigne, Avril, 52–63
Lavigne, John, 54
Lavigne, Judy (nee Loshaw), 53, 54–55, 59, 60
Lavigne, Matt, 54
Lavigne, Michelle, 54
LeCrae, 91, 92, 94, 252–55, 256–60, 266
Lee, Amy, 76, 77, 78, 81–82
Lefevre, Mylon, 47–48, 167
Lennon, John, 27, 189, 258–59
Levine, Jared, 249
Levitan, Ken, 65, 66
Lewis, Crystal, 266–67, 272–73
Lewis, C. S., 162
Lifehouse, 10, 11, 163
Living Sacrifice, 79

Loeffler, Joe, 122
Loeffler, Pete, 122, 124, 126
Loeffler, Sam, 122, 125, 127
Los Angeles Times, 101
Love Song, 12, 13
Luther, Martin, 18
Luttrell, Jase, 211
Lynch, David, 42

M

MacIntosh, Mike, 17–18
Madonna, 36, 41, 42, 63, 147, 220
Maher, Bill, 19, 144
Mallette, Pattie, 225–26, 227, 228, 231
Manfred, Rob, 89
Mannheim Steamroller, 10, 11
Maranatha! Music, 12–14, 18
Marilyn Manson, 128, 176
Marshall, Winston, 165, 169
Martin, Chris, 184
Mary Mary, 10, 23, 71, 238–39
Mase, 209–11
M-Audio, 240–41
Maust, Matt, 160–61
Max, Kevin, 285–87, 316n5
Maxim (magazine), 62
MCA, 122
McCartney, Jesse, 238
McCormick, Neil, 66–67
MC Hammer, 7
McIntyre, Philip, 30
McKeehan, Toby, 172
McNeal, Reggie, 25
Mead, Sister, Janet, 101
Medd, Stephen, 55, 57–58
Meece, David, 246
Megadeth, 139–41, 143, 208, 293
MercyMe, 2, 19, 20, 23, 99, 101–8
Michael, George, 247
Microsoft, 243–44

Millard, Bart, 19–20, 21, 98, 99, 101–3, 105–6, 107
Mintz, Alan, 249
Moby, 240
Moody, Ben, 76–82
Moral Majority, 8
Moring, Mark, 152–53
Mosely, Jeff, 235
Mosley, Lacey, 196, 197–201
Mosley Music Group, 188
Mr Hudson, 165
MTV, 5, 19, 20, 35, 36–37, 41, 48, 50, 51, 61, 94, 108, 111, 116, 123, 196, 209
MTV Video Music Awards (aka VMAs), 41–42, 45–46
Mulholland Drive (film), 42
Mumford, Eleanor, 163, 164–65
Mumford, John, 163, 164–65
Mumford, Marcus, 163–64, 165, 166, 168–71
Mumford & Sons, 162, 163–70, 293
Murray, Anne, 10
Mushnick, Phil, 88–89
Mustaine, Dave, 139–43, 208
Mustard Seed Faith, 12
MxPx, 144

N

Nas, 97
Nashville, Tennessee, 7, 10, 46, 65–66, 117, 157, 182, 186, 192, 205–6, 212, 234, 249, 254, 287
NBC, 54, 57
Newlyweds, The (TV series), 50–51
Newsweek, 31
Newton-John, Olivia, 9
New York Post, 88
New York Times, 90, 226–27
Nirvana, 199
Noebel, David, 255–56

Nordeman, Nichole, 4
Norman, Larry, 100–101, 168, 174–75

O

Obama, Barack, 88, 207
O'Brien, Brendan, 184
O Brother, Where Art Thou? (film), 10, 11
O'Conner, Flannery, 214
Octone (label), 196
Olivarus, Kathryn (of *Yale Daily News*), 230–31
Omartian, Michael, 23, 246
Omartian, Stormie, 246
120 Minutes, 123
OneRepublic, 185–88
Orrico, Stacie, 108–15, 266, 287
Out of Eden, 266

P–Q

Page Six magazine, 38
Paglia, Camille, 41–42
Paisley, Brad, 144
Parable, 12, 14, 129
Paramore, 3, 190–94, 196
Parr, Claire (nee West), 20
Parton, Dolly, 84
Passion of the Christ, The (film), 75, 143–50
Paste magazine, 16, 158
Patillo, Leon, 18
Pauley, Jane, 57
P. Diddy, 209
Peacock, Charlie, 15, 17, 129–31, 280
Pearcey, Nancy, 253, 255
Pearcey, Rick, 253
Perry, Katy, 33–41, 118, 187, 232, 237, 260, 273
Petra, 161
Picotte, Tom, 57
Pillar, 3
Pinnick, Doug, 90

Piper, John, 258, 259
Pitchfork Media, 158–59
Pittman, Brian, 172
Plugged In magazine, 51, 60–61, 68, 74, 170–71, 227
P.O.D., 10, 11, 19, 173
Politically Incorrect (TV show), 19, 144
Polnareff, Michel, 261
Pop Matters, 166–67, 168
Powell, Mac, 212
Presley, Elvis, xii, 42, 47, 69, 84, 85, 225, 258
Prince, 4, 161, 261–64
Provident (Label Group), 10

R

rapture theology, 17
Rapzilla, 95
RCA, 66
Reach Records, 252
Reagan, Ronald, 8
Reid, L. A., 56, 57, 58
Relevant magazine, 64, 166
Relient K, 171, 174–75, 177, 275
Re:think (label), 15, 130–31
Reunion (label), 117
Reznor, Trent, 147
Richard, Cliff, 216, 221
Righteous Brothers, 163
Rihanna, 188, 206
R. Kelly, 7–8
Roaring Lambs (Briner), 287–88
Roberts, Oral, 258
Robertson, Pat, 258–59
Robertson, Robbie, 249–50
Roc-A-Fella Records, 71, 73
Rock & Roll Rebellion, The (Joseph), 1
Rock 'n' Roll Worship Circus, 283
Rolling Stone (magazine), 21, 35, 37, 53, 62–63, 75–76, 92, 158, 162, 167, 183–84, 205, 206, 229, 274, 280

Rolling Stones, 22, 170, 174
Rubin, Rick, 147
Run-D.M.C., 7
Russell, Jonnie, 160

S

San Diego CityBeat, 159
Sandoval, Sonny, 19
Santana, 18
Sawyer, Diane, 147
Schaeffer, Francis, 253, 255
Schaeffer, Franky, 133
Scharen, Christian, 70, 162, 163–64, 169
Scheuchzer, Mike, 105
Schulz, Charles, 160–61
Schumer, Ben, 166–67, 168
Seals, Pat, 199
Seawind, 23
Sensibility Music, 117
Serletic, Matt, 111
Session, David, 182–83
Short, Robert L., 161
Shrek (film), 250
Simon, Paul, 173
Simpson, Ashlee, 48–49, 51–52
Simpson, Jessica, 48–51, 52, 108
Simpson, Joe, 48–50, 51, 52
Simpson, Tina, 50
Simpsons, The (TV show) 4–5
Sims, Tommy, 23
Sixpence None the Richer, 66, 112, 122, 123, 173, 185
60 Minutes, 5, 203–4
Slade, Isaac, 178, 180, 181–82, 183, 184
Smith, Michael W., 16, 20, 23, 107, 282
Smithouser, Loren Eaton Bob, 74–75
Solid Rock (label), 174
Sparks, Jordin, 26, 31, 232, 233
Sparrow Records (now EMICMG), 10, 11, 15, 130–31, 273

Spears, Britney, 41, 48, 58, 62, 108, 116
Spearses (parents of Britney Spears), 237
Spin (magazine), 157–58, 167
Squint Entertainment, 122–23
Stahl, Lesley, 204
Stampley, Micah, 76
Stanley, Ralph, 167
Staple Singers, 84
Stapp, Scott, 143–57
Stapp, Steven (father of Scott), 145, 151, 154–55
Star Magazine, 28
Steinbeck, John, 168, 169, 170
Stellar Awards, 71
Stern, Howard, 19, 41
Stevens, Cat, 161
Stewart, Rod, 246
Sting, 224
Strangerthings.com, 77
Streisand, Barbra, 194
Strickland, KaDee, 229
Stryper, 2, 15, 161
Studdard, Ruben, 26, 31
Styll, John, 23
Sullivan, Caroline, 272
Summer, Donna, 18, 246
Swaggart, Jimmy, 70
Sweet Comfort Band, 12, 246
Swift, Andrea Gardner (mother of Taylor), 205
Swift, Scott Kingsley (father of Taylor), 205
Swift, Taylor, 203, 204–8
Switchfoot, 2, 3, 6, 7, 14–16, 23, 34, 112, 127–38, 167, 173

T

Tackett, Del, 256
Tait, Michael, 285
Taylor, James, 291
Taylor, Steve, 23, 122–23, 174–75, 254

Tedder, Ryan, 185–89
Tegan and Sara, 191
Telegraph (UK), 66–67, 206
Thiessen, Matt, 171, 172–77
Third Day, 212, 282
Thomas, B. J., 15
Timbaland, 177–78
Timberlake, Justin, 102, 227
TobyMac, 212, 213, 285, 287
Tooth & Nail Records, 289
Total Truth (Pearcey), 253, 255
Trance (music), 240, 241, 245
Tranter, Nicki, 217–19
Trebek, Alex, 9–10
Tribalmixes.com, 239–40
Trinity Broadcasting Network, 30
Tucker, Chris, 147
Turner, Steve, 253, 254
Twain, Shania, 57
12 Stones, 10
Twenty Øne Piløts, 274–81, 293

U

Ugwu, Reggie, 92–93
Ulrich, Lars, 140
Underwood, Carrie, 26, 31, 32
United Artists Records, 13
Universal, 3
USA Today, 5, 217
Usher, 227
U2, 6, 15, 67, 69, 75, 140, 158, 189, 221, 250, 254

V

Van De Bogart, Wayne, 55
VH1, 5, 20, 108
Vibe magazine, 210
Vicious, Sid, 176
View, The, 229
Vineyard (Church/movement), 162–63, 164

Virgin Records, 108–11, 114, 285–87
Voice, The (TV show), 261

W–X

Waliszewski, Bob, 51–52, 60–61
Walters, Barbara, 230
Warner Bros., 157
Warped Tour, 172–73
Washington, Harold, 88
Way, The (Jesus music band), 12
Welsh, David, 178, 184
West, Kanye, 7, 71–76, 86, 89, 95, 255
White, John Paul, 117–18
Wilder, Matthew, 250
Willett, Nathan, 160, 161
Williams, Hayley, 190–92, 193, 194–96
Williams, Joy, 116–21
Willman, Chris, 76–77, 80, 81
Wimber, John, 162–63
Winans, the, 247
Wind-Up Records, 81, 153
Word Records, 10, 111, 123, 125, 273, 287
"worldview," 255–56
worship movement, 239, 284
worship music, 179, 239, 244, 260, 282, 284
Wright Entertainment Group, 30
Wysocki, Ben, 178–79, 180–81

Y–Z

Yahoo.com, 196
Yahoo! News, 30, 267–68
Yetton, Nate, 117
Yoh (of DJBooth), 95–96
York, Taylor, 192–93, 195
YouTube, 171, 226, 259, 267–68, 270